CLINICAL ETHICS CONSULTATION

Medical Law and Ethics

Series Editor
Sheila McLean, Director of the Institute of Law and Ethics in Medicine,
School of Law, University of Glasgow

The 21st century seems likely to witness some of the most major developments in medicine and healthcare ever seen. At the same time, the debate about the extent to which science and/or medicine should lead the moral agenda continues, as do questions about the appropriate role for law.

This series brings together some of the best contemporary academic commentators to tackle these dilemmas in a challenging, informed and inquiring manner. The scope of the series is purposely wide, including contributions from a variety of disciplines such as law, philosophy and social sciences.

Other titles in the series

Ethical Issues of Human Genetic Databases
A Challenge to Classical Health Research Ethics?
Bernice Elger
ISBN 978-0-7546-7492-4

Issues in Human Rights Protection of Intellectually Disabled Persons
Andreas Dimopoulos
ISBN 978-0-7546-7760-4

The Legal, Medical and Cultural Regulation of the Body
Transformation and Transgression
Edited by Stephen W. Smith and Ronan Deazley
ISBN 978-0-7546-7736-9

Bioequity – Property and the Human Body
Nils Hoppe
ISBN 978-0-7546-7280-7

Altruism Reconsidered
Exploring New Approaches to Property in Human Tissue
Edited by Michael Steinmann, Peter Sýkora and Urban Wiesing
ISBN 978-0-7546-7270-8

Clinical Ethics Consultation
Theories and Methods, Implementation, Evaluation

Edited by

JAN SCHILDMANN
Ruhr-University Bochum, Germany

JOHN-STEWART GORDON
Queen's University Kingston, Canada

and

JOCHEN VOLLMANN
Ruhr-University Bochum, Germany

LONDON AND NEW YORK

First published 2010 by Ashgate Publishing

Published 2016 by Routledge
2 Park Square, Milton Park, Abingdon, Oxon OX14 4RN
711 Third Avenue, New York, NY 10017, USA

Routledge is an imprint of the Taylor & Francis Group, an informa business

Copyright © Jan Schildmann, John-Stewart Gordon and Jochen Vollmann 2010

Jan Schildmann, John-Stewart Gordon and Jochen Vollmann have asserted their right under the Copyright, Designs and Patents Act, 1988, to be identified as the editors of this work.

All rights reserved. No part of this book may be reprinted or reproduced or utilised in any form or by any electronic, mechanical, or other means, now known or hereafter invented, including photocopying and recording, or in any information storage or retrieval system, without permission in writing from the publishers.

Notice:
Product or corporate names may be trademarks or registered trademarks, and are used only for identification and explanation without intent to infringe.

British Library Cataloguing in Publication Data
Clinical ethics consultation : theories and methods,
  implementation, evaluation. -- (Medical law and ethics)
  1. Medical ethics consultation. 2. Medical ethics
  consultation--Evaluation. 3. Medical ethics consultation--
  Case studies.
  I. Series II. Schildmann, Jan, 1974- III. Gordon,
  John-Stewart, 1976- IV. Vollmann, Jochen.
  174.2-dc22

Library of Congress Cataloging-in-Publication Data
Clinical ethics consultation : theories and methods, implementation, evaluation / [edited] by Jan Schildmann, John-Stewart Gordon, and Jochen Vollmann.
    p. ; cm. -- (Medical law and ethics)
  Includes bibliographical references and index.
  ISBN 978-1-4094-0511-5 (hbk)
1. Medical ethics consultation. I. Schildmann, Jan, 1974- II. Gordon, John-Stewart, 1976- III. Vollmann, Jochen. IV. Series: Medical law and ethics.
  [DNLM: 1. Ethics, Clinical. 2. Ethical Theory. 3. Ethics Committees, Clinical.
  4. Ethics Consultation. WB 60 C6408 2010]
  R724.C52545 2010
  174.2--dc22
                                                                   2010021622

ISBN 9781409405115 (hbk)
ISBN 9781138254466 (pbk)

Contents

List of Tables and Figure		*vii*
List of Contributors		*ix*

1 Introduction 1
   Jan Schildmann, John-Stewart Gordon and Jochen Vollmann

PART I   THEORIES AND METHODS   9

2 Ethics as a Method? 11
   John-Stewart Gordon

3 Ethics – Empiricism – Consultation:
   Defining a Complex Relationship 21
   Uwe Fahr and Markus Rothhaar

4 Philosophical Foundations of Clinical Ethics:
   A Hermeneutic Perspective 37
   Guy Widdershoven and Bert Molewijk

5 Discourse Ethics and Ethics Consultation 53
   Uwe Fahr

6 Implementation of Clinical Ethics Consultation in Conflict with
   Professional Conscience? Suggestions for Reconciliation 65
   László Kovács

7 Ethics Consultation: Facilitating Reflection on Professional
   Norms in Medicine 79
   Christiane Stüber

PART II   IMPLEMENTATION   89

8 The Implementation Process of Clinical Ethics Consultation:
   Concepts, Resistance, Recommendations 91
   Jochen Vollmann

9	What Does the Ethical Expertise of a Moral Philosopher Involve in Clinical Ethics Consultancy? *Beate Herrmann*	107
10	Moving Towards Clinical Ethics Consultation in Italy: Practical Experience, Foundational and Methodological Considerations *Nunziata Comoretto*	119
11	Demands and Needs in Clinical Ethics Consultation in Georgia *Nino Chikhladze and Nato Pitskhelauri*	131
12	Clinical Ethics Consultation in Croatia *Ana Borovecki*	139
13	Clinical Ethics in the Netherlands: Moral Case Deliberation in Health Care Organizations *Margreet Stolper, Sandra van der Dam, Guy Widdershoven and Bert Molewijk*	149
14	Clinical Ethics Consultation and Bedside Rationing *Daniel Strech*	161

PART III	**EVALUATION OF CLINICAL ETHICS CONSULTATION**	**173**
15	Experience in Ethical Decision-making and Attitudes Towards Ethics Consultation of Regional Hospital Physicians in Bulgaria *Silviya Aleksandrova*	175
16	Ethical Decision-making in Nursing Homes: A Literature Study *Georg Bollig*	187
17	Evaluation of Clinical Ethics Consultation: A Systematic Review and Critical Appraisal of Research Methods and Outcome Criteria *Jan Schildmann and Jochen Vollmann*	203

Index   *217*

List of Tables and Figure

Tables

8.1	Three Levels of Clinical-ethical Institutionalization	95
8.2	Steps to Implement Clinical Ethics Consultation	98
15.1	General and Socio-demographic Data of the Responding Physicians	178
15.2	Discussion of Ethical Problems in Physicians' Practice	179
15.3	Occurrence and Types of Ethical Dilemmas Encountered in Physicians' Practice	179
15.4	Occurrence and Types of Ethical Dilemmas Encountered in Physicians' Practice by Specialty	180
15.5	Perceived Need and Main Sources of Advice/Help in Solving Ethical Problems	181
15.6	Attitudes of Responding Physicians Towards Ethics Consultation	182
15.7	What Qualities and Skills Should an Ethics Consultant Possess?	183
17.1	Relevance Criteria and Respective Exclusion Criteria	206
17.2	MeSH and Textwords Used for the Search Algorithm	207
17.3	Methods of Data Collection in Quantitative Studies	208
17.4	Outcomes of CEC as Investigated in Quantitative Studies	209

Figure

16.1	A Three-step Approach to Ethical Deliberation and Decision-making in Nursing Homes	198

List of Contributors

Silviya Aleksandrova, MA in Medicine at the Medical University of Pleven, Bulgaria (1996), Masters in Bioethics at the Catholic University of Louvain, Belgium (2004), PhD in Public Health (2008). Currently Dr Aleksandrova is assistant professor in public health and medical ethics at the Medical University of Pleven and conducts lectures and seminars with medical students, nurses, midwives, laboratory technicians, rehabilitators and social workers. She is a member of the European Clinical Ethics Network, of the UNESCO Chair in Bioethics International Scientific Committee, of the World Association for Medical Law and of Bulgarian professional organisations. Dr Aleksandrova published the monograph, *Hospice Care – Management and Ethics*, for which she received the high scientific achievement award of the Bulgarian Association of Scientists (2004). She has also published, as a single author, the textbooks *Medical Ethics* (2007, in Bulgarian) and *Bioethics: Basic Course* (2008, in English). Dr Aleksandrova is co-author of the textbook, *Social Medicine* (2002, 2006, 2009) and the practical guideline, *Epilepsy – The Sacred Disease* (2005). She has published articles on medical ethics, hospice care and public health in national and international scientific journals.

Georg Bollig, MAS, MD, DEAA, is a physician and researcher. After completing medical studies at the universities of Cologne, Vienna and Seattle, he became a specialist in anaesthesiology, pain therapy and palliative care. He holds a diploma from the European Academy of Anaesthesiology (DEAA) and received a Master's degree in Palliative Care and Organisational Ethics from the University Klagenfurt/IFF Vienna. Dr Bollig has worked in various fields of science and has published books and articles on anaesthesiology, pain therapy, emergency medicine, nursing home medicine and palliative care. He is a member of a working group from the German Association for Palliative Medicine (DGP) on palliative medicine for non-cancer patients and board member on the Norwegian Palliative Association (NPA). Currently he works both clinically as a consultant physician with palliative and nursing home medicine in a specialised palliative care unit in the Bergen Red Cross Nursing Home in Bergen, Norway, and as a researcher on ethics and end-of-life decision-making in nursing homes in the Department of Surgical Sciences, Haukeland University Hospital, University of Bergen, Norway.

Ana Borovecki, BA, PhD, MD, is a researcher in medical ethics, a physician and philosopher by training. Following her studies in medicine, philosophy and comparative literature at the School of Medicine and the School of Philosophy at the University of Zagreb, Croatia, she received her European Masters degree in Bioethics from the Catholic University of Louvain, Belgium and her PhD degree from Radboud University Nijemgen, the Netherlands. She has completed clinical training in clinical pharmacology and is currently working as an assistant professor at the Andrija Stampar School of Public Health at the School of Medicine, University of Zagreb. Dr Borovecki has published on ethics committees, the physician-patient relationship and on patients' rights and the teaching of ethics and communication in medicine in the *Journal of Medical Ethics*, *Medicine Healthcare and Philosophy*, *British Medical Journal* and several other journals. In addition she has co-edited three books on research ethics, clinical ethics consultation and public health and ethics.

Nino Chikhladze, MD, PhD. After ten years working in internal medicine Dr Chikhladze joined the Faculty of Medicine at Tbilisi State University where, currently, she is an associate professor in the Department of Public Health. She has taught medical ethics to undergraduate students and bioethics and medical law to postgraduate students at Tbilisi State University. Dr Chikhladze is a member of the faculty research ethics committee and has been a visiting professor at the University of Paris-VIII in the Faculty of Sociology. Dr Chikhladze has published on the history of medical ethics, ethics and social justice in *Georgian Medical News*, *Annals of Biomedical Research and Education* and other journals.

Nunziata Comoretto, MD, PhD, is a researcher in bioethics and an assistant professor. Following her medical studies and her MD in Legal Medicine at the University of Udine, she received her PhD in Bioethics from the Catholic University of the Sacred Heart, Rome. She has been a visiting scholar at the Center for Clinical Bioethics, Georgetown University, Washington, DC and joined the Institute of Bioethics of the Catholic University of the Sacred Heart as a researcher in bioethics. She teaches bioethics and clinical ethics at the Catholic University School of Nursing, and is also a clinical ethics consultant at the Policlinico Gemelli University Hospital. Dr Comoretto has published on the ethics of end-of-life care issues and the physician-patient relationship in peer-reviewed journals including *Medicina e Morale* and *Child Development & Disabilities*. In addition she has contributed chapters to books on clinical ethics foundation and methods.

Uwe Fahr, MA, PhD, is a philosopher, ethics consultant and researcher in medical ethics. He studied philosophy, sociology and psychoanalysis at the Johann Wolfgang Goethe University in Frankfurt. He has written a doctoral thesis on 'death by request' and received his PhD from the same university. Dr Fahr worked for several years as an editor for the nursing magazine *Pflege aktuell*. After his PhD he studied adult education at the University of Kaiserslautern and from 2001 to 2004 he worked at the University of Basel Institute of Applied Ethics and Medical Ethics as a researcher and teacher of medical ethics. Since 2005 he has worked as an ethics consultant at the University Hospitals of the

University of Erlangen-Nurnberg. He is a researcher at the Institute for the History of Medicine and Medical Ethics and teaches philosophy at the Institute of Philosophy of the University of Erlangen-Nurnberg. His main research topics are ethics consultation in hospitals and clinics, philosophical consultation and the foundation of medical ethics. Dr Fahr has published several articles about ethics consultation, the ethics of end-of-life care issues and clinical ethics committees. In addition he has co-edited two books on end-of-life decision-making and clinical ethics committees (*Yearbook Ethics in Clinics 2008*). For more information, see www.uwefahr.de.

John-Stewart Gordon, MA in philosophy and history at Konstanz University (2001), PhD in philosophy at Göttingen University (2005). Currently, he is visiting Professor in philosophy at Queen's University in Kingston, Canada. He is member of the board of *Bioethics* and area-editor of *The Internet Encyclopedia of Philosophy* (IEP). He has published two books as a single author, *Aristoteles über Gerechtigkeit: Das V. Buch der Nikomachischen Ethik* (Alber Press 2007) and *Bemerkungen zum Begründungstrilemma* (Lit Press 2007). Furthermore, he is single editor of *Morality and Justice* (Rowman & Littlefield 2009) and co-editor of *Bioethics and Culture* (Cambridge University Press 2010). In addition, he has published peer-reviewed articles in journals/encyclopedia such as *Bioethics*, *Journal for Business, Economics, and Ethics* or *IEP*. He has taught philosophy and bioethics at Tübingen University, Ruhr-University Bochum, Duisburg-Essen University, and Queen's University Kingston.

Beate Herrmann, MA in philosophy and political science at Heidelberg University, PhD, currently works as a clinical ethics consultant at the Heidelberg University Hospital, Medical Department. Dr Herrmann was a doctoral fellow in the Research Training Group (Graduiertenkolleg) 'Bioethik' at the Interdepartmental Center for Ethics in the Sciences and Humanities (IZEW), University of Tübingen, and received her PhD in philosophy in 2007. She was a scientific assistant at the IZEW and at the Institute for Ethics and History of Medicine, University of Tübingen. She is the single author of the forthcoming book, *Der menschliche Körper zwischen Vermarktung und Unverfügbarkeit: Grundlinien einer Ethik der Selbstverfügung* (Karl Alber 2009), and co-editor of the book, *Wem gehört der menschliche Körper? Ethische, rechtliche und soziale Aspekte der Kommerzialisierung des menschlichen Körpers und seiner Teile* (together with Thomas Potthast and Uta Müller, Mentis 2009). She has published peer-reviewed articles in several journals and books on distributive justice in organ commercialisation, clinical ethics and ethics consultation. She has taught philosophy and bioethics at Leipzig University and Heidelberg University.

László Kovács, PhD in Bioethics from the University of Tübingen, European Masters in Bioethics, an MA in Applied Ethics from the Catholic University of Louvain and an MA in Catholic Theology from the Theological College of

Eger. Currently he is chair assistant at the Chair of Ethics in Life Sciences at the University of Tübingen and scientific assistant of the Institute for History and Ethics of Medicine. Dr Kovács' PhD thesis was on the ethics of human genetics and this field of research is still one of his major interests. Since then he has been a pastoral worker at the stroke unit and the Department of Radio-oncology at the University Hospital in Tübingen, where he has contributed to ethical deliberations on withholding and withdrawing life-sustaining treatment. Furthermore, he is working on the ethics of treatment limitation in neonatal intensive care. Dr Kovács is author and editor of several books on topics such as the influence of metaphors on human genetics (*Medizin – Macht – Metaphern*), on the nature of genetic information in different disciplines (*Was bedeutet 'Genetische Information'?*), and on the theoretical foundation and practical tasks of bioethics (*Wie funktioniert Bioethik?*).

Bert Molewijk MA, PhD, studied psychiatric nursing (RN) and theory of health care sciences (MA, specialising in ethics) at Maastricht University and completed his PhD on empirical ethics ('Patient autonomy and individualised evidence-based risk information') at the University of Leiden. After a post-doctoral post at the Ethics Institute in Utrecht ('Implicit Normativity of Technology'), in 2003 he returned to Maastricht University as Program Leader of Moral Deliberation and Clinical Ethics. Currently he is assistant professor at the Department of Medical Humanities of the EMGO Institute for Health and Care Research, VU Medical Center. He is co-founder and coordinator of the Dutch Network for Clinical Moral Deliberation and the European Clinical Ethics Network. He is chairing a Health Ethics Committee in elderly care and is a member of a National Review Board for scientific research in mental health care. He has published on clinical ethics, moral deliberation and empirical ethics.

Markus Rothhaar, PhD, is currently a researcher in medical ethics and bioethics at the University of Erlangen-Nuremberg. He studied philosophy, history and biology at the universities of Saarbrücken, Heidelberg and Tübingen and received his PhD in Philosophy at the University of Tübingen (2000). Following an appointment as parliamentary assistant at the European Parliament in Brussels, he worked as a *Koordinierender Referent* to the German Bundestag's *Enquete-Kommission Ethik und Recht der modernen Medizin* (Study Commission on Law and Ethics of Modern Medicine) until 2006. Dr Rothhaar has published on the philosophical aspects of biopolitics, the concept of human dignity, embryonic stem cell research and end-of-life issues. He has taught philosophy and bioethics at the universities of Tübingen, Berlin (Charité) and Potsdam.

Jan Schildmann, MA, MD, is a researcher in medical ethics and a physician. Following his medical studies at the Charité Medical School, Berlin, he received his MA in Medical Law and Ethics from King's College, University of London. After completing his clinical training in medical oncology and palliative care, he joined the Department of Medical Ethics and History of Medicine, Ruhr-University Bochum, where he leads a research group on the ethical and empirical aspect at the end-of-life. He has published more than 50 articles and co-edited three books on topics in clinical ethics, empirical ethics, research ethics and the teaching of ethics and communication in medicine. Dr Schildmann has received several awards for his work including prizes from the International Balint Society and the European Society for Philosophy in Healthcare and Medicine (ESPHM).

Margreet Stolper, MA, has studied psychomotoric therapy (BA) and health science (MA) at Maastricht University. For several years she combined working as a researcher at Maastricht University and as a psychomotoric therapist in a psychiatric hospital in the Netherlands. Ms Stolper is currently working towards her PhD on 'moral competence and the influence of moral case deliberation' at the Department of Medical Humanities of the EMGO Institute for Health and Care Research, VU University Medical Centre, Amsterdam. In addition to this, she manages Moral Deliberation projects in several health care institutions which include a course for health care professionals to become facilitators in Moral Case Deliberation. She has also published in this field.

Daniel Strech, MD, PhD, is a researcher in medical ethics and health policy analysis at Hannover Medical School (Germany). Following his studies in medicine and philosophy in Düsseldorf (Germany), Nantes and Montpellier (both France), he worked as a psychiatrist at the Charité Medical School, Berlin. He received a postdoctoral research stipend for the research training group in 'Bioethics' sponsored by the German Research Society (DFG) and afterwards joined the Department of Medical Ethics and History of Medicine, University of Tübingen, as a researcher in public health ethics. In 2008 he was appointed to a professorship in medical ethics at Hannover Medical School. Daniel Strech has published on the ethics of evidence-based medicine, the methodology of systematic reviews of empirical bioethics, bedside rationing and priority setting in the *Journal of Medical Ethics*, *BMC Medical Ethics*, *Health Policy*, *Clinical Epidemiology* and other journals.

Christiane Stüber, M.Soc.Sc., is a researcher in philosophy and medical ethics. She studied at the universities of Leipzig (Germany), Swansea (UK) and Cape Town (South Africa) and holds a Master of Social Science in Philosophy. Her non-academic work includes an internship at a local newspaper in Gotha, work for Transparency International (a Berlin-based NGO), freelance journalism for various magazines in Cape Town and political activism in her current hometown of Lichtenberg. Her academic work includes research assistance and teaching at the University of Leipzig. Currently she is finishing her PhD thesis on professional ethics in hospitals.

Sandra van der Dam, MA, was originally trained as a residential social worker. After her bachelor's degree, she continued studying sociology at the University of Amsterdam. She specialised in sociology of care and policy and received her MA in 2000. Her first job was as an innovation worker at the National Institute of Care and Welfare. From 2004 to 2006 she worked as a scientific researcher monitoring the population of marginalised hard-drug users in a town in the south of the Netherlands. In 2006 she commenced research towards a PhD at Maastricht University (CAPHRI institute), evaluating a moral case deliberation project in two institutions for care for the elderly.

Jochen Vollmann, MD, PhD, is professor and director of the Institute for Medical Ethics and History of Medicine and Chair of the Centre for Medical Ethics, Ruhr-University Bochum, Germany. He completed a clinical training in psychiatry and psychotherapy at the University Hospitals in Gießen, Munich and Freiburg, and wrote his habilitation thesis on ethical problems of informed consent in psychiatry at the Free University of Berlin. Professor Vollmann was visiting fellow at the Kennedy Institute of Ethics, Georgetown University, Washington, DC (1994/1995), visiting professor at the San Francisco School of Medicine, University of California and at the Mount Sinai School of Medicine, New York (1999/2000), at the Institute for the Medical Humanities UTMB, Texas (2001) and at the Centre for Values, Ethics and the Law in Medicine at the University of Sydney (2004, 2008, 2009 and 2010). He was honoured with the Prize for Brain Research in Geriatrics by the University of Witten/Herdecke in 1999 and with the Stehr-Boldt-Prize for Medical Ethics of the University of Zürich in 2001. Professor Vollmann's research interests include informed consent and capacity assessment, ethics and psychiatry, end-of-life decision-making, advance directives, medical professionalism, clinical ethics committees and clinical ethics consultation.

Guy Widdershoven, PhD, studied philosophy, mathematics and political science at the University of Amsterdam. The subject of his PhD was philosophy of action (1987). Until March 2009, he was Professor of Ethics of Health Care at the Faculty of Health, Medicine and Life Sciences of Maastricht University and scientific director of the School for Public Health and Primary Care (CAPHRI) of the same university. Currently he is Professor of Medical Philosophy and Ethics and Head of the Department of Medical Humanities of the EMGO Institute for Health and Care Research, VU Medical Center. He is also scientific director of the national research school CaRe (Netherlands School of Primary Care Research). He is president of the European Association of Centres for Medical Ethics (EACME). He has published on hermeneutic ethics and ethical issues in chronic care, especially in psychiatry and elderly care, and end-of-life decisions.

Chapter 1
Introduction

Jan Schildmann, John-Stewart Gordon and Jochen Vollmann

Clinical Ethics Consultation – A Brief Introduction

Clinical ethics consultation[1] (CEC) has been implemented in many hospitals and other clinical settings. A representative survey conducted in the United States indicates that CEC services are available in more than 80 per cent of hospitals.[2] In Europe the UK Clinical Ethics Network lists almost 100 CEC structures on their website (www.ethics-network.org.uk) and latest available data from Germany show that there are CEC structures in more than 300 health care institutions.[3] The steady rise of new diagnostic and treatment options and questions regarding an ethically justified application (and limitation) of these possibilities has been cited as one important trigger for this development. The diversity of values in modern society and its various communities as well as the legal and ethical emphasis of patients' autonomy are other important factors in this respect. Following the implementation of the first CEC structures in US hospitals in the 1970s two decades passed before CEC was implemented in health care institutions in Europe. Differences such as cultural characteristics, legal aspects and the funding of the health care systems not only between the USA and Europe but also between the European countries mean that CEC had to be adapted to the specific contexts. This is especially valid for the very recent development of the implementation of CEC structures in the so-called 'transitional countries' in Eastern Europe, of which there are a number of case studies presented in this book.

CEC – whether it takes place in the USA, in one of the European countries or in any other part in the world – is a multi- or even interdisciplinary enterprise. Medical ethicists, physicians, philosophers, nurses, social scientists, theologians and many more professions contribute to CEC. The diverse disciplinary background of

---

1   In this book the term 'clinical ethics consultation' (CEC) is widely used in the sense of services offered by individuals or groups which have been set up to address the ethical issues involved in clinical practice and/or in specific clinical cases. In the light of different theoretical and methodical approaches to CEC the authors of the different chapters provide definitions of specific concepts of CEC.

2   Fox, E., Myers, S. and Pearlman, R.A. 2007. Ethics consultation in United States: A national survey. *American Journal of Bioethics*, 7, 13–25.

3   Dörries, A. and Hespe-Jungesblut, K. 2007. Bundesweite Umfrage zur Implementierung Klinischer Ethikberatung in Krankenhäusern. *Ethik in der Medizin*, 19, 148–56.

those doing CEC may be one reason for the variety of CEC services we encounter in practice. Differences not only relate to organizational aspects but also to the theoretical and methodological premises of CEC and the aims of the different services. Until now there has been little detailed description of the above-mentioned aspects of CEC in the literature and even less systematic analysis of the similarities and differences of the existing CEC structures. The time-consuming practice of setting up and doing CEC may be one reason contributing to the relative scarcity of literature on CEC. In the multidisciplinary field of clinical ethics it seems also a task on its own to describe one's CEC activities in a way that is accessible and intelligible to others. This may be even more valid for CEC structures which seem to be somewhat intermediate between the realm of philosophical ethical reflection and the world of busy clinical practice.

Information about CEC with respect to its theoretical premises, methodology and the aims of CEC structures is important for a number of reasons. First of all such descriptions can facilitate the discussion of those involved in CEC and thereby stimulate our thinking about our own concepts and practice regarding CEC. Secondly, descriptions of the practice of CEC and its underlying foundations are the necessary basis for a comparative analysis. Such an analysis again may lead to the important issue of evaluation of CEC. Many CEC structures which have been implemented in recent years receive considerable funding for staff and for educational purposes and it is very likely that at some stage these services will be called upon to account for the impact they have on daily clinical practice.

The great number of CEC activities in many European countries during the last decade, the few existing possibilities to discuss the conceptual and practical aspects of this work, and the scarcity of literature, were our main reasons for organizing the conference, *Clinical Ethics Consultation: Theories & Methods – Implementation – Evaluation*, which took place from 11–15 February 2008 at the Institute for Medical Ethics and History of Medicine, Ruhr-University Bochum. The main aim of the project was to provide a forum for researchers from different European countries and disciplines who are involved in CEC and to facilitate discussion on the theories and methods underlying CEC as well as the exchange of ideas regarding the issues of implementation and evaluation of CEC. This book contains a selection of presented papers. All chapters have been peer-reviewed with a focus on interdisciplinary perspectives on theoretical and practical aspects of CEC.

Part I: Theories and Methods

The appropriateness of different theories and methods is at the centre of current interdisciplinary debate on CEC. In the first section of this book philosophers and medical ethicists provide their accounts of theoretical and methodical aspects of CEC. The envisaged roles, qualifications and tasks of the clinical ethicist indicate clearly that the questions and answers on theories and methods are also relevant for the practice of CEC.

The first chapter in this section, by John-Stewart Gordon, is concerned with a particular approach to ethical problem-solving called 'ethics as a method'. The first part contains an analysis of three ethical approaches – principle ethics, casuistry, and mid-level ethical theories – with regard to their strengths and weaknesses concerning CEC. The second part provides an account of a dynamic method of ethical decision-making, which generally appeals to Aristotle's concept of ethical reasoning and presents a brief framework on ethical decision-making in CEC. The third part deals with the appropriate role of an ethicist in the context of CEC.

Uwe Fahr and Markus Rothhaar argue in Chapter 3 that empirical research is important for the development of ethics consultation, but it also poses a challenge. In their chapter, they present different conceptual constellations based on different models of the relationship of ethics and empiricism in medicine and bioethics. By means of conceptual analysis they explore the significance of empirical social research for ethics consultation and its future development. The authors come to the conclusion that social science research and approaches which form the basis for norms must be separated. They must be converged within the context of inter- and trans-disciplinary research, in order to enable studies on clinical ethics consultation. In particular, the development of suitable evaluation instruments and their requirements presupposes the development of philosophical social science models of consultation.

In Chapter 4 Guy Widdershoven and Bert Molewijk claim that clinical ethics has been developed, not as a theoretical endeavour, but as a practical process of dealing with ethical issues in health care, engaging practitioners in adopting new views and vocabularies. However, according to them, it is possible, and necessary, to reflect on the foundations of clinical ethics from a philosophical point of view. Based on the conceptual foundation and their longstanding experience with CEC in practice they reflect on clinical ethics from a hermeneutic perspective. Philosophical hermeneutics stresses that ethics is a form of practical understanding. This ideally takes place in a dialogue in which experiences are exchanged and perspectives merged. Moral deliberation is presented as an example of clinical ethics as dialogue and presupposes that the participants have moral knowledge, and aims to develop this knowledge further. According to hermeneutic philosophy, the ethicist should act as a facilitator, fostering the process of moral deliberation. However, according to their view, hermeneutic philosophy does not provide a set of instructions for clinical ethics; it rather explains what the practice of clinical ethics is about. It helps ethicists and other participants in practice to focus on practical experiences as a source for moral inquiry.

Uwe Fahr argues in Chapter 5 that by using the theory of discourse ethics one can better understand what ethics consultation is about. Discourse ethics is able to explain the ethical foundation of ethics consultation. It shows that one has to differentiate between practical discourse and ethical theory. It may be that the arguments of discourse ethics, trying to make plausible that ethics has a cognitive basis, are untrue. Nonetheless, if one accepts the claim that ethics has a cognitive basis, one can, according to Fahr, use the difference between ethical discourse and ethical theory to claim that one does not need an ethical theory in order to structure one's method in case deliberation. Using the complex justification model of discourse ethics, Fahr's aim is to argue that the main point in establishing ethics consultation and practical discourses is to institutionalize them. If they are established according to the contra-factual presuppositions inherent in the communication community it becomes more probable that agreement about general norms can be reached.

László Kovács, in Chapter 6, makes the case that conscience is a fundamental point of reference even though it is little understood in clinical ethics. Using conscience in moral decision-making is the subject of much debate. Some ethicists suggest unifying medical services by establishing treatment standards, pushing the fallible conscience into the role of personal opinion. Others insist upon the beneficial role of conscience in moral decision-making. Such controversies focus mainly on the content of professional conscience and neglect the dynamics of it. In Kovács' view, CEC is challenging to the use of conscience by its very existence, but depending on the way of implementation and the basic attitudes of ethics consultants it can also improve physicians' professional commitment. CEC should not be seen as a 'better alternative' than conscience to solving moral discrepancies, but as a means to strengthen the medical professional's conscience for clinical decision-making.

Christiane Stüber, in Chapter 7, examines the professional ethics of health care professionals and their relationships of trust with patients in German hospitals through the lens of moral philosophy. After discussing two contemporary theories of trust, the concept of the 'decent agent' is introduced to explore to what extent medical staff can reasonably be expected to comply with professional norms. Stüber argues that CEC can provide an appropriate setting for medical staff to reflect upon the contents of traditional professional norms and their contemporary relevance for good patient care. CEC will have a positive effect on the maintenance of hospital patients' trust in medical staff, and will strengthen professionals' confidence in their own capacity to live up to professional norms.

Part II: Implementation

Setting up CEC structures in health care institutions is not an easy task. On this background the second section of this book not only provides insight in experiences of ethics consultants from five different countries but also touches on the important question of factors which positively support the process of implementation of CEC structures on different levels.

In Chapter 8, Jochen Vollmann provides an overview of factors relevant to the process of implementation of CEC. Based on his longstanding practical experience as a clinical ethics consultant and on his own research, Vollmann focuses on the interplay between the level of clinical case analysis and the organizational level. To make CEC a lively, accepted and valuable contribution, the so-called 'bottom-up' and 'top-down' approaches should both be present in institutions in which CEC structures are set up. In addition it is necessary to define the aims of CEC for each institution to make sure that the implemented CEC structure is sufficiently specific for the respective purpose and mission. As pointed out by the author the implementation of CEC is also affected by the political and societal contexts – an aspect which is illustrated by the development of CEC structures in the so-called 'transitional countries' of Eastern Europe.

Beate Herrmann, in Chapter 9, claims that in the context of clinical ethics consultation, the primary task of the consultant is often seen as moderating and mediating the communication between different agents in order to facilitate discussion and to achieve a consensus. Against this widely held position, it is argued that the term 'ethics consultancy' refers to the fact that it is not simply a question of those involved reaching a general consensus about further action or about one particular course of action. Rather, this consensus should be 'ethically qualified' in a more closely defined sense. Herrmann gives a definition of the ethical expertise of the moral philosopher in the context of clinical ethics consultation. Therefore, she outlines a typology of competences and presents their usefulness for the consultation processes. In this regard the relationship of ethical expertise and moral judgement will be examined in detail.

In her chapter, Nunziata Comoretto stresses that CEC is still a new phenomenon in Italy. However, the Institute of Bioethics of the Catholic University of the Sacred Heart is the oldest such institute within a medical school in Italy. It performs CECs at a tertiary-care academic centre in Rome. Since the beginning of the consulting activity, defining a decision-making approach for CEC has been one of the most important problems to solve. Their methodology can be labelled as a casuistic approach, supported by a person-centred ethical theory. According to their experience, ethical theory has a key role in solving clinical ethics problems, as a framework to provide the appropriate description of an action. Ethical theory is also a common starting point to explain the source of moral disagreement and almost always to resolve the dispute. The main hypothesis is that decision-making in clinical ethics could be better achieved not merely by applying a methodology, but by developing ethical virtues, especially the virtue of prudence. Further, ethical decision-making in the clinical context cannot be independent of a strong physician-patient relationship, which is based on mutual trust. In that perspective, ethical theory, according to her view, gives a strong foundation to ethical action, and the philosophy of medicine to relational ethics.

Nino Chikhladze and Nato Pitskhelauri present the first of two case studies on CEC implementation in the above-mentioned 'transitional countries'. They describe developments at the macro level, such as the establishment of the National Council on Bioethics, as well as legal developments related to the establishment of clinical ethics committees. Despite these changes with respect to the framework, the authors observe little implementation of CEC structures in Georgia. Lack of information about patients' rights and scarce opportunities for training in medical ethics for health care professionals are among a number of factors cited by the authors as possible explanations for the discrepancy between the perceived need for CEC and the limited number of activities in the field so far.

Ana Borovecki's is the second case study from Eastern Europe. Borovecki deals with the need for CEC as it has been described in the literature and the challenges with respect to the implementation of the respective structures. In her analysis Borovecki describes the loss of trust in medical practice, corruption and low educational levels of patients as characteristics of a society in which the implementation of CEC may be nothing more than 'a tool for alibi ethics or a tool for crisis management'. As a measure of preventive ethics the potential challenges to CEC are explored and possible strategies for the implementation of CEC are described.

Margreet Stolper et al. have developed a range of CEC initiatives in different clinical settings. In contrast to the situation of the 'transitional countries', the implementation of CEC has a rather long tradition in the Netherlands. However, the authors describe their concept of moral case deliberation. The method is characterized by a systematic reflection on moral questions generated in clinical practice in order to increase the moral competency of health care professionals. The training of moral case deliberation facilitators as well as aspects of organizational challenges are at the centre of this case study.

Daniel Strech argues that the topic of allocation of resources should have a place in the field of CEC. Following a summary of empirical research on the practice of bedside rationing in various countries the author suggests that CEC as a transparent and structured approach to resource allocation may support clinicians who are confronted with these tough decisions. Following this line of argument, Strech presents a framework 'clinical ethics consultation and bedside rationing' which focuses on the possible tasks for CEC in the context of scarce resources at the hospital level.

Part III: Evaluation of Clinical Ethics Consultation

In many cases the demand for implementation of CEC structures has been accompanied by a call for evaluation of these interventions. The final section of this book presents original work and a systematic review on evaluation of CEC. The methodical challenges related to the evaluation of an ethical intervention and possible approaches to handle normative and empirical challenges form part of all contributions in this section.

Silviya Aleksandrova examines the evaluation of physicians' experiences with CEC structures. In her report of a cross-sectional survey conducted in four hospitals in Bulgaria, Aleksandrova presents findings on the current practice of physicians' decision-making with respect to ethical challenges. In addition to this valuable information, which may serve as a baseline for the potential contribution of CEC with respect to decision-making in clinical practice, the study gives a picture of physicians' expectations regarding the competences of clinical ethics consultants.

Georg Bollig examines the ethical challenges in nursing homes as well as the strategies used to deal with these issues in Norway. In general, eliciting information about the practice in a particular field is a prerequisite when planning an evaluation study. This is particularly true if the field is rather new as is the case for CEC in nursing homes. Based on his research, Bollig distinguishes 'everyday ethical issues' (e.g., eliciting informed consent) and 'big ethical issues' such as end-of-life decisions. The author suggests the implementation of 'ethics peer groups' as well as external ethics consultation to facilitate minor and major ethical conflicts in nursing homes.

Jan Schildmann and Jochen Vollman provide an overview on methodological aspects of the evaluation of CEC. The authors point out that many evaluation studies provide little information on common quality criteria of empirical research such as validity or reliability of the measurement instruments used to determine the outcomes of CEC. In addition the chapter explores conceptual difficulties with respect to the use of outcome criteria in quantitative studies. These studies are designed to provide generalizable data on the impact of CEC, an intervention that deals with highly individual and context-sensitive aspects of clinical practice. The analysis of current challenges on evaluation of CEC refers back to underlying concepts and methods of CEC as they are discussed in the first chapter of this book.

We hope that this book will support the work of representatives from different health care professions as well as other disciplines who contribute to the work of clinical ethics committees or other forms of CEC services. In addition, the combination of conceptual and empirical work in this book should be relevant to current research on theoretical and methodological aspects of CEC. We are very thankful to all the authors for their chapters and their willingness to contribute to this volume. We also thank the German Federal Ministry of Education and Research for funding this project (FK 01 GP 0681), without which this book would not exist.

PART I
Theories and Methods

This section on theories and methods deals with different possible approaches in CEC and is therefore of great importance with regard to philosophical reasoning. The main question is how we should solve complex cases in clinical ethics, that is, which ethical theory, approach or method is most suitable in order to make an empirically based, well-informed ethical decision. The second major question is whether clinical ethicists should be ethicists by education (e.g., Gordon, Comoretto) or rather, well-trained facilitators with some ethical knowledge (e.g., Widdershoven and Molewijk, Stolper et al.). The chapters in this section address both vital questions by presenting interesting and differing responses. The combination of theories and methods, implementation and evaluation of CEC in this volume shows the close connection between philosophical reasoning and empirical findings in medicine. Clinical ethics, however, can be criticised for not appealing to theories and methods appropriately, which is a defect that arises when people evaluate empirical findings in a rather loose way that reveals their lack of profound ethical knowledge. On the other hand, philosophers – in particular ethicists – show hardly any interest in the problems of health care professionals in the clinical context. This is mainly due to the fact that many ethicists think that empirical research in ethics leads more or less into the trap of the naturalistic fallacy. This particular issue is addressed in the volume. The volume offers a forum for theorists and practitioners alike who try to make use of empirical data and research for ethical analyses in CEC.

Chapter 2
Ethics as a Method?

John-Stewart Gordon

Introduction

One of the most important theoretical issues with regard to clinical ethics consultation (CEC) is the vital question of how to justify particular decisions in the context of ethical counselling in medicine. This chapter has three parts. First, I briefly examine three types of ethical approaches – principle ethics, casuistry, and mid-level ethical theories – with regard to their contribution for the theoretical foundation and performance of CEC. Secondly, I present a first outline of a more dynamic account for ethical decision-making in CEC. Thirdly, I discuss the role of the ethicist in CEC.

The following considerations are based on the general assumption that the complexity of human life is so great that one rigid ethical theory is simply unable to cover all aspects of the moral life for ethical decision-making. That is, even illuminating (classical) ethical theories cannot claim to be the only source of moral deliberation. It is apparent, by applying these approaches, that they are usually more plausible if applied to some limited range of morality rather than to all of it. One possible way to avoid this is to adopt a dynamic ethical method of reasoning. In the end, one should be able to use this dynamic method in order to determine and evaluate the relevant aspects of a particular case and to combine them in a sound, coherent and justified way for ethical decision-making in CEC.

Evaluation of Three Types of Ethical Theories

Principle Ethics and CEC

Breaking bad news at the bedside, physician-assisted suicide or cases where one person can save the lives of many (e.g., the numbers debate)[1] are, in general,

---

1 The classic example is the case in which one terminally ill person is still alive, although she will die soon, but there are three other people who will die prior to the death of the terminally ill person unless they receive her donor organs. They could be saved at the expense of the terminally ill person. Should the terminally ill person be forced to donate her organs and hence predecease the others? Is this ethically justified, or has the terminally ill person even a moral duty to donate her organs?

complex cases where people are faced with difficult problems. These problems cannot be completely resolved by the rough application of a deductive Kantian or utilitarian model of principle ethics.

Take the following well-known example of a person who wants to commit suicide as paradigmatic in the Kantian assessment. Suppose, Kant says, a man is so tired of his unhappy life that he wants to commit suicide (e.g., this may be due to his ill-health). Before doing so, he should ask himself whether such an action goes against his duty to his own self. Can he consistently will to make a universal rule out of the maxim: 'Whenever life gets difficult, and there seems more of a possibility of pain than pleasure, one should commit suicide'? According to Kant, the man cannot universalize his maxim because:

> A system of nature by whose law the very same feeling whose function is to stimulate the furtherance of life should actually destroy life would contradict itself and consequently could not subsist as a system of nature. (Kant 1964: 89)

To act inconsistently is, for Kant, to act irrationally, and to act irrationally with respect to a moral matter is to act immorally.

However, it seems obvious, at least in the above-mentioned case, that this strict line of argumentation is inappropriate for CEC. The rough application of one moral principle in order to cope with different and complex cases may be good in theory but somewhat awkward in practice. Additionally, Kant rejects the idea of paying any attention to anthropology (in the broad sense of the term) and to appreciate the relevant circumstances of cases (see Kant's *Groundwork*, Preface). It is also difficult to apply the categorical imperative to particular cases, especially with regard to most clinical cases, since Kant does not provide the reader with clear guidelines of how to do so. However, Kant's ethics is especially strong when applying the second formula of the categorical imperative[2] (the formula of humanity as an end in itself) in one particular type of medical case where the principles of autonomy, non-maleficence and justice are sacrificed on behalf of the utilitarian ideal of the greatest good for the greatest number (e.g., the Tuskegee Study, human radiation experiments). Thus, the second formula is good for protecting the patients' rights against deficient lines of argumentation by being a reasonable shield against all kinds of forms of exploitation of human beings.

Although utilitarian ethical approaches pay more attention to anthropological data and appreciate the circumstances of each particular case more than do Kantian-oriented approaches (see, for instance, Mill 1998), they fall short of, at least, three main aspects: First, nearly all utilitarian approaches are faced, more or less, with the problem of the protection of minorities or minority rights. Secondly, the narrow limitation to the consequences of particular acts seems somewhat inappropriate

---

2 'Act in such a way that you always treat humanity, whether in your own person or in the person of any other, never simply as a means, but always at the same time as an end'. (Kant 1964: 66–7).

given the fact that the person's motives for acting are not considered, at all. And thirdly, all consequences are oriented towards the greatest good for the greatest number, which may seem right for most cases but holds many dangers for the rest.

It seems that the advantages of Kant's theory compensate for the disadvantages of utilitarian approaches and vice versa. There is a gap between both ethical theories which rests on two different ways of reasoning: deontological and consequential reasoning. The following typical aspects of principle ethics are important features for ethical decision-making in CEC:

1. Prohibition of exploitation of human beings.
2. The criteria for acting should be universalizable.
3. The concept of utility should be considered (first, with regard to the patient, and second, with regard to other people); and
4. The patient's motives and the consequences of actions should be reviewed and evaluated.

Casuistry and CEC

Principle ethics is a top-down model of ethical decision-making while casuistry is a bottom-up model of ethical reasoning. Casuists such as Jonsen and Toulmin (1990) try to examine the whole ethical range of the particular case and, thus, casuistry is considered as very case-sensitive. In general, they do not rest their ethical reasoning on abstract universal norms or general rules but on the particular circumstances of each case. Casuists claim that the proposed action-guiding force of universal principles, etc., is misleading since it pretends a kind of certainty which is lacking. Instead, one should detect paradigmatic cases and analogies in order to have a good basis for ethical decision-making. However, it seems somewhat open how one should determine what a paradigmatic case really is; one may object that the process of determining paradigmatic cases presupposes a kind of general reasoning to detect them. Another main objection is that casuistry is almost a matter of cultural- and community-bound values and expectations and, hence, is relative in nature. This may cause harm for some people if, in general, no one acknowledges some universal moral principles that protect those people (e.g., human rights).

Faced with the above-mentioned case of a person who wants to commit suicide because of his ill-health, casuists first try to detect other cases with the same or nearly the same background and, secondly, they examine whether the patient's wish is in accord with the cultural values of the community. Thirdly, they analyse further particulars, such as the relationship between the person and his family and try to integrate the results in their ethical reasoning. In the end, they weigh the relevant reasons for and against the patient's wish to commit suicide and provide a conclusion. This way of ethical reasoning is case-sensitive and community-bound so that casuists in other communities may decide differently with regard to similar cases.

People who make ethical decisions in CEC usually want to present well-justified reasons for their decisions. 'Well-justified' in this context means that other people can universally agree with these reasons. They have the strong feeling that it is not a matter of contingent facts, such as the dependency on a particular community, but, rather, there are universal claims, which make important ethical decisions accessible to all people with regard to the same situation. CEC needs more action-guiding force than casuistry can offer. There are some important typical aspects of casuistic reasoning, which should be part of CEC: (1) case-sensitivity, (2) detecting and examination of paradigmatic cases and analogies, and (3) partial integration of cultural- and community-bound values and expectations (including the close examination of the values of the patient and the family).

Principlism and CEC

Beauchamp and Childress, who are the founders of mid-level principles in biomedical ethics, developed an ethical framework in order to solve clinical problems (Beauchamp and Childress 2001). Their conception had been used worldwide as a guide for ethical decision-making by physicians and ethicists alike and it seems obvious that their common morality approach is especially valuable with regard to CEC.

The common morality is the starting point and the constraining framework of principlism. It 'contains moral norms that bind all persons in all places; no norms are more basic in the moral life' (Beauchamp and Childress 2001: 3). These moral norms are universal prima facie principles such as the principles of autonomy, non-maleficence, beneficence and justice. They rest on the shared considered judgements of morally serious persons (i.e., the coherence model of justification). The particular moralities contain non-universal moral norms, which rest on, for example, cultural, religious or institutional sources. These norms are concrete and rich in substance, unlike the universal principles, which are abstract and content-thin. The methods of specification[3] and balancing[4] are the main tools to enrich the abstract and content-thin universal principles with empirical data that stem

---

3 Beauchamp and Childress define 'specification' as 'a process of reducing the indeterminateness of abstract norms and providing them with action-guiding content' (2001: 16).

4 According to Beauchamp and Childress, the method of balancing is 'especially important for reaching judgments in individual cases' and 'consists of deliberation and judgments about the relative weight and strength of moral norms' (2001: 18). This means that balancing has something to do with providing good reasons for justified norms. Beauchamp and Childress mention six conditions against the objection that the method of balancing is too intuitive and open-ended:

1. The overriding norm is more reasonable
2. The infringement's justifying objective must be achievable
3. The infringement is morally preferable
4. The infringement must be in accord with the primary goal of action
5. Minimization of the infringement's possible negative effects, and
6. Impartiality in action (Beauchamp and Childress 2001: 19–20).

from the particular moralities. That is, people who are part of different particular moralities may specify and balance the universal moral principles differently by virtue of the different empirical data and sources. The most developed particular morality is closest to common morality.

At first sight, principlism seems to be a good candidate for CEC since it combines all, or at least most, advantages of the above-mentioned top-down and bottom-up models. However, at second glance, it remains somewhat unclear how one should make ethical decisions by using the approach of Beauchamp and Childress. Gert and Clouser may be right by claiming that the mid-level principles are merely 'checkpoints' and are still too abstract to be a useful guide in ethical decision-making (Gert and Clouser 1990). Physicians and other people using their approach might be overstrained by applying principlism to particular clinical cases because the framework lacks an additional organizing principle, which would be of great help for an easy application of the approach. In addition, a sound model of CEC should not be limited to one culture but open for different cross-cultural settings. It seems that the four-principle approach is not that sensitive, although Beauchamp and Childress stress that their approach is open for different particular moralities. The reason is, for example, that their principle of autonomy contains the conception of individual informed consent. In different cultural settings the principle of autonomy is not specified by the norm of individual informed consent but by the norm of family or community informed consent (this is typical of societies such as those of China, Japan, and sub-Saharan African countries). Beauchamp and Childress seem to suggest in their writings that only the specified norm of individual informed consent is appropriate for ethical decision-making, especially in clinical cases.

The following typical aspects of principlism are important features for ethical decision-making in CEC: (1) The concept of universal prima facie mid-level principles, (2) the methods of specification and balancing; and (3) the idea of common morality and particular moralities.

Ethics as a Method

Preliminary Remarks

Aristotle is certainly right in claiming that it is impossible to be as precise in ethical matters as in fields such as mathematics (see Aristotle EN I). This idea is based on the fact that the complexity of moral life is so substantive that one is unable to provide precise and simple answers to difficult ethical issues. A sound ethical theory should fulfil two main conditions: first, a sound logical justification, and secondly, a reasonable applicability of the proposed theory in practical matters. Most approaches make one foundational feature (e.g., utility, duty) or a class of features in the case of principlism (autonomy, non-maleficence, beneficence, justice) 'absolute', and apply a concept that is normally plausible within a limited range of morality to morality at large, thereby undermining the plausibility of the particular ethical theory. Consider the following example. From a utilitarian standpoint 'breaking bad news' can be either ethically justified or not, dependent on the consequences of the particular action. From the Kantian approach, instead, one is always obligated to tell the truth no matter what the consequences are (see Kant's famous writing, 'On a supposed right to tell lies from benevolent motives'). The rough application of the deductive utilitarian and Kantian ethics leads in many cases to counterintuitive conclusions. The conception of 'ethics as a method' pays more attention to the circumstances of the particular case, which is especially valuable for CEC by being a dynamic way of ethical reasoning and decision-making. Ethical decisions of rational people may, of course, vary within certain limits, which rest on different cultures or religions – but not everything is ethically justified (see the chapter by Comoretto in this volume).

How to Make Sound Ethical Decisions in CEC

Case description   One of the most important aspects with regard to a sound ethical decision is the lack of information about the particular case. Thus, one has to ensure that all useful information should be provided for ethical decision-making. A keen gathering of information by interrogating the patient and the family is required. To do this, a list of key questions may help the interrogator to determine the particular conditions of each case, such as: who, where, what, when, why, how.

What is technically possible?   The expertise of the physician is necessary to answer this vital question before one is able to examine the moral problems of the particular case. The physician has to take all possible treatments into account and he or she has to inform the patient and the family about the pros and cons, irrespective of his or her normative judgement on what is medically indicated (i.e., there is no medical pre-selection of certain particular 'futile' treatments at this stage). Actually, this is the foundation of all decisions. All ethical decision-making is bound by the empirical findings of the particular case.

Determination and evaluation of moral problems   Normally, the physician and his or her medical staff are able to determine and evaluate moral problems in simple cases by virtue of their practical experiences and additional knowledge in medical ethics. The determination and evaluation of moral problems in all other cases should be accompanied by either a medical professional with special and extended knowledge in medical ethics or a professional (medical) ethicist (see below). To determine and to evaluate all morally problematic aspects of a particular and complex case is a difficult task, which should (normally) be done by a person who is trained to do so. The following simplified and somewhat idealized procedure is recommended for CEC:

1. The physician and ethicist should talk to the patient (gathering and clarifying information).
2. The physician and ethicist should talk to the family and other persons involved (gathering and clarifying information).
3. The physician/medical staff and ethicist should discuss the particular case in order to determine and to evaluate the case along ethical aspects (ethical reasoning$_1$).
4. The physician and ethicist should talk to the patient and the family (ethical reasoning$_2$).
5. The patient's and family's process of decision-making.
6. The final decision.

The third and fourth steps are decisive for CEC because here is the place where the ethical discourse comes to the fore. The ethicist's task is to offer a possible and sound solution to moral problems in a particular case and to discuss the ideas with the physician and medical staff. It is obvious that a simple application of a rigid ethical theory is inappropriate for CEC; a dynamic way of ethical reasoning, which ensures flexibility, should be adopted with regard to CEC in order to guarantee a sound process of ethical decision-making.

The dynamic way of ethical reasoning With regard to difficult moral cases, the ethicist has to determine which typical aspects of the above-mentioned important features of principle ethics, casuistry and principlism should be considered for the evaluation of the particular case and ethical decision-making in CEC:

- The prohibition of exploitation of human beings.
- The criteria for acting should be universalizable.
- The concept of utility should be considered.
- The patient's motives and the consequences of actions concerning the particular case should be reviewed and evaluated.
- Case-sensitivity is required.
- Detecting and examination of paradigmatic cases and analogies.
- The part-integration of cultural- and community-bound values and expectations (including the close examination of the values of the patient and the family).
- The idea of universal prima facie mid-level principles.
- The methods of specification and balancing.
- The idea of common morality and particular moralities.

This type of ethical reasoning rests on the concept of prudence (see also Aristotle EN VI). One has to consider the special circumstances of the particular case and to combine them with an overall concept of human well-being in order to provide a sound CEC. It is unreasonable to think that one is able to solve every moral issue by just one rigid ethical theory. The ethicist has to be cautious to ensure a sound, rational and coherent process of ethical decision-making in association with the physician and the patient in order to provide an applicable way of moral problem-solving. The physician, in turn, has to be kind and responsive in his or her social interaction with patients, especially during the CEC (i.e., having good communication skills). Harsh and awkward words of the physician and medical staff, uttered by mistake, or, even worse, by having in a rude way which would be a moral vice can do more harm to the patient than one may assume.

The Role of the Ethicist in CEC

Years ago most physicians erroneously believed that they were able to solve any moral problem with regard to clinical cases. This overambitious self-image was mainly based on paternalistic reasoning, which had lasted hundreds of years and shaped their self-conception as a god-like healer. Times have changed and nowadays many physicians accept the fact that a lot of clinical cases are more complex and more difficult than they can handle; they have started to recognize that they are (partly) unable to deal with these more complex cases in a reasonable way. Many physicians are now open to receiving help from outside their own medical profession, which is a great success for the patients.

This professional help was provided by ethicists who knew how to determine and to analyse ethical cases. A new era had begun – the medical ethicist was born. However, setting the history of the medical ethicist aside, one main point remains of vital importance, which concerns the role and the professional education of the person who is doing CEC (see also the chapters by Herrmann, and Stolper et al. in this volume). It is certainly right that most clinical cases can be solved by physicians and other health care personnel, but more complex cases call for persons with additional ethical knowledge, for example, physicians with additional expertise in medical ethics. However, some clinical cases remain that are most complex and very difficult to handle. These are the so-called hard cases. In order to cope with such cases, one certainly needs professional ethical help from outside the medical profession, unless the physician himself has a broad and deep knowledge of medical ethics, in order to ensure that the particular case can be solved appropriately.

It is quite controversial whether the medical ethicist should have a broad and deep knowledge in medical ethics and, additionally, in the main field of ethics and ethical theory *or* whether the medical ethicist should have just sufficient knowledge in medical ethics, etc. The former type of medical ethicist probably needs a professional education in ethics and medical ethics, that is, he or she has studied at university, while the latter type of a medical ethicist will be able to attend a crash course in medical ethics or to attend some weekend courses in order to acquire his or her knowledge. In most cases, the latter type will do good work, but in so-called hard cases – against the background of the application of the proposed dynamic model of ethical reasoning – one should certainly trust only a full professional in medical ethics, who is able to determine all the moral problems of the particular case and to analyse thoroughly the complex ethical issues which may arise from the case in question.[5]

Likewise, if one goes to the general practitioner, who has, in general, sufficient knowledge and helps one in most cases, one should not expect him or her to conduct difficult surgery. Consider another example. If one wants to fly across the Atlantic, then under normal circumstances one should not engage an inexperienced hobby pilot who knows how to fly small planes but not large aircraft. In short, take the golden midway and find people who are really able to help the patient in providing ethical assistance on different levels with regard to the magnitude of the particular case.

Conclusions

The process of ethical reasoning in CEC is dialectical and interactive. Different reasons, views and ethical stances may clash. The difficult task is to determine all ethical conflicts, to evaluate them and to provide feasible solutions for the particular case. This can be achieved by a dynamic and flexible method that responds adequately to the moral requirements of complex clinical cases in CEC. The proposed method is one possible way to do so.

Acknowledgements

I am grateful to the participants of the international conference on clinical ethics consultation for their comments to my presentation and, in particular, with regard

---

5 Another recent model with regard to teaching ethics and the role of the ethicist in CEC was developed by Molewijk and colleagues (see Molewijk et al. 2008). Their model of 'moral case deliberation' is a contextual approach to CEC, which is based on pragmatic-hermeneutical and dialogical ethics. Here, the ethicist 'functions as a non-directive facilitator as opposed to an expert and concentrates on the quality of the deliberation process and the meaningfulness of the moral issues' (Molewijk et al. 2008: 120). The participants, i.e., the health care professionals of 'teaching ethics in the clinic', should be equipped with, first, some ethical knowledge, secondly, the capabilities to create a moral dialogue with colleagues, and thirdly, communications skills, reasoning skills, and virtues. Molewijk et al. do not discuss the role of the ethicist in moral case deliberation in detail, although they see the problem at stake by posing some interesting questions at the end of their article: 'Should ethicists persist in a procedural moderator role or should there be room for ethicists to bring in their moral judgements when situations are considered morally wrong? (...) Should ethicists justify or criticise substantial decisions of the healthcare professionals? Should they ultimately leave the hospital and let the healthcare professionals do their own moral case deliberation?' (Molewijk et al. 2008: 123). However, their approach of moral case deliberation and the questions reveal that the role of the ethicist as a facilitator is rather minor in comparison to my proposed account with regard to the role of ethicists in CEC.

to the helpful comments of two reviewers. Furthermore, I am grateful to the participants of the International Bioethics Retreat meeting in Paris with regard to their comments to a revised version of my presentation. I am also very grateful to the 'Heinrich und Alma Vogelsang-Stiftung' for funding my travel and expenses to Paris.

References

Aristotle, EN I. Artistotle. 1995. Nicomachean Ethics, in *The Complete Works of Aristotle*, edited by J. Barnes. Volume II, 5th edition. Princeton, NJ: Princeton University Press.

Beauchamp, T. and Childress, J. 2001. *Principles of Biomedical Ethics*. 5th edition. Oxford: Oxford University Press.

Gert, B. and Clouser, K. 1990. A critique of principlism. *Journal of Medicine and Philosophy*, 15(2), 219–36.

Jonsen, A. and Toulmin, S. 1990. *The Abuse of Casuistry: A History of Moral Reasoning*. 2nd edition. Berkeley, CA: University of California Press.

Kant, I. 1889. *Critique of Practical Reason and Other Works on the Theory of Ethics* (trans. by T. Abbott). 4th edition. London: Kongmans, Green and Co.

Kant, I. 1964. *Groundwork of the Metaphysic of Morals* (trans. by H. Paton). New York: Harper Perennial.

Mill, J.S. 1998. *Utilitarianism*, edited by G. Sher. 2nd edition. Oxford: Oxford University Press.

Molewijk, A.C., Abma, T., Stolper, M. and Widdershoven, G.A.M. 2008. Teaching ethics in the clinic: The theory and practice of moral case deliberation. *Journal of Medical Ethics*, 34, 120–24.

Chapter 3
Ethics – Empiricism – Consultation: Defining a Complex Relationship

Uwe Fahr and Markus Rothhaar

Introduction

Starting about ten to 15 years ago, something like an 'empirical turn' could be observed in medical ethics and bioethics (cf. Borry et al. 2005).[1] Numerous social-science-oriented studies on medical-ethics issues or on the development of ethics consultation are testimony to this. Many of these studies offer interesting and relevant information: They report, e.g., on the incidence of active euthanasia in response to patients' explicit demands (cf., e.g., Bosshard et al. 2005, Bosshard 2006) or present the results of evaluation studies of ethics consultations (cf. Schildmann and Vollmann in this volume). Inter- and transdisciplinary approaches are essential for this kind of research, as the contributions in this volume show. Altogether, medical ethics and bioethics only seem meaningful in concert with philosophers, social scientists, theologians, physicians, biologists and other scientific disciplines.

However, it must be admitted that the necessary reflection on methods does not appear to be developing with the same momentum as empirical research itself (for a discussion, compare also Düwell 2005 and van den Daele 2008) This becomes even more problematic because the lack of reflection on the relationship of social-science-oriented research and normative discussions can lead to lack of clarity in the status of empirical statements within the context of medical-ethical research.

The dividing line here is whether or not empirical research in its emphatic sense can be considered relevant to the actual normative question. For even if one argues that empirical surveys in themselves cannot contribute anything to answering normative questions, one can nevertheless deem such surveys important, e.g., for identifying ethical problems in day-to-day clinical work and/or

---

[1] It is not unlikely that the 'empirical turn' ultimately has sociological reasons, in so far as for medical ethicists with an academic background in medicine the methodology of the empirical social sciences often seems more easily accessible than philosophical methodology in the narrower sense. In addition it does not seem to be an uncommon opinion that empirical studies in medical ethics have greater chances of being allocated research funds due to the fact that they deliver supposedly tangible results.

for describing them more precisely. Theories that go beyond this are confronted with the complex problem of establishing a relationship of empirical and normative theory formation that evades the widespread criticism of drawing an actually or supposedly unacceptable conclusion from description to normativity.

This balancing act between socio-scientific, ethical and normative formation of theory becomes even more critical when the issue is research on clinical ethics consultation. In this case, we must not only reflect on the relationship of empirical research and the formation of medical-ethical theory. Rather, both areas in this case must be put into relation to yet another consultation theory that must be based on social science research. Clinical ethics consultation is rooted both in consultation theory as well as in the setting where it provides consultation: ethics within the framework of a hospital.

With this as background, in subsequent paragraphs we shall point out several ambiguities in the term 'empiricism'. Next, we intend to outline what we mean by normativity and descriptivity from our point of view – we shall do this in the awareness that already this step would require a considerable argumentative effort that would transcend the scope of this contribution. On this basis we shall sketch different ethical theories which conceptualize the relationship of normativity and descriptivity in the context which interests us here. In a further section we shall comment on the significance of these theories for grasping more precisely what ethics consultation is about. Finally, we shall outline the areas in which empirical research seems to be indispensable for ethics consultation.

Ambiguities in the Term 'Empiricism'

Before discussing the individual concepts in more detail, it is first necessary to clarify which forms of empiricism we mean in this context.

Originally the term 'empirics' simply meant experience, in particular sensory perception, i.e., experience we make with our senses. However, from the late sixteenth century on, with the advent of early modern science, the concept took on a narrower meaning. Empiricism in this context no longer simply meant sensory perception but rather a specific method: the systematic knowledge of nature acquired by means of sensory data gained through experiments posing specific questions. Science, which was evolving with this concept of experience, pushed into the background the emphatic concepts of experience that still played a major role in Hegel's *Phenomenology of Spirit*. Experiences such as readers perhaps made upon reading *Critique of Pure Reason* or upon reading Marcel Proust were increasingly marginalized and relegated to the private sphere as non-committal aesthetic pursuits.

The development of psychology, sociology and the critical social sciences in the nineteenth century was increasingly accompanied by an establishment of methodical and regimented experience also in these areas of knowledge. It is therefore no accident that medical ethics found its social science methodology primarily in psychology and sociology. This repertoire of research methods evolving from social theory and sociology is oriented on scientific models of research (induction), but at the same time it differs from these due to their research subject. Their research field is not nature, but the social world. This fundamentally different research subject has now justifiably become the occasion for extensive scientific-theoretical fundamental controversies, which we cannot go into further now (cf. Seiffert 1996, Schnell et al. 2005). Up to this day, at least in the social sciences, the analytical-inductive research method has not been able to claim to be the sole research method. Along with it there are other research methods such as the phenomenological research method or the hermeneutical research method which have yielded results in 'qualitative' social research. What is central to the analytical-inductive research method is that it does distinguish between unobservable 'constructs' on the one hand and 'operational definitions', which translate those constructs into an observation language.

Despite these controversies, there is certainly a broad consensus to be found when one ascertains: the activity of empirical social studies consists mainly in the collection and interpretation of data about social facts – no matter how problematic the relationship of collecting and interpreting may be here and how difficult it may be to determine what 'social facts' actually are in the ontological and epistemic sense. These 'social facts' must be determined in planning every single research project: they can range from the constructs of family structures, prejudices, socialization processes to company culture, from organization structure, orientation patterns of subcultures to subsystems of society.

It is only in more recent times that the emphatic experience concept – once refuted – is becoming more accessible again within the context of so-called qualitative research. Contrary to the criticism of the traditional experience concept – that it merely reflects individual idiosyncrasies – this qualitative research itself seeks methodical regulation, allowing a validation of hypotheses and assertions.

The contributions in this anthology reflect the range of the concept of empiricism, by using quite different forms of experience for the development of ethics consultation. For example, Ana Borovecki relates in her contribution what experiences ethics consultants in Croatia make in establishing ethics consultation. She cites studies on the attitudes of Croatian physicians and discusses the significance of ethical reflection for ethics consultation, based on studies of the French philosopher Boite (Chapter 12). Stolper et al. demonstrate the systematization of experience with certain models of ethics consultation using the example of a model of moral case deliberation in Dutch health care organizations (Chapter 13). Especially the philosophical justification attempts of the moral-philosophical principles of ethics consultation refer to experience in the emphatic sense. Hence, Widdershoven and Molewijk, for instance, refer in their contribution to the concept of Gadamer's 'fusion of horizons' and from that attempt to derive that practical experiences are a source for moral inquiry (Chapter 4). In his contribution, Fahr also refers to the thesis formulated in discourse ethics that moral statements make a claim to truth but can only realize this claim in a way limited in place and time in the community of those conducting the moral argument: an experience which, according to Fahr, would substantially change the basic principle of ethics consultation and lead to caution towards self-assured moral assertions (Chapter 5).

With which topics does empirical medical ethics and bioethics research primarily concern itself? To analyse this systematically, we would suggest distinguishing between several large groups of study topics:

1. Data collection on *practices, methods and decision-making processes* at the location, i.e., in the hospital, in the nursing home, in the entire health care system, etc.
2. The *results and consequences* of methods, regulations and decisions.
3. Data collection of *ethically relevant attitudes, opinions, behaviours, wishes, estimations* of the involved players, those affected etc. and/or including transformation processes of ethically relevant attitudes.
4. The *evaluations of measures* to change practices, decisions, attitudes, etc. (e.g., of ethics consultation).

Here 'mixed forms' are not only conceivable, they are generally the rule. One obvious question, not seldom posed, is how the attitudes of the consultation participants influence the actual decision-making processes.

Besides these research fields of 'empirical ethics' in the narrower sense, there are other fields and approaches of social research which concern themselves with ethics and also often include empirical research. What we mean here is a type of social research that studies processes of genesis, of effecting and actually implementing norms in social systems (such as the social psychology of Mead or the developmental psychology of Kohlberg). Thus, this type of social research concerns itself with the genesis and facticity of moral conceptions. This form of empirical social research goes beyond the previously described research, because it is not merely satisfied with just 'ensuring individual details' (Seiffert 1996: 232). Rather, it seeks to 'inductively derive general statements from facts that have been empirically established' (Seiffert 1996: 232).

In summary, we can say that empirical research can characterize analytical-inductive methods as well as phenomenological, hermeneutic or other research based on 'qualitative' methods. It can be satisfied with simply ascertaining individual facts or it can seek to formulate general theories. Besides these forms of empirical science, there are finally the emphatic concepts of 'experience' as they have time and again distinguished themselves in philosophy in contrast to the regulating research methods of social science as the critical, correcting authority.

Normativity and Descriptivity

Ethics – understood as a sub-discipline of philosophy – is a science of the conditions of validity of normative assertions;[2] depending on the theoretical viewpoint it is even a science which sets norms and gives reasons for them (normative ethics). In contrast, empirical social research is a descriptive science: it describes a social reality of what is actually done and proposes hypotheses of why it is done. The operationalized constructs are not only studied, they are viewed in the context of other social facts, in order to establish relationships between these facts such as a causal relationship.

Empirical research projects which have the purpose of informing the participants about relevant aspects of an occurrence, an approach, an organization or about the views of the participants and, if necessary, to make these practices, approaches or views accessible for critical assessment, do not pose any substantial problems with respect to the relationship of descriptivity and ethical normativity. It is different, however, with theories that want to attribute a relevance beyond that to the empirically gained findings for the normative level. They have to grapple with the classic problem of the relationship of normativity and descriptivity, of 'ought' and 'is'.

If the researcher seeks to assign reality itself a normative severity, i.e., to make reality in its facticity the orientation factor, they must go beyond the claim of descriptivity in applying empirical theory. If the empirically described social reality is itself assigned relevance on the normative level and the empirically collected data are in any way assigned normative relevance, it will have to face fundamental philosophical objections. It will usually be exposed to the 'is-ought fallacy' as pointed out by David Hume, and have to respond to it.[3] Part of the methodical reflection of an 'empirical ethicist' is thus devoted to refuting this reproach and showing to what extent it is irrelevant for his proposed theory regarding the relationship of empiricism and ethics.

Models of the Relationship of Normativity and Descriptivity

In the following section we shall discuss a few models of the relationship of normativity and descriptivity,[4] which from our viewpoint are relevant for the

---

2 'Descriptive ethics', which first evolved in the twentieth century, is not a philosophical discipline, but rather a social science discipline.

3 We prefer here the term 'is-ought fallacy' instead of the term 'naturalistic fallacy', since at least in G.E. Moore's classic formulation of the naturalistic fallacy the focus is much more on whether the concept 'good' may be equated with any natural attribute such as 'desire'.

4 Hope (1999) and Sugarman and Sulmasy (2001) make similar mention of the types and examples of empirical research in ethics presented in this chapter. However, neither

medical-ethical discourse or have become significant in it. We shall briefly outline the consequentialist, deontological, discourse-ethical and hermeneutic models and elaborate on the strengths and weaknesses of each.

Empiricism in Consequentialist Ethics Models

Within a consequentialist ethics model, it is of course indispensable to refer to empirical data, especially data that is prognostic in character. It also clearly does not fall under the objection of an is-ought fallacy, in so far as this reference is contained in the underlying – but not empirically gained – normative principle, namely the evaluation of actions according to their observable, agent-neutral consequences.

What we mean by this relatively abstract statement is doubtlessly most obvious in the so-called empirical 'slippery-slope' arguments. Slippery-slope arguments are by definition consequentialist arguments which assess the moral rightness or wrongness – often of legal regulations – according to their possible consequences. *That* commandments and prohibitions are to be assessed as to their possible consequences is not an empirically derived principle, but rather a purely normative principle. *Whether* the feared or desired consequences will really occur or not is a question which can only and alone be answered using the instruments of empirical social research. When for instance in the euthanasia debate it is asserted as a slippery slope argument that the allowance of active euthanasia on demand would lead to an increase in the number of killings without the patient demanding it, but this could not be confirmed in the respective survey statistics in countries where active euthanasia is allowed, this argument would be *empirically* disproved (or in the opposite case *empirically* confirmed).[5]

Dieter Birnbacher takes a rather exceptional stance in the context of this ethics model. In his essay 'Ethics and Social Science: Which Kind of Co-operation?' (Birnbacher 1999) he asserts that empirical research which goes beyond the 'classical' consequentialist paradigms of collecting data, beyond the statements on the consequences of actions and/or regulations, is of crucial importance for both theoretical and applied ethics. One of the questions he uses to illustrate this is which reason for protecting the environment is the most 'effective' from a social psychology viewpoint, in order to achieve environmental protection goals which are desirable for purely utilitarian reasons. Birnbacher elaborates that an anthropocentric utilitarian justification is apparently not motivating enough for psychological reasons. Therefore an 'ecocentric' and consequently non-utilitarian justification must be propagated to the masses of the population in order to attain goals which are actually utilitarian in nature (cf. Birnbacher 1999: 327). Birnbacher

---

author makes any connection to the respective underlying causal models or any meta-ethical reflection on their validity.

5   Here on the other hand it would be necessary to first consider which time periods should be included in order to make relevant statements.

argues analogously when he draws on the empirical social sciences, especially the insights of empirical social psychology, to resolve 'fundamental questions of general ethics' (Birnbacher 1999: 330) such as differentiating between acts of commission and acts of omission or considering the problem of a general theory of justice (cf. Birnbacher 1999: 330–35). Here, too, Birnbacher asserts that a direct recourse to the utilitarian principle of utility maximization on the basis of conflicting (social) psychology-, anthropology- and culture-related patterns of thought and behaviour in the population – which even includes, e.g., differentiating between acts of commission and omission, meaningless from Birnbacher's utilitarian viewpoint, would be downright counterproductive for the desired utility maximization. A sufficiently subtle utilitarianism must therefore take into account such patterns of thought and behaviour that are irrational according to utilitarian standards, and must do so precisely because of its desired utility maximization.

From this brief outline it becomes clear, however, that Birnbacher's asserted fundamental significance of the empirical social sciences to resolve 'fundamental questions of general ethics' cannot do so beyond the narrower consequentialist approach. Indeed, all of his considerations presuppose the very specific consequentialist theory programme of a utilitarianism that is psychologically, anthropologically and culturally adapted to aiming for an ultimate utility maximization. In light of this and in light of the fact that this theory programme goes beyond these boundaries to an in part actually manipulative social technique, it is nonetheless irritating when rather hermeneutically oriented ethicists such as Albert Musschenga characterize Birnbacher's considerations as almost a kind of proof of principle for the general relevance of empirical social research in ethics (cf. Musschenga 2005: 477 f.).

Empiricism in Deontological Ethics Models

Even strictly deontological ethics approaches usually cannot do without some kind of reference to the empirical circumstances of the action. This especially applies where norms or values – and indeed for good ethical reasons, which as such are not empirical in nature – depend on empirical validity conditions. In particular, deontological ethics based on the 'right to self-determination' must take this into account, because for the right to self-determination there are without doubt specific empirical realization or validity conditions: being informed, competency, the existence of alternatives and freedom from external pressure,[6]

---

6 However, caution is advised in using the term 'freedom from external pressure'. In the biotheical and medical ethical discourse in Germany there is indeed a tendency to set the requirement for this criterion so high that no decision would count any more as 'self-determined' under real conditions. In this way the gate is ultimately opened for creating a new paternalism. The question of how this criterion is exactly formulated is thus an important ethical task. It is, however, primarily a normative problem, which empiricism can only help solve in a limited way.

to name only the most important. Of course, theoretically one could conceive of a very abstract theory of self-determination which refrains from formulating such criteria and instead simply declares that the decision of a person when they have been given at least two options is by definition 'self-determined'. Such a theory was proposed by, e.g., Thomas Hobbes, who considers it a completely free and self-determined decision to submit to slavery rather than be killed. According to Hobbes, when a cruel perpetrator renders you unable to fight and threatens to kill you, the choice of becoming a slave over death would be something like a free choice (Hobbes 1994: 127). Moreover, Hobbes even goes as far as to hold this bondage under certain conditions for a valid contract, just because it came about due to 'free self-determination' (Hobbes 1994: 128). Such an abstract concept of 'self-determination' will surely have to be rejected for very good *ethical* reasons.

If one does reject it, empirical research can make an especially important contribution to analysing which social or legal practices would best meet the above-mentioned criteria in what way and which would not, and it can provide instruments and information which enable criticism where these criteria are only insufficiently met. That can provide valuable information especially for a legislator or an author of guidelines, whose aim with their regulations is to implement the respect for patient autonomy in practice in the best possible way.

The implementation of this principle depends even more strongly on empiricism where an expression of will is not (no longer) possible, but rather where one must fall back on the pre-formulated will (in the form of an advanced directive) or on surrogate decision-making. If one does not question in principle – which could of course be possible – that both can be seen as expression of the right to self-determination, then it is evident that we depend on empirical research to the greatest extent when we want to find out which interpretation or investigation methods are best suited to securing the autonomy of the affected person. Also here a meaningful interaction between empiricism and normative theory can be observed in so far as the latter is needed to determine the fundamental status of surrogate decision-making and advanced directives and to formulate normative postulates on how to handle these. Empiricism, in turn, is required to conceive and quite concretely develop one (or more) best practice guidelines and/or to criticize unsatisfactory ones.

If, for instance, as the findings of the survey carried out by Wolfram Höfling and Anna Schäfer among guardianship judges (Höfling und Schäfer 2007) showed, there is a high degree of chance and arbitrariness in those judges' decisions on the supposed will or on the implementation of advanced directives, it can be very important information for a legislator who reflects on the provisions of the advanced directives and the supposed will of the patient. This information can help him or her decide which role the guardianship court should play in a planned regulation. As studies from the US indicate (cf. Shalowitz et al. 2006), the same is true particularly if the speculations of the next of kin about the patient's suspected will differ massively from the wishes of the affected patient – as they do in a considerable number of cases.

In such considerations the main concern is usually how, i.e., with which rules and organization forms, certain deontological norms such as the protection of human life or respect of self-determination can be granted qualified validity in social and legal practice. Hence, the level on which empirical social research becomes significant in this context is normally not the ethical level of the individual but primarily the level of the legislator, of the author of guidelines, of the person responsible for the organization and structure of processes, etc.

Nonetheless, empirical research which takes place in the context of a deontological ethics model can also be relevant for clinical ethics consultation. One reason for this is that clinical ethics consultation itself is often concerned with organizing and structuring clinical processes – either by being confronted with them or by playing an active role in forming them. Another reason is that the kind of empirical background knowledge as described here can of course be relevant for the ethics consultant in concrete cases.

Discourse Ethics Model

Discourse ethics does not perceive itself to be 'normative ethics', but rather as philosophical ethics in the emphatic sense, which seeks to defend the cognitive claim of making moral judgements against scepticism and non-cognitivism (Habermas 1990b). The fact that discourse ethics also points out a number of argumentation conditions in this context does not make it belong to the domain of normative ethics. Rather, what it does is point out necessary (transcendental) conditions of meaningful moral speech as such. Different variants of discourse ethics thus refer in different ways to the empirical social sciences.

For Jürgen Habermas, empirical theories are above all interesting that lay strong claims to being universalistic. Philosophy serves here in particular as a stand-in for the reconstructive sciences (Habermas 1990a). 'Starting primarily from the intuitive knowledge of competent subjects – competent in terms of judgement, action, and language – and secondarily from systematic knowledge handed down by culture, the reconstructive sciences explain the presumably universal bases of rational experience and judgement, as well as of action and linguistic communication' (Habermas 1990a: 15). For cognitivistic ethics, the developmental psychology of moral judgement represents such an interesting theory, which has time and again given rise to intensive disputes in discourse ethics (cf., e.g., Habermas 1990c).

In discourse ethics – at least in the variant of Jürgen Habermas – normative ethics' is relegated to the practical discourse of morally committed citizens. Even philosophers and social scientists cannot act as experts there, in so far as the actual aim is to agree upon moral norms that should govern the social interaction of those involved and of those affected by such a norm with reference to their actions. In the context of this practical discourse the social scientist is only an expert to the extent that they can analyse and present, e.g., the framework conditions, usage of terms or the perceptions of the participants. However, wherever this goes beyond that into a normative area, they can no longer speak as an expert, but only as a committed citizen, who just like everyone else must attempt to provide moral arguments for the norms they suggest.

Viewed in this way, the hypothesis at least does not seem inadmissible that discourse ethics takes up some of the different concepts of empirical research mentioned above. For discourse ethics as philosophical justification programme of cognitivistic ethics, empirical theories are especially interesting that aim at general statements which thus can support even the fallaciously understood theory programme of discourse ethics. In the practical discourses themselves, however, social research becomes interesting, which is concerned with determining individual details. From this perspective it does make a difference in the context of practical discourse whether those participating in the discourse are sufficiently informed about the concrete circumstances.

Hermeneutic Model

Van der Scheer and Widdershoven have developed a model based on social research that aims to make a substantial contribution to medical ethics (van der Scheer and Widdershoven 2004). Already at the beginning of their contribution they start with a fundamental presupposition. They emphasize the difference between the so-called abstract ethical theories of philosophical tradition on the one hand and the concrete issues of practical ethics on the other. Precisely contrary to the assumptions of discourse ethics, the authors assert that moral philosophy is capable of giving practical guidance in topical moral issues. Moral philosophers such as Kant or the moral-philosophical investigation of moral language (Richard M. Hare is probably meant) represent examples of abstract ethical theory, which lack this strength.

Already this presupposition appears problematic. It remains unclear why just these theories should not have the strength to provide practical guidance. The categorical imperative of Kant seeks to differentiate moral maxims from immoral maxims, and the concrete implementation of Kant's ethics contains a plethora of instructions for moral action. However, it also remains unclear how the desideratum of practical ethics – its moral philosophical foundation – can be taken seriously, when meta-ethical studies are met with the inapplicable expectation of how to solve practical problems of action.

The authors distinguish three forms of 'empirical research *in* ethics' (van der Scheer and Widdershoven 2004: 72). Empirical research in ethics is thus to be distinguished from descriptive ethics. Accordingly, ethics and empiricism can be combined with each other in the following way. First there is the 'parallel combination' according to which empirical research and ethics each have their specific tasks, which cannot be reduced to each other. Secondly, the there is the 'symbiotic relationship'. Here, empirical research and ethics influence each other, for instance by putting certain topics on the agenda of ethical discussion and by applying certain results obtained in one discipline to another.

Thirdly, there is an 'integrated' empirical-ethical approach that would bring forth a new discipline (Molewijk et al 2004). The integrated empirical-ethical approach makes it possible that 'empirical research about normative practices can generate ethical theories with normative consequences' (van der Scheer and Widdershoven 2004: 72; Molewijk et al 2004). This approach is now linked with a pragmatic approach in ethics, which in turn asserts that 'the most important work in integrated empirical ethics consists in the search for rules and guidelines for further action, a search which occurs in dialogue with the practice as it has been investigated' (van der Scheer and Widdershoven 2004: 72).

The authors themselves argue that the approach is criticized for wrongly diminishing the difference between 'is' and 'ought' (van der Scheer and Widdershoven 2004: 73). Secondly, a loss of normativity is attested. As central objection it is emphasized that the justification of the good or the right cannot be the subject of empirical research. The authors themselves name as further objection that they could be confronted with ethical relativism.

This integrative approach represents the most ambitious attempt in the context of the models presented here with respect to the relationship of empiricism and ethics, to bridge the gap between 'is' and 'ought'. However, it remains to be said that a convincing presentation of the approach does not yet exist in so far as the authors have not succeeded in plausibly refuting the objections they themselves have posed.

Ethics Consultation and Empirical Research

Empirical social research on ethics consultation must do justice to the two-sided anchoring (Engel et al. 2007: 35) of consultation. Ethics consultation is *consultation* on *ethical* conflict cases in the hospital. This entails that empirical research on ethics consultation has to do with two different models in which the concept of normativity is used differently. In the case of the clinical ethics consultant this means that the consultant requires both consulting competence and competence in ethical issues.

Just as in medical ethics and bioethics, one must distinguish also in consultation theory between the normative level and socio-scientific research. Empirical social research can make a contribution to clarifying consultation models of ethics consultation. As advisor, the ethics consultant uses a model of consultation whose development, justification and presentation are part of consultation theory. They may do this in a deliberate or unreflected manner and in doing so ignore important insights of consultation theory – as consultant they are in any case integrated into this consultation theory. Such a consultation theory always has a normative dimension in the sense that it describes, e.g., approaches/methods and links them with expectations of effects. It can thus become a critical measure – a norm – for the consultation performance of the consultant. However, such a model will always have to undergo revisions in the light of empirical experience.

Empirical social research cannot make *any* contribution to founding norms or values that play a role in ethics consultation. It describes which norms, values or rules are applied, but not which ones *ought to be* applied. The dispute about this is in itself part of the practical discourse or – as far as possible – of a normative ethical theory. That is also the reason why the debate on the moral-philosophical principles of ethics consultation is assigned such importance. How this can happen, whether hermeneutically (Widdershoven and Molewijk in this volume), in an ethics discourse (Fahr in this volume) or casuistically (Comoretto in this volume) or in yet another way is therefore just as open as the role of the ethics consultant in the consultations (Widdershoven and Molewijk, Fahr in this volume).

Social research can *describe* the ethic-moral competences of today's practising ethics consultants, but the form this competence *ought to* have is a matter of contention and does not belong to the domain of social research. The form of this competence ranges from the assertion of a heightened moral insightfulness and the awareness of the morally justified course of action in the consultation case (Meyers 2007) or the differentiated interpretation of the moral expertise of the moral philosopher in ethics consultation (Herrmann in this volume) and from the knowledge of heuristics and methods of improving a moral judgement and a parenthesizing of the moral judgement (Fahr 2008) up to complete abstinence of the moral judgement in the consultation process (for the so-called pure facilitation approach compare Widdershoven and Molewijk in this volume, Aulisio et al. 2003). It will usually encompass knowledge of directives, guidelines and legal regulations. It remains an open question in the debate whether the competence of moral judgement can be conceived purely formally (e.g., as in the theory of Lawrence Kohlberg) and thus is accessible to research or whether it should be oriented on content with the aim of assessing the results of ethics consultations in the light of an overriding criterion. However, social research on its own will not be able to generate such an overriding criterion.

Empirical social research will become indispensable especially in the development of evaluation methods of ethics consultation. The evaluation studies presented here by Schildmann (Schildmann and Vollmann in this volume) provide first indications which in the future must be elaborated further in detail. Ethics consultation can be evaluated under the most diverse aspects as consultation and thus made accessible to empirical research. For instance, *the concept of consultation* as well as its *effectiveness*, its *efficiency* and also its *usefulness* can serve as objects of evaluation of ethics consultation. Especially for the evaluation of the effectiveness a more detailed description of the intervention forms of ethics consultants is needed. Expectations are associated with these interventions concerning which effects are included in them. These effects must be described in an effect model that describes interventions and the expected effects and develops a theoretical model why these effects can be expected. Such an effect model, that moreover represents a desideratum of research, opens up a wide horizon of empirical research. Empirical social research can inform about the status of development of ethics committees and ethics consultations in hospitals and clinics (cf., e.g., the indications, if few in number, in Frewer and Fahr 2007). It is without question that socio-scientific surveys about the prevalence of ethics committees, number, duration and frequency of ethics consultations and similar topics represent important information sources. It makes the respective activities visible and can thus elaborate problems of ethics consultation. Suitable solutions can become visible and possibly generalized.

Conclusion

Especially the medical-ethical models in the narrower sense, which advocate a new relationship of normativity and descriptivity, do not succeed in clearly showing that they are not committing the *is-ought* fallacy. Other models conceptualize the relationship of empiricism and ethics in a far more complicated way and point out that empirical social science can make a contribution to ethics – whereby in any case the meaning of the term 'ethics' must be determined in more detail.

It is less 'ethics' that poses a problem for empirical research of ethics consultation but rather the fact that to this day the formation of a consultation theory model for ethics consultation has been inadequate. The absence of suitable effect models, the inadequate description of advisory intervention measures, the lack of clarity about the goal of ethics consultation and similar consultation-theoretical desiderata pose considerable problems for empirical research.

On the other hand, what ethics consultation can expect from social research is a critical clarification regarding its 'ethical' dimension. To be sure, social science cannot take over the function of generating and justifying norms, values and moral rules that play a role in ethics consultation. It can, however, describe the concrete forms of implementation of moral organization culture, in the framework of which the ethics consultant does their work (cf. also Meyers 2007: Chapters 2 and 3). This can enable the ethics consultant who is not merely seeking acceptance to learn to view their work with the necessary critical gaze in order not to get taken in by the hidden values of the 'organization hospital'. To avoid becoming an acceptance broker and stop-gap for the often dramatic communication deficits in the modern hospital, the ethics consultant faces the challenge of having to make these hidden values visible instead of sharing them without criticism.

References

Aulisio, M.P., Arnold, R.M. and Youngner, S.J. (eds). 2003. *Ethics Consultation: From Theory to Practice*. Baltimore, MA: Johns Hopkins University Press.

Birnbacher, D. 1999. Ethics and social science: Which kind of co-operation? *Ethical Theory and Moral Practice*, 2, 319–36.

Borry P., Schotsmans, P. and Dierickx, K. 2005. The birth of the empirical turn in bioethics. *Bioethics*, 19, 49–71.

Bosshard, G. 2006. Ärztliche Entscheidungsfindung am Lebensende im internationalen Vergleich, in *Entscheidungen am Lebensende in der modernen Medizin: Ethik, Recht, Ökonomie und Klinik*, edited by J. Schildmann, U. Fahr and J. Vollmann. Münster: Lit Verlag, 199–211.

Bosshard, G., Nilstun, T., Bilsen, J. et al. 2005. Forgoing treatment at the end of life in six European countries. *Archives of Internal Medicine*, 165, 401–7.

Düwell, M. 2005. Sozialwissenschaften, Gesellschaftstheorie und Ethik. *Jahrbuch für Wissenschaft und Ethik*, 10, 5–22.

Engel, F., Nestmann, F. and Sickendick, U. 2007. *Das Handbuch der Beratung. Band 1: Disziplinen und Zugänge.* Tübingen: DGVT-Verlag.

Fahr, U. 2008. Die Aufgaben des Klinischen Ethikberaters aus erwachsenenpädagogischer Sicht, in *Klinische Ethikberatung an Universitätskliniken*, edited by D. Groß, A.T. May and A. Simon. Münster: Lit-Verlag, 69–79.

Frewer, A. and Fahr, U. 2007. Clinical ethics and confidentiality: Opinions of experts and ethics committees. *HEC Forum*, 4, 277–91.

Habermas, J. 1990a. Philosophy as Stand-In and Interpreter, in *Moral Consciousness and Communicative Action*, edited by J. Habermas. Cambridge: Polity Press.

Habermas, J. 1990b. Discourse Ethics: Notes on a Program of Philosophical Justification, in *Moral Consciousness and Communicative Action*, J. Habermas. Cambridge: Polity Press.

Habermas, J. 1990c. Moral Consciousness and Communicative Action, in *Moral Consciousness and Communicative Action*, edited by J. Habermas. Cambridge: Polity Press.

Hobbes, T. 1994. *The Elements of Law Natural and Politic.* Oxford: Oxford University Press.

Höfling, W. and Schäfer, A. 2007. *Leben und Sterben in Richterhand.* Tübingen: Mohr Siebeck.

Hope, T. 1999. Empirical medical ethics. *Journal of Medical Ethics*, 3, 219–20.

Meyers, C. 2007. *A Practical Guide to Clinical Ethics Consulting: Expertise, Ethos, and Power.* Plymouth: Rowman & Littlefield Publishers.

Molewijk, B., Stiggelbout, A.E., Otten, W., Dupius, H.M. and Kievit, J. 2004. Empirical data and moral theory: A plea for integrated empirical ethics. *Medicine, Health Care and Philosophy*, 7, 55–69.

Musschenga, A.W. 2005. Empirical ethics, context-sensitivity and contextualism. *Journal of Medicine and Philosophy*, 30, 467–90.

Schnell, R., Hill, P.B. and Essere, E. 2005. *Methoden der empirischen Sozialforschung.* 7. völlig überarbeitete Auflage. Munich: Oldenburg Wissenschaftsverlag.

Seiffert, H. 1996. *Einführung in die Wissenschaftstheorie 1. Sprachanalyse. Deduktion. Induktion in der Natur- und Sozialwissenschaft.* 12. Auflage. Munich: C.H.Beck.

Shalowitz, D.I., Garrett-Mayer, E. and Wendler, D. 2006. The accuracy of surrogate decision makers: A systematic review. *Archives of Internal Medicine*, 166, 493–7.

Sugarman, J. and Sulmasy, D. 2001. *Methods in Medical Ethics*. Washington, DC: Georgetown University Press.

van den Daele, W. 2008. Soziologische Aufklärung und moralische Geltung: Empirische Argumente im bioethischen Diskurs, in *Praxis in der Ethik. Zur Methodenreflexion in der anwendungsorientierten Moralphilosophie*, edited by M. Zichy and H. Grimm. Berlin: de Gruyter, 119–51.

van der Scheer, L. and Widdershoven, G. 2004. Integrated empirical ethics: Loss of normativity? *Medicine, Health Care and Philosophy*, 7, 71–9.

Chapter 4
Philosophical Foundations of Clinical Ethics: A Hermeneutic Perspective

Guy Widdershoven and Bert Molewijk

Introduction

Clinical ethics has become a major trend in health care. Since the middle of the twentieth century, medical technology has made much progress, resulting in the possibility of keeping patients alive who in earlier times would surely have died. This has created uncertainty about whether such technologies should actually be applied. Moreover, the democratization of Western societies and the professionalization of the patient movement have resulted in a decline of the authority of the doctor, and have put the wishes of the patient more to the front. More recently, the rise of evidence-based medicine and quality management policies have led to more emphasis on transparency, reflection and justification. As a result of these developments, ethics has become a central issue in medicine. Health care professionals increasingly ask for specific advice about treatment and care, not only regarding technical aspects, but also from a moral perspective. This has led to the establishment of clinical ethical committees, supporting decision-making in difficult cases, to the rise of professionals in clinical ethics who can be called in to give advice, and to the development of moral deliberation activities, in which a group of professionals reflects on a case, facilitated by an ethicist.

Over the past few decades, clinical ethicists have established ways of dealing with ethical issues suited to problems in health care. They have elaborated ways of discussing cases, and tools to structure the discussion. They have learned how to address ethical issues and find solutions which worked for the participants in practice. Clinical ethics has been developed, not as a theoretical endeavour, but as a practical process of dealing with the situation, engaging practitioners in adopting new views and vocabularies. Clinical ethicists have followed and built upon the structure of clinical practice, responding to its particularities and intricacies.

The specific contextual and practical nature of clinical ethics differs from the more traditional academic and medical ethics domains. The latter are much more explicit with respect to their theoretical frameworks and their epistemological views. Clinical ethics seems much less explicit with respect to its theoretical and philosophical backgrounds. This raises questions about the philosophical foundations of clinical ethics. Can and should clinical ethics be justified from a philosophical perspective? We believe it can and should. In this chapter we present a specific approach to clinical ethics: hermeneutic philosophy. We discuss central elements of hermeneutic philosophy, and show their relevance for clinical ethics by focusing on a concrete example, the development of a moral deliberation project in a psychiatric hospital in the Netherlands. This moral deliberation project was inspired by hermeneutic philosophy. The aim of this chapter is to show the possibility and importance of a philosophical foundation of clinical ethics in general, and to demonstrate both the theoretical and the practical strengths of hermeneutic philosophy for clinical ethics in particular.

Hermeneutic Philosophy

Hermeneutic philosophy deals with the preconditions of understanding (the Greek verb *hermeneuo* means interpreting messages and texts). It was developed by Heidegger (1927) and Gadamer (1960). According to Heidegger, understanding should be regarded in the context of human existence as being-in-the-world. Against Descartes, who defines *res cogitans* against *res extensa* as an intellect without space and time, Heidegger stresses that human existence is always in space and time. Before abstract and universal thought is possible, human existence is positioned in the world. Heidegger calls this 'being-in-the-world'.

According to Heidegger, being-in-the-world has two sides. The first side of being-in-the-world is finding oneself moved; the second side is moving oneself. Finding oneself moved is related to the basic characteristic of being-in-the-mood. Moods show that human existence implies finding oneself thrown into the world. Moving oneself is related to the basic characteristic of understanding. Understanding implies knowing how to handle things. It is oriented towards the future. Whereas being-in-the-mood is related to human existence as being thrown into the world, understanding is related to projecting and planning. Understanding means 'seeing as': one sees a chair as something to sit in, or a book as something to read. Understanding is prior to seeing a thing as a meaningless object. One has to abstract from the already known context and use of a chair or a book if one wants to regard them just as objects.

According to Heidegger, understanding is based upon pre-understandings. In order to make sense of a chair or a book, we already have to be able to handle them. Cultures which do not make use of chairs or books will not be able to make sense of them. This implies that understanding does not start from scratch. Interpretation is not a matter of grasping what is there without any preconditions or preconceptions. On the contrary: every interpretation is based upon a primordial view which is embedded in one's knowledge of how to handle the situation. Does this not bring us in a circle? We seem only to be able to understand, if we already understand. Heidegger acknowledges that there is a circle here, yet he stresses that it is not a vicious circle. In the process of understanding, preconceptions can prove to be fruitful. Although we can only understand a chair or a book by having preconceptions, the process of interpretation can lead to a refinement of our preconceptions. A chair can be more comfortable than we imagined (or less); a book can provide us with new ways of looking at the world. This process is called the hermeneutic circle. It has the form of a spiral, according to Gadamer (1960).

From a hermeneutic perspective, philosophical thinking is also a matter of understanding. It is rooted in human existence. Philosophy presupposes everyday experience of the world. Philosophy is contextual and historical. Like any interpretation, philosophy starts from preconceptions, which cannot be surpassed, but which serve as a basis for thinking. These preconceptions are given with our immersion in language and history. According to Gadamer, there is no absolute starting point for philosophy which may enable us to formulate a universal truth. Every philosophical argument makes use of a language that is already there. This does not mean that philosophy is relativistic. Although human reason requires language, this is not an obstacle for our thinking (Gadamer 1977: 90). Language enables us to communicate with others and to express our experiences in new ways. The existence of a variety of languages with different conceptual structures shows that human thinking is not a mere reflection of the world. This does not mean that concepts are idiosyncratic. According to Gadamer, the plurality of languages can be regarded as variations of one 'logic of experience' (Gadamer 1960: 412). Gadamer stresses that the plurality of languages is actually the basis for the growth of understanding:

> It would be wrong to conclude from the variety of languages, that rationality is divided. The opposite is true. The finitude, the particularity of our being, which is visible in the variety of languages, is the condition for the infinite conversation towards truth, that we are. (Gadamer 1967: 111)

According to Gadamer, philosophical hermeneutics is a theory of experience. Hermeneutics makes explicit various aspects of experience, as a process of understanding the world through applying and refining one's preconceptions, and learning from conversation with others. This process of understanding is at work in every human endeavour. Hermeneutic philosophy can help to clarify what is at stake in specific interpretive practices, such as clinical ethics. In order to make explicit fundamental aspects of interpretation, hermeneutics has to depart from experience itself. Hermeneutics has to make use of practical examples, embodying contextual and historical ways of understanding. According to Aristotle, only in actual experiences does the process of understanding take place. There is no moral truth independent of experience; the meaning and construction of morality is inherently contextual and temporal (EN, 1096b 32–5). Therefore, we will base our hermeneutic foundation of clinical ethics on a concrete example of a moral deliberation project, stemming from our own clinical ethical experiences. Although this example is particular, the interpretation is aimed at identifying aspects of clinical ethical practice which are of more general relevance, not by abstracting from the individuality of our own experience, but by elucidating elements which can be recognized by others. The interpretation is also aimed at demonstrating the practical and theoretical usefulness of hermeneutics as a philosophical foundation for clinical ethics.

A Moral Deliberation Project in a Psychiatric Hospital

Within this section we describe experiences in the first two years of a four-year moral deliberation project inspired by hermeneutic philosophy. Within a moral deliberation project, the involved clinical ethicist has four different roles: a facilitator for moral case deliberations, a trainer for health care professionals to become facilitators themselves, a project manager responsible for the moral deliberation project, and a researcher who evaluates the results and progresses of the project. All our moral deliberation projects are monitored and facilitated by interactive process and outcomes research (Abma et al. 2008, Molewijk et al. 2008b, 2008c, Widdershoven et al. 2009). Hermeneutic philosophy inspires and guides the ground attitude of the clinical ethicist in all four different roles. We first describe the moral deliberation project and also present a moral case which has been discussed during a moral case deliberation session. In the next sections we then reflect on the role of hermeneutic philosophy therein.

A moral case deliberation consists of a meeting with health-care-givers who systematically reflect on one of their moral questions within a concrete clinical case from their practice (Molewijk et al. 2008a, 2008b, Steinkamp and Gordijn 2003, Verkerk et al. 2004). Most questions concern 'What should we consider as the morally right thing to do in this specific situation and how should we do it in a morally right way?' Besides focusing on right arguments (e.g., for behaving in a certain way), a moral case deliberation also focuses on actual right behaviour in current contexts, and on being a morally right person. The reflection, which takes usually one to two hours, is facilitated by a trained facilitator and structured by means of a selected conversation method. The facilitator, an ethicist or someone who is trained in clinical ethics and conversation methods, does not give substantial advice and does not morally justify or legitimize a specific decision. The expertise of the facilitator consists of fostering a constructive dialogue among the participants, keeping an eye on the moral dimension of the case, supporting the joint deliberation process, and helping the group in planning actions in order to improve the quality of care. Three central, often co-existing, goals of moral case deliberation are: (1) to reflect on the case and to improve the quality of care within that case; (2) to reflect on what it means to be a good professional and to enhance the professional's moral competencies, (3) to reflect on institutional or organizational issues and to improve the quality of care at that level (Molewijk et al. 2008c).

Moral deliberation can be done on an incidental basis. In order to have longer lasting results, however, it has to be organized in a more structured way. This is done in so-called moral deliberation *projects* in which ethicists work together with participants in practice to develop and implement moral deliberation as a structural activity. These projects typically last three to six years. GGNet, a large mental health care institution in the east of the Netherlands, is one of the leaders in the Netherlands with respect to the structural implementation of moral deliberation. The moral deliberation group within GGNet is responsible for the facilitation and implementation of these moral deliberations. The implementation of a moral deliberation project consists of several phases (Molewijk et al. 2008b, 2008c). After an investigation of the moral culture and ethics policy of the institution, the ethicist and the stakeholders shape a project plan. The moral deliberation group will then start facilitating moral deliberations among teams. Next, a core group of employees who have experienced moral deliberation as participants are trained as facilitators who can manage two different conversation methods for moral deliberation (Molewijk et al. 2008a). During a period of half a year, trainees participate in six special training sessions of four hours combined with homework (reading, writing and many practical exercises in their own team). Finally, the focus shifts to the implementation and embedding of structural attention for moral issues within the institution.

In GGNet, the moral deliberation project was evaluated after two years, in order to establish effects and to improve the implementation process (Molewijk et al. 2008c). At that time, the first phases of the project were well under way. The project plan was made, and moral deliberation sessions had been organized on a structural basis on various wards. The phase of training experienced employees to become facilitators had not yet been started. The project showed positive results, with good evaluations of the moral deliberation sessions and their relevance for the daily work of participants (Molewijk et al. 2008c). Participants especially appreciated the fact that they could share experiences of difficult cases, and that the discussion improved the awareness of their own behaviour and thinking as well as the awareness of perspectives of others. Moreover, they reported an improvement in cooperation and dialogue among professionals of various disciplines. Through the methodology and the codes of conduct of the moral deliberation sessions, participants experienced that they became more open-minded and constructive, while remaining critical. The participants were positive about the role of the ethicist as facilitator. They appreciated that the facilitator created an open atmosphere, encouraged communication and reflection, and structured the session, without determining its content (Molewijk et al. 2008c).

In one of the sessions, a case about preventive seclusion was discussed. A nurse from an acute emergency department submitted the case, concerning a young man who had been admitted to the ward for five days. On his fifth day, the nurse came back from holidays. During that day she and her female colleague decided to put the young man into the seclusion room in order to prevent aggressive escalations and to maintain the general safety on the ward. However, the nurse had a serious and sincere concern with respect to the moral justification of the decision to put the young man in the seclusion room. During the moral deliberation session, which took 90 minutes and which was facilitated by an ethicist, the participants first paid attention to the factual aspects of the case and the background of her worry whether she had done the morally right thing. Through a first inquiry with respect to the case, the ethicist and the participants helped the nurse to formulate her core moral question, which functioned as the specific starting-point for the collective moral inquiry: 'Was it morally justified to put the man in the seclusion room at that time?' They reflected upon the concrete case through non-judgemental questioning and with respect for the nurse's and others' interpretation of the situation. Next, the participants discussed the existing views among the participants regarding the question whether the decision was morally justified. Various, sometimes opposite, justificatory arguments were made explicit and examined, and also the conceptual analysis of the detailed aspects of actually making a decision, and the morally right timing for this specific decision, were challenged. The participants became aware that the decisive reason for the seclusion had not been the potential threat of the patient as such (which is the standard medical and legal criterion for seclusion and therefore often pops up at first as 'the' argument), but the lack of good communication with the young man, the nurses' risk assessment with respect to the upcoming evening shift, and the lack of any relationship with the young man because of the nurse having been away on holiday. The situation was perceived as potentially dangerous, because there was little insight into the patient's possible reactions. Thus, the danger was not so much in the patient; it was the result of the specific staff situation and the (a lack of) interaction with the patient. A better information transfer during changes of the shift and communication with the patient might have been an alternative to putting the patient in seclusion.

During the evaluation of this moral deliberation session, participants mentioned that they appreciated the fact that a colleague could openly doubt whether she did the right thing; they considered this as a professional attitude. Furthermore, they felt that the attitude of the ethicist and the specific codes of conduct related to the conversation method (i.e., a Socratic dialogue) gave enough security to examine each other's presuppositions in more depth. They learned that the process of making a decision is more complex and has more nuances than is often suggested. They appreciated that they had developed a new view on the role of danger and the relationship between communication and danger. As a result, they decided to be especially critical when justifications for using the seclusion room are brought up. They also decided to improve the staff composition with respect to the continuity of staff members who already have a relationship with the clients.

Finally, they also realized that making moral judgements is closely connected to the pre-understandings of the situation. They became aware of the fact that one single act can be interpreted in many different (or even opposite) ways. They also became aware that things and acts and words have no static universal meanings. This brings us back to the role of meaning and pre-understanding and the way hermeneutic philosophy deals with this.

Perspectives and Dialogue

According to philosophical hermeneutics, understanding is based upon pre-understandings. We always see the world from a certain point of view. Normally, we are not aware of this. We are oriented towards the world, and do not reflect upon our own position within that world. We become aware of (the limits of) our view when our understanding fails or is examined through a critical or naïve question. This may happen when we try to sit down in a chair in a museum, and are warned by the guard that the object is not to be used, since it is a work of art. At that moment, our pre-understanding that chairs are for sitting is challenged. Another illustration of challenging our pre-understandings, but now in the opposite direction, can be found in a garden with contemporary statues in the Smithsonian Institution in Washington (USA), where, next to a work of art consisting of a circle of chairs, a sign says: 'You are allowed to sit on this work of art'. This sign defies the expectation of the visitor that a work of art is not to be used in an ordinary way. Indeed, one can see people who sit down on one of the chairs look around first, to make sure that they are not acting against any regulations. Thus, they are urged to reflect on their presuppositions. This is in line with the hermeneutic idea that works of art can make us aware of and reflect on our being-in-the-world.

Within moral case deliberation, our being-in-the-world is examined on purpose. This occurs not only by means of other perspectives on the case, but also by means of the attitude of the facilitator and the codes of conduct of the conversation methods. The facilitator is especially sensitive to the particularity of meanings and meaning-making. For example, he or she may make explicit the specific way the participants interpret 'danger' by asking them: 'What is danger in this situation according to you?' Or: 'What constitutes "danger" in this specific situation for you personally?' When we are confronted with a limitation of our perspective, we learn to see that our view is not the only view possible, and, moreover, that it may not be the most relevant one. There are other perspectives, which may be more proper in the specific situation. This means that we are invited to reconsider our own perspective, and to become open to other perspectives. Thus, when one reads the sign that says that visitors are allowed to sit on a work of art, one may become aware that the distinction between art (which is purely for contemplation) and tools (which are for use) is artificial, and does not do justice to the many ways in which art functions in daily life. As a result, one may come to see that art is not something for museums only, but is present everywhere. If works of art can be used as chairs, so chairs can be regarded as works of art; they are not only useful for sitting, but also express aspects of human life. As a consequence, one may experience the world around oneself (including one's own furniture) in a new way.

The process of becoming open to another perspective does not mean that one changes a wrong view for the right one. The idea of 'the' right view would imply that an understanding without pre-understandings would be possible. Hermeneutic philosophy is critical of objectivism (there is one good perspective, from which the matter under consideration can be fully grasped); yet it does not imply relativism (all perspectives are different and equally valid). Hermeneutics goes beyond the opposition between objectivism and relativism (Bernstein 1983). Although all knowledge is bound to a certain perspective, this perspective can be widened in interaction with other perspectives. One can learn to understand the other, not by leaving one's own point of view behind, but by broadening one's perspective so that the viewpoints meet and merge. The result is a process of fusion of horizons, in which one does not remain what one was before (Gadamer 1960). What would then be needed, in order for a fusion of horizons to succeed? A hermeneutic approach would require that one both acknowledges that the perspective of the other is different from one's own, and is interested in bridging the gap between the two. These two aspects are crucial elements of a dialogue. In a dialogue, people are open for and prepared to learn from differences in perspective. 'To reach an understanding in a dialogue is not merely a matter of asserting one's own point of view, but a change into a communion in which one does not remain what one was' (Gadamer 1960: 379).

The facilitator of a moral case deliberation actively tries to avoid objectivism by explaining to the participants of the deliberation that we should not strive for one moral truth. Participants should be encouraged to give up the belief that there exists one single answer to the question: What is morally justified? If participants believe that, in the end, there is one single answer or meaning, they will often start to argue or debate because they want to find the only possible answer or meaning. Only if participants learn to let go of the initial drive to convince the other can they become sensitive to various meanings and perspectives. At that moment, they will be able to listen actively, to start a true inquiry into meaning and judgements, and to start to learn.

According to hermeneutic philosophy, growth of understanding comes about through a confrontation of perspectives in a critical yet respectful and open dialogue. This basic hermeneutic principle can be recognized in the moral deliberation project described above, both with respect to how the moral case deliberation is organized and facilitated, and with respect to what participants reported as the results of the moral case deliberation. Through interviews, focus groups and evaluation questionnaires, we found that the participants valued moral deliberation positively because it gave them the opportunity to become aware of their own perspective and to learn from meeting other perspectives (Molewijk et al. 2008c). They experienced the process as open, but also critical. They did not just take over the views proposed by others, but examined them critically. The example of the moral deliberation session about preventive seclusion shows that, through an open dialogue, the participants became aware that the situation was more complex than the legal system presupposes. They realized that legal criteria (like danger) do not suffice to explain and judge specific instances of coercion, since concrete circumstances, such as the (lack of) communication between nurse and patient, are crucial for understanding and judging the nurse's interventions. The participants realized that legal criteria alone are not decisive in decisions about coercion. This does not mean that legal criteria become irrelevant. During the moral deliberation session, danger is not dismissed as a criterion; the participants come to see that the interpretation of danger is dependent on the communication with the patient, and that communication may result in a diminishing of danger. Thus, danger is not an objective criterion; it is part of the communicative process.

Play and Ritual

One might be tempted to think that a dialogical process of fusion of horizons during a moral case deliberation is primarily a matter of argumentation and discursive deliberation. Although arguments and discussions can be a vehicle for mutual understanding, they are not the sole way to reach it. Moreover, the working of arguments and deliberations should not be reduced to a matter of exchange of information and logical reasoning. An argument is only convincing if it motivates the other to see the world differently and to act upon this. A dialogue is not a mutual expression of points of view, but a process in which one invites the other to see one's point of view as relevant, and is prepared to accept the perspective of the other as relevant.

A fusion of horizons requires interplay between two parties. One can only become open to another perspective if one is invited to take part in it, in the same way as a person is invited to a dance. The invitation should neither be coercive nor show a lack of engagement. A proper invitation is conducive, not because it is overpowering, but because it is polite and honourable to the person invited. The invitation is a prequel to the dance itself, showing a process of tuning, in which both parties respond to one another in a ritualistic way. During the dance, this process continues, and makes the dancers feel part of a larger unity. The interplay is not merely a matter of tuning between individuals. The rhythm of the music and the example of others is important in bringing about a practice of joint movements.

The notion of play refers back to what was said before about being-in-the-mood and understanding. Play is being moved and moving at the same time (Gadamer 1960). Play is fundamental for human life and human existence. The movement in play is not a conscious decision of the one who plays, the player finds himself moving before he has made any decision. Someone who picks up a ball, and bounces it, becomes part of the process of bouncing, in interaction with the ball. This fundamental hermeneutic process is at work in every interpretation. If one reads a book or watches a movie, one becomes immersed, tuning in with the rhythm of the work. One does not read separate lines or look at distinct cuts, but participates in the world created by the book or the movie. The same goes for a dialogue during a moral case deliberation. In a true dialogue, the participants find themselves immersed in a joint world which is not a projection of any of the participants, but the basis for individual contributions. The role of play in dialogue does not mean that argumentation and discussion have no content. It does mean, however, that the development of shared views is not a matter of finding the right content through coherent and logical reasoning only and then communicating it, but that what is right in content can only be established in and through a process of commitment and communication that is carried forward by means of play and ritual. In other words, within moral case deliberation, process and content (i.e., 'outcomes') are interwoven in a complex way. This is demonstrated by the fact that establishing a true dialogue among participants of a moral case deliberation is both a process and a result, a means and a goal. And especially through a good dialogue, content matters become qualified and meaningful results.

In the evaluation of the moral case deliberation sessions, the participants mentioned that they experienced more openness towards one another, while they remained critical of what was being said. The combination of openness and critical attitude can be interpreted in terms of play. In play, spontaneity and seriousness go together. The participants respond directly towards one another, without premeditation. At the same time, the play requires full attention. According to the participants the moral case deliberation furthered cooperation in the team. This can also be interpreted in terms of play: the moral deliberation sessions are vehicles for furthering interaction and joint movements. The elaboration of the relationship between danger and communication during the discussion about preventive seclusion provides a concrete example of joint immersion in a process of meaning-making. The new view on danger is not invented by one of the participants; it results from an interaction in which all parties are focused on each other and on the issue at hand, just as players are focused both on the other players and on the aim of the game.

The hermeneutic notions of play and ritual can help to understand the need for a structural embedding of moral deliberation in health care organizations. As a game becomes easier and more attractive when it is practised regularly, moral deliberation becomes more fluid and more relevant through exercise. The structured way of discussing cases and the quality of the dialogical process together provide the participants with a scenario for dealing with moral problems, just as a ritual provides an order of steps for organizing a common practice. This scenario of an attitude of dialogue and structure also contributes to decision-making processes and interdisciplinary communication *after* the specific moral case deliberation.

Phronesis and Practical Understanding

One of the claims of hermeneutic philosophy is that understanding starts with actual experience, not with theories or concepts. Theories and concepts are useful, but ultimately they should be based upon and useful for concrete practices. Hermeneutics endorses Aristotle's view of ethics as practical philosophy. According to Aristotle, moral knowledge originates from reflections on and within concrete situations. There is no moral truth independent from experience. The meaning and construction of morality is inherently contextual and temporal. Aristotle is critical of Plato's idea of the good as absolute. He doubts whether all things can be called good in the same way. Moreover, he says that even if this would be the case, it would not be useful for us as humans: 'Even if the good that is ascribed to various things would form a unity or exist on its own, this would not be achievable for human beings' (EN, 1096b 32–5).

According to Aristotle, practical philosophy starts from experience. This means that people need to have experience in order to study ethics. The study of ethics is not for young persons, because they lack experience. Practical philosophy requires practical experience. Only people who are trained and educated in moral life are sensitive to ethical issues and open to moral philosophy. For Aristotle, there is a circle between ethics and practice. Ethics presupposes a moral practice, yet ethics can contribute to this practice, by clarifying why it is good. Ethics makes explicit what is already implicit in practice. It clarifies what people actually do when they act rightly (Gadamer 1978: 95). Aristotle stresses that experienced people have knowledge of what is right and wrong. This knowledge is not general, but concrete. Experienced people know what is good in specific situations. This kind of knowledge is called *phronesis*, or practical understanding. *Phronesis* enables a person to see what action is suited to concrete circumstances. It is knowledge of things that change (in contrast to *sofia*, which is knowledge of things that do not change). This does not mean that *phronesis* lacks general principles. It does mean that general principles have to be applied to concrete circumstances. This is not a matter of logical deduction. *Phronesis* requires deliberation and choice (EN, 1140a 25ff). An example of this can be found in the judge who applies a law with prudence. By taking the situation into account, the judge does not do away with the principle of justice, but applies it properly (EN, 1137b 25–30). *Phronesis* is knowledge of the concrete, not as the opposite of the general, but as its incarnation (Gadamer 1960: 296, 1978: 97).

In order to acquire *phronesis*, people have to learn to distinguish concrete situations. They have to become sensitive to the particularity of practical problems. This sensitivity can be developed through practice. A judge has to be involved with many cases in order to learn how to apply the principle of justice. Examples from others can also be helpful. By seeing and hearing how more experienced people act, one may learn to understand the situation and develop ways of dealing with it. This requires more than just copying the behaviour of others. One actually has to understand why the action is right and be able to set an example oneself. This understanding is not merely a rational insight but is closely related to the development of a character.

Moral deliberation presupposes that the participants have moral knowledge, and can contribute to develop this knowledge further. Moral deliberation according to hermeneutics always starts with concrete experiences (and not with hypothetical thought experiments or concepts or theories from ethics). Even in the reasoning process on a case, hypothetical questions such as 'Imagine that this young man did this and that' are avoided. Hypothetical cases and hypothetical reasoning are avoided since they do not start from experience. We only know for sure that a certain kind of reasoning is true if participants in an actual case really reason in that way. We only know whether that actual reasoning does make sense and is valid if we know the given circumstances and are able to reflect upon both the reasoning and the circumstances. So the focus is on the concrete situation in the case at hand and on actual experiences. The participants are invited to reflect on the case, and give their judgment. In the evaluation of the moral deliberation project, the participants appreciated sharing experiences about difficult cases. They felt that their practical understanding and their *phronesis* were respected and challenged, rather than replaced by abstract knowledge and theory. The deliberation about preventive seclusion did not focus on the notion of danger in an abstract sense, but on the meaning of danger in a situation where communication was not optimal. The discussion resulted in a growth of practical understanding concerning danger in such situations. This also implies a better understanding of the complexity of a criterion such as danger, which is not only relevant for the case under consideration, but of wider importance. Thus the participants learned about danger in general through discussing a particular situation. This is also demonstrated in participants' behaviour in subsequent moral case deliberations: the quality of the dialogue, the moral inquiry and the art of asking good questions clearly improved since they became sensitive to meaning-making processes and their connection with developing moral judgements.

The Role of the Ethicist

If the focus of clinical ethics is on the moral knowledge and expertise of participants in practice, one may wonder what role the ethicist plays. Clearly, this is not the role of a final authority, declaring what is right or wrong in practice. According to hermeneutic philosophy, ethicists should not provide solutions, point at 'the' moral answer and justify certain decisions by means of abstract concepts, theories and logical argumentation. As a matter of fact, according to the epistemological account of hermeneutic philosophy, ethicists are simply not able to do so. According to hermeneutic philosophy, the ethicist should act as a facilitator, fostering the process of moral deliberation. The role of the facilitator can also be played by practitioners, provided that they have experience with moral deliberation and are trained appropriately. The role of facilitator is sometimes described as answering the question who is the appropriate decision-maker (ASBH Task Force 1998, Aulisio et al. 2003). From a hermeneutic perspective, this is a limited interpretation of facilitating. Rather than establishing who has the authority to decide in a procedural and formal-legal way, the ethicist as facilitator focuses on what is good care and what is a good person. In other words, the facilitator helps the participants to learn to reflect upon a case and learn from one another. She acts like the coach of a team, who helps the players by providing structure and stimulating the participants to use their skills and cooperate in order to reach their goal. Of course, when it comes to decision-making authority, there are certain formal legal rules and responsibilities and people should gain knowledge about that kind of 'objective knowledge'. However, reflecting about good care and good characters involves a much deeper learning process which focuses on the constituents of meaning-making and moral judgments. According to hermeneutic philosophy, the ethicist should help the health care professional to develop their own *phronesis*.

As a facilitator, the ethicist needs to have knowledge of and experience in guiding group processes. However, she also needs to have moral knowledge and expertise herself. She has to be sensitive to the issues which are brought up in the presentation of and the discussion about the case. In order to help making explicit moral considerations, the ethicist has to have experience with the practice under consideration. The clinical ethicist has to invest in getting to know what is at stake in the work of the practitioners.

The ethicist as a facilitator focuses on the experiences and views of the participants in practice, yet this focus is not free from pre-understandings. The ethicist necessarily has a perspective on the case herself. This means that the ethicist will not accept uncritically what participants in a practice think or claim. The ethicist will try to make sense of what practitioners express from her own perspective, and critically examine ideas expressed by the group. This is not an external critique, however, but an element of a dialogical learning process, in which both the ethicist and the practitioners change. The more the ethicist becomes familiar with the practice under consideration, and involved in a dialogue with the practitioners, the more she becomes part of the learning process herself.

Facilitating reflection is not only a matter of chairing moral deliberation sessions. Moral deliberation has to become part of the organization. The sessions have to be experienced as useful by practitioners, so that they are willing to invest their time. Moral deliberation also has to be regarded as important by the managers and the board of directors. This requires continuous action, in which the ethicist will have to involve various stakeholders from the organization.

During the moral deliberation project in GGNet, the ethicist acted as a facilitator of moral deliberation sessions. In their evaluation of the sessions, the participants expressed appreciation of the facilitation by the ethicist. They highly valued the open atmosphere, but also the structuring of the session. In GGNet, the ethicist played a central role in the process of implementing moral deliberation, being part of the moral deliberation group, and helping the group to set up moral deliberations. Because the moral deliberation group involved a close cooperation between the ethicist and professionals from the organization, moral deliberation became a structural component of the work, and relevant for practice. An indication of this is the fact that participants of the moral deliberation sessions evaluated the meetings as relevant for their daily work on the ward.

Conclusion

We may conclude that the experience of the participants in the moral case deliberation sessions is in line with the basic tenets of hermeneutic philosophy. Becoming aware of one's own perspective and learning that others have different perspectives is regarded as fruitful. The sessions are not experienced as instances for argumentation and discussion, but as joint enterprises aimed at finding out what is relevant for the case at hand. The participants are immersed in the process, like players in a play. The structure of the sessions provides a secure base for the participants, not as a set of logical steps, but as a ritual supporting the joint process of critical moral inquiry and mutual understanding. This results in new conceptualizations of the issues at stake in the case, such as danger. It makes the participants view their practice differently, and provides new ways of acting in the future. The deliberation both presupposes moral sensitivity and moral knowledge on the side of the participants and at the same time helps to develop these further. The ethicist functions as a facilitator, being immersed in and responding to developments during the process.

One might say our analysis is biased, because the moral deliberation project which we presented as an example was itself based upon hermeneutic philosophy. In response to this, we would like to emphasize that although the project was inspired by hermeneutics, it was developed with practitioners, making use of their experience and trying to meet their needs. The project was motivated by hermeneutic ideas, but these were tested for their relevance in practice, and tuned to the situation. The evaluation of the project referred to in this chapter (Molewijk et al. 2008c) used open questions focusing on concrete experiences, which the participants answered without any explicit knowledge of hermeneutic concepts. The questionnaire and the interview questions were developed through interaction with the various stakeholders within the hospital. The participants themselves explained how they experienced the sessions and appreciated the influence of the project on their daily work. Furthermore, (interpretations of the) results of the evaluation study have been discussed with the involved stakeholders in order to check their validity and to respect the ongoing cooperation (i.e., the evaluation study ended where it began: in interactions with the involved stakeholders of the hospital) (Abma et al. 2008). Hermeneutic philosophy does not and cannot produce moral deliberations or moral deliberation projects. On the contrary, only concrete examples of moral deliberation (projects) can show what hermeneutic dialogue actually means. The hermeneutic elements which we discussed in this chapter are not artefacts from our own philosophical convictions; they were experienced during the process and recognized by the health care practitioners we worked with. Although our moral case deliberations and the project management of our project are guided by ideas from hermeneutic philosophy, our approach is not unique in focusing upon concrete experiences of practitioners and stimulating reflection through dialogue. Many forms of clinical ethics organize discussions about concrete cases, and bring about learning processes by furthering an exchange of perspectives. In doing so, they practically embody the logic of hermeneutic understanding which we have elaborated in this chapter.

What is the relevance of making the hermeneutic aspects of clinical ethics explicit? In what sense does it help clinical ethicists to do their work better? Hermeneutic philosophy does not provide a set of instructions for clinical ethics;

it rather explains what the practice of clinical ethics is about. It helps ethicists and other participants in practice to focus on practical experiences as a source for moral inquiry. Although hermeneutic philosophy does not prescribe a specific method for clinical ethics, it does provide many insights which can be of practical use for clinical ethicists, both with respect to the substantial dealing with ethical cases and with respect to setting up a clinical ethics project in a health care institution. Finally, it may help to correct simplistic reductionist views of clinical ethics and unjustified demands put upon it. Clinical ethics does not provide the right answer to ethical problems. It does, however, support individual professionals in becoming more sensitive to moral issues and groups of professionals in dealing with difficult situations by improving communication and dialogical learning.

References

Abma, T., Molewijk, A.C. and Widdershoven, G.A.M. 2008. Good care in ongoing dialogue: Improving the quality of care through moral deliberation and responsive evaluation. *Health Care Analysis*, 17(3), 217–35.

ASBH Task Force on Standards for Bioethics Consultation. 1998. *Core Competencies for Health Care Ethics Consultation. The Report of the American Society for Bioethics and Humanities*. Glenview, IL.

Aulisio, M.P., Arnold, R.M. and Youngner, S.J. (eds). 2003. *Ethics Consultation: From Theory to Practice*. Baltimore and London: The John Hopkins University Press.

Bernstein, R.J. 1983. *Beyond Objectivism and Relativism*. Oxford: Oxford University Press.

Gadamer, H.-G. 1960. *Wahrheit und Methode*. Tübingen: J.C.B. Mohr.

Gadamer, H.-G. 1967. *Kleine Schriften I, Philosophie, Hermeneutik*. Tübingen: J.C.B. Mohr.

Gadamer, H.-G. 1977. *Kleine Schriften IV, Variationen*. Tübingen: J.C.B. Mohr.

Gadamer, H.-G. 1978. *Die Idee des Guten zwischen Plato und Aristoteles*. Heidelberg: Carl Winter Universitätsverlag.

Heidegger, M. 1927. *Sein und Zeit*. Tübingen: Max Niemeyer Verlag.

Molewijk, A.C., Abma, T., Stolper, M. and Widdershoven, G.A.M. 2008a. Teaching ethics in the clinic: The theory and practice of moral case deliberation. *Journal of Medical Ethics*, 34, 120–24.

Molewijk, B., Verkerk, M., Milius, H. and Widdershoven, G.A.M. 2008b. Implementing moral case deliberation in a psychiatric hospital: Process and outcome. *Medicine, Health Care and Philosophy*, 11, 43–56.

Molewijk, B., van Zadelhoff, E., Lendemeijer, B. and Widdershoven, G.A.M. 2008c. Implementing moral case deliberation in Dutch health care: Improving moral competency of professionals and the quality of care. *Biomedica Forum*, 1, 57–65.

Steinkamp, N. and Gordijn, B. 2003. Ethical case deliberation on the ward: A comparison of four models. *Medicine, Health Care and Philosophy*, 6, 235–46.

Verkerk, M.A., Lindemann, H., Maekelberghe, E., Feenstra, E.E., Hartoungh, M. and De Bree, R. 2004. Enhancing reflection: An interpersonal exercise in ethics education. *Hastings Center Report*, 34(6), 31–8.

Widdershoven, G.A.M. 2005. Interpretation and dialogue in hermeneutic ethics, in *Case Analysis in Clinical Ethics*, edited by R. Ashcroft, A. Lucassen, M. Parker, M. Verkerk and G.A.M. Widdershoven. Cambridge: Cambridge University Press, 57–76.

Widdershoven, G.A.M., Abma, T. and Molewijk, A.C. 2009. Empirical ethics as a dialogical practice. *Bioethics*, 23(4), 236–48.

Chapter 5
Discourse Ethics and Ethics Consultation

Uwe Fahr

Introduction

What is ethics consultation about? The answer seems to be very easy and indeed tautological: ethics consultation is about ethics. However, what does the term 'ethics' indicate in the context of ethics consultation? It seems that 'ethics' could mean quite different ideas or conceptions in clinical practice and in moral philosophy. Most people seem to think that ethics in a clinical setting is about specific issues such as death and dying, organ transplantation or difficulties between physicians and nurses. From a moral philosopher's point of view, 'ethics' is about more theoretical problems: How could Kant's theory of practical reason be adequately understood? Are utilitarianism and consequentialism better theories to understand human action and human practice? How could the moral language be adequately conceptualized? The main focus of 'ethics' in philosophy is on foundational problems. It is a theory about human practices, although it is not about all human practices. There are practices such as artistic practices, for example composing music, and there are practices such as producing knowledge, for example in scientific practices. The former are the subject matter of aesthetics; the latter are the subject matter of a theory of knowledge. Both theories may be useful and necessary for a theory of morality, but ethics is about a specific kind of human behaviour, about acts and deeds.

The first lesson to be learned in ethics consultation is that these consultations are not about ethics, at least not in the sense a moral philosopher understands 'ethics'. None of the philosophical questions in which philosophers are interested are discussed in ethics consultations. The ethics consultant goes into the hospital and discusses treatment decisions with physicians, nurses and sometimes patients and their relatives. Questions may arise such as: Should the ventilation be stopped? Does a patient have the right to stop his dialysis even though if he does he is going to die within days or weeks? Or imagine the following situation: a female patient had a schizophrenic episode, then some years later she was told that her feet have to be amputated to save her life. The patient does not consent to the amputation. In the period of time since the schizophrenic episode, it became arguable whether she was fully aware of what she was doing. Should the operation be performed? The ethics consultant believes that these cases have an 'ethical' aspect and that the persons affected are in need of help.

In this respect there seems to be a misunderstanding between the ethics consultant and the philosopher. The former uses the word 'ethics' in a way that cannot be called a philosophical one. Using a case description, my aim is to describe more accurately in which way 'ethics' is used in ethics consultation. Having done this we have to address two different issues. First we have to look for the impact of consultation methods on the client. Second we have to ask for the basis of the moral values put forward in an ethics consultation.

What Happens in an Ethics Consultation?

Although I am very sceptical about case narratives in ethics (Fahr 2007), I would like to start with a short story:

> A physician called an ethics consultant by phone for consultation. He described to the consultant the following scene. He had to care for a 90-year-old woman. Immediately before she was to undergo heart surgery, she made an advance directive. She told the physicians that she does not want any artificial nutrition in the case where her brain has been damaged severely and she was no longer able to live a self-determined life or communicate with her relatives. After the surgery, she suffered a severe apoplectic stroke destroying large areas of her brain. The physician told the consultant that he was sure that the precondition in the advance directive was now fulfilled. However, he also said that he had got into difficulty with following her wishes. He could treat her with an artificial nutrition tube very easily. Not to do so just meant that she was going to starve. In the other case, she would go on to live for several more years as a severely handicapped patient in a nursing home, her ability to make contact with her relatives lost. The consultant met with the physician and the relatives and they discussed how the treatment could or should go on in this situation. It was a very stressful and emotional situation, because the patient was a loved one to the relatives and they had do decide if they wanted to go on with treatment or not. Discussing the treatment plan, the consultant stressed the central role of the patient's will and her wishes, thinking of the central guidelines of the German Medical Association and some legal decisions during the last few decades in Germany. It was obvious that this was a common basis for the participants. The consultant went on asking the relatives about the patient and her wishes. What kind of person is she? After 15 minutes the participants had a shared picture of the patient and although it was obvious that she would die without artificial nutrition all participants decided to stop feeding.

Although I am fully aware that a case narrative is not the same as the case itself, I would like to use this story to give a more accurate account of ethics consultation. Everybody may use their own experiences in ethics consultation to see if my account is accurate or not. Some remarks may be useful to make my point more clear.

Firstly, it may be true that this story tells more about my views of ethical problems or about my patterns of perceptions (*Wahrnehmungsmuster*), my patterns of emotions (*Emotionsmuster*) or my patterns of interpretation (*Deutungsmuster*) (see also Fahr 2008b). Nonetheless we need a starting point for every discussion and in the time given we have no better starting point than case narratives. Secondly, I think that not only the case narrative but the 'real situation' can be described as a kind of drama with several characters (*dramatis personae*). It may be that there are some characters that are not at the scene. There may be some persons affected by the decision who are not present, for example, other patients in a similar medical situation, or a relative the consultant did not meet during the consultation process. Thirdly, the discussion in the case description was not about ethical theory, norms or moral rules. It was about the question of how to apply given moral rules to a situation in which action was imminent. It was a moral question of the kind: What should I do? Shall I (the physician) obey the patient's wish or not? Shall we (the relatives) consent to further treatment or not? Who has to take the (moral and legal) responsibility for the decision? Sometimes there are various moral rules, values or norms at stake, sometimes the discussion is more about assuring the physician that his or her decision is accepted by the relatives or the surrogates. In addition, there was no discussion about the validity of moral judgements, about philosophical problems of autonomy – not even about the notorious equivocality of 'autonomy' – or ethical relativism. The participants just used their personal morally relevant convictions and the established legal and moral framework.

The example given shows that in ethics consultation the word 'ethics' is used in a specific way that should be described more clearly because 'ethics' in ethics consultation is not the same as 'ethics' in philosophy. How then could 'ethics' in ethics consultation be described more accurately?

Phenomenology of Morals

It is notoriously difficult to describe adequately what is going on in an ethics consultation. One could imagine a more empirical way to do such a description. One solution would be to transcribe the ethics consultations of various consultants and compare their methods and their strategies, for example, their methods of consultation, their strategies to establish themselves as experts in 'ethics', the consultation techniques they use, etc. Such a description would give us a sketch of ethics consultations and could be compared with other forms of consultations. It would help us to understand more thoroughly in which way terms such as 'ethics' were used in ethics consultations. My aim here is not a sociological study of ethics consultations. For this reason I take another way to reach the aim of describing what 'ethics' in ethics consultation is. It may be useful to describe the 'ethical' aspect in ethics consultation from a more phenomenological point of view.

If we look at any given ethics consultation in more detail, we can see that there is *confusion* or *perplexity* at the beginning of the discussion. We would never discuss any moral problems in ordinary life if we knew how to act all the time. At times, our moral beliefs become suddenly questionable or they just do not answer to the given situation in which acting is inevitable. This is the reason why we ask: what should I do? This question is the starting point for further reflection. In such situations, the persons affected are often seeking advice from friends, colleagues or other persons close to them. If they are no longer able to help, there may be an expert with specialized knowledge who may be able to give advice for such kinds of situations. To act as an ethics consultant means to see the situation with the eyes of the person affected and to help the client search for a way of acting that is suitable to the situation and to the general ideas of 'good' or 'right' acting in such situations. The person affected would not feel comfortable if the consultant solved the problem for him or her, in the manner one might solve problems with the client's computer. The person seeking advice would be no longer accountable if he or she just followed the counsellor's advice.

In a more general way, Habermas – in accordance with Peter Strawson – points out that 'the world of moral phenomena can be grasped only in the performative attitude of participants in interaction, that resentment and personal emotional responses in general point to suprapersonal standards for judging norms and commands (...)' (Habermas 1992: 50). Using this attitude we can see the perplexity of the physician in the narrated case as a starting point. We could see his expectations of his patient's expectations: He thinks that his patient expects him to respect her will and wishes. Furthermore he may see himself with the eyes of colleagues or other patients, saying that it would be *unfair and unmoral* to let one of his patients starve, and he himself may think in the same way. There may be also some fear of legal liability. He wants reassurance that he is choosing the *right* action, if he accepts his patient's wishes. It is the fact that the participants and the affected in a clinical situation become aware of 'suprapersonal standards' that are binding for them and that these standards are not clear. Their own skills seem to be not developed enough to make the situation more transparent. To overcome this confusion it seems necessary to become more aware of the 'suprapersonal standards' of the participants and the affected. Ethics consultation seems to be about these standards. An ethics consultation could be called a *moral* deliberation because all participants claim more general values, rules or norms. They may not have a shared set of values, but they all claim validity for their values, rules, norms and arguments.

A sociological description of the ethics consultation would be of great interest. It could show that such situations are situations of moral perplexity and that the moral values of participants and those affected are at stake. We have to take the performative attitude, not the attitude of an observer of the drama, to see the claims of validity of all participants in this drama. It brings into sight that the participants are convinced of their claims of values, rules, norms, etc. These values, norms or rules have an inherent relation to 'suprapersonal standards'. As ethics consultants we are part of the scene; we bring in our personal view of the 'suprapersonal standards', but we have no better insight into what is 'right' or 'wrong' in the situation (see also Fahr 2008a).

Two questions have to be answered now. Firstly, what kind of 'suprapersonal standards' can be used in ethics consultation, or what is the foundation of *ethics* consultation? Secondly, in which way does the consultation process affect the method of deliberation used by the ethics consultant?

Method of Deliberation

Ethics consultation is founded in counselling *and* in 'ethics'. The consultant needs specialized training and knowledge in counselling and in philosophical ethics. He or she should be an expert regarding counselling processes and philosophical theories about morality. However, counsellors normally are aware that they have to use their clients' standards for the counselling process and not their own. Due to this fact the ethics consultant seems to be confronted with a tension between philosophical ethics and 'ethics' in ethic consultations. The ethics consultant has to deal with the problem of whether he or she should follow his or her own standards or the standards of his or her clients. Ethics consultants try to solve this problem using an implicit or an explicit method. According to the foundation of ethics consultation in counselling and ethics, the consultant could use counselling methods or methods of ethical theories. The aim of counselling methods is to moderate and to coordinate the process of deliberation of a morally relevant issue (the 'case').

It seems that ethics consultants quite often see themselves as experts in regard to moral judgement and that they believe that they are better decision-makers than the physicians, nurses, patients or relatives. Often ethics consultants seek for methods in ethical theories, which could help them to judge the situation more adequately than the participants. They seek for consultation methods in philosophical and ethical methodology. Such theories are those like so-called 'principlism', or other theories of mid-level so-called principles. Regarding the 'ethical' side of ethics consultations, various methods have been suggested (for example, Steinkamp and Gordijn 2003).

I would like to show that we can better understand the ethical foundations of ethics consultation if we do not believe that the ethics consultant should use a specialized ethical theory which can help him or her to develop the 'right' solution. My argument is that otherwise ethics consultants confound counselling and ethics.

The aims of methods can be classified into three different dimensions. A method can improve *the general structure of ethics consultation* in hospitals, or it can improve the *process of deliberation*, and, thirdly, it could be possible that a method improves the *general 'outcome'* of the deliberation process (Simon 2008). Clinical ethicists often focused on this third dimension. A consultation method could improve an ethical deliberation in two of the three dimensions.

For example, if a method implies clarification of whom the client (the patient? the physician? the nurses? the relatives? all of them?), the counsellor may tend to clarify at the beginning of a consultation process what kind of mandate he or she has for the consultation (structure). If a method implies that every person affected who is participating in a deliberation process should be heard and should have the possibility to speak during the process of deliberation, this will help to identify persons who will be frightened by hierarchies, who are helpless or lacking knowledge. The consultant may have the duty to help the weakest in the discussion (process).

It is arguable, however, whether there is a consultation method which could be useful to reach a better (in the sense of ethically better) outcome of the deliberation process. Ethicists tend to think that method should guarantee the best possible 'ethical outcome' (Meyers 2007: 17). Using an ethical theory like that of Beauchamp and Childress, they hope to reach this aim. They need a different ethical discourse, in which these 'principles' are justified. Most philosophers seem to believe that this discourse is the philosophical discourse of normative ethics. However, the theory of Beauchamp and Childress shows that this cannot be true. These 'principles' are neither generally accepted by philosophers nor is there a general agreement among philosophers how these principles should be interpreted. Moreover, the ethical theory of principlism is 'American', in the sense that the authors often use American legal cases which have no validity, for example, in Germany or Switzerland.

Christopher Meyers suggested that we can use a modified form of principlism. Going back to the real basis of principlism, to the thought of William D. Ross, he suggests an ethical theory of eight fundamental duties. Using a procedure based on these duties, he believes that it is possible to *come closer to the best ethical outcome.* However, it is not clear how he can know that the outcome comes closer to the *best* one. We could classify an outcome as close to the best one only if we knew which solution would be the best one. Then we could compare the best solution with the proposed ones. This done, we would be able to find out which solution would be the closest one. But this procedure is not feasible, because we do not know the *best outcome*. All that we can know in an ethical deliberation is that at the end of the deliberation process we come up with a plan of action that *seems to be* more adequate and better justified than the one we started with. We are able to know this, because during the discussion we are able to learn that our first plans and justifications were not convincing. Now we have more elaborated and more sophisticated plans and justifications. Furthermore, it may be that at the end of the deliberation process we agree more upon interpretations and perceptions of the given situation, and it may be that we have learned why other participants have quite different feelings in this situation (Meyers 2007).

I have to answer an objection which may come up here. One may say that the method criticized comes close to what is called the 'authoritarian approach' (ASBH 2003) and that most ethics consultants actually follow the 'ethics facilitation approach' which was recommended by the American Society for

Bioethics and Humanities. My answer is twofold. Firstly, we would need much more social research about ethics consultations to learn more about the way consultations were performed by consultants. It may be that in the clinical setting the facilitation approach is not accepted enough and consultants tend to the more authoritarian approach. My impression is that (at least in German practices of ethics consultation) there is great pressure on ethics consultants to find the 'best outcome', and not only to do their job in the best manner one could expect. On the other hand, as far as I can see, there is no attempt to explain in what way the facilitation approach has an ethical basis. The facilitation approach 'recognizes the boundaries for morally acceptable solutions normally set by the context in which ethics consultation is done' (ASBH 2003: 172). My argument is that the 'suprapersonal standards' which come into sight if one takes the performative attitude are related to standards transcendent of the context. The facilitation approach is not able to explain how this is possible.

The problems of ethical theories as the basis for ethics consultations show that we should not seek for a counselling method in 'ethics' because there is no general consensus about a normative ethical theory such as 'principlism' or 'consequentialism'. If this is true we could not apply an ethical theory in ethics consultation. Instead of such a theory we could use the 'suprapersonal standards' of our clients, and a useful method of ethics consultation would clarify useful means of counselling interventions that are able to clarify implicit 'suprapersonal standards' of participants and other persons affected.

Ethics Consultation – Practical Discourse – Ethical Theory

It is still not clear in which kind of 'ethics' ethics consultation is founded. To maintain that the ethics consultant should use the 'suprapersonal standards' of his or her clients seems to open ethics consultation for relativism. I like to suggest that in Habermas's version of discourse ethics some useful terminological differentiation can be found which could help to understand better how the ethics consultant can help his or her client to come closer to ethically better solutions.

First of all Habermas reformulated the *principle of universalization* (U) of Immanuel Kant as a so-called bridging principle. It is called a bridging principle because it bridges the gap between *maxims* on the one hand and a *general will* on the other hand. According to Habermas, this principle is the only moral principle and it is 'conceived as a rule of argumentation and is part of the logic of practical discourses' (Habermas 1992: 93). In Habermas, version (U) is stated as follows:

> (U) *All* affected can accept the consequences and the side effect its *general* observance can be anticipated to have for the satisfaction of *everyone's* interests (and these consequences are preferred to those of known alternative possibilities for regulation). (Habermas 1992: 65)

In this way Habermas clearly differentiates *practical discourses* from *ethical theory*. As far as I can see there is no place for such a thing as *normative ethics* in his theory. What is normally called normative ethics, for example, attempts to show how we should clarify our moral convictions or let theme guide our behaviour – let us say, for example: Peter Singer's utilitarianism or Rawls' theory of justice – is nothing other than 'a contribution to a discourse among citizens' (Habermas 1992: 94). In this regard Habermas makes clear that no one – including moral philosophers – has any exceptional access to *the moral truth or rightness*.

Every participant in a practical discourse can claim validity for his or her suggestions, but it is the communication community that has to accept these claims as valid. It is principle (D) of discourse ethics that brings this idea into the justification programme of discourse ethics. Principle (D) reads as follows: '(D) Only those norms can claim to be valid that meet (or could meet) with the approval of all affected in their capacity as participants in a practical discourse' (Habermas 1992: 66). As Habermas points out, this principle 'stipulates the basic idea of a moral theory but does not form part of a logic of argumentation' (Habermas 1992: 93). What ethical theory is about is justifying such a rule. Using transcendental-pragmatic arguments, discourse ethics is an attempt to justify this rule. It is not the place here to scrutinize discourse ethics as a theory and programme to justify the cognitive sense of moral judgements. I grant that one could be sceptical about the possibility of transcendental arguments. Nonetheless discourse ethics helps to differentiate between ethics consultation, practical discourse and ethical theory.

Ethics consultation is about a single case, starting from the moral perplexity of and moral conflicts among persons affected. By agreeing to reach for a solution via deliberation and argumentation they agree to abstain from violence or force, from fabrication and beguilement. Participants bring in their personal commitments to various and sometimes conflicting values or moral rules. From this background they have to describe the situation carefully. *Practical discourse* is the discourse held in society about general moral rules, values or any other 'substantive principles or basic norms' (Habermas 1992: 93). Practical discourse is the place where moral argumentation takes place. It is the place where I strive to convince others that my values or moral conceptions are acceptable because good arguments are able to support them. *Ethical theory* on the other hand tries (for example) to justify (or to criticize) the cognitive sense of ethics. Its opponent is not another citizen trying to make plausible his or her moral convictions. For example, the opponent of the cognitive moral philosopher is the sceptical moral philosopher, who is generally sceptical about the possibility that morality is anything else than a power game without any chance to claim validity, or just the expression of personal emotions.

If we accept this differentiation it becomes clear that the ethical basis of ethics consultation could not be found in ethical theory. The ethical basis could be found in the practical discourses of society. The philosopher (and the medical ethicist who normally is not even a philosopher) is no more than a participant in this practical discourse with the same rights and duties.

In my narrative, the consultant used established guidelines and the legal framework in Germany. I think that these guidelines and legal judgments are part of a more general ethical discourse in which the members of a given society seek to justify generally accepted norms, values, etc. It may be that the discourse is not wholly free and fair in Germany. It is not difficult to see that a small expert group assigned to a working group by the German Medical Association brings their personal prejudices, personal beliefs and theoretical conceptions into the guidelines. However these guidelines are often widely discussed in German society and mostly they are accepted by physicians, patients, journalists, ethicists and so on after some time, or they are modified as a consequence of thorough critique of citizens. I acknowledge that this is a very weak ethical basis for ethics consultation, but I think it is the best one we have given the times and the society.

Practical Discourses as Power Games

It seems to me obvious that all practical discourses or ethics consultations are flawed. It is not only that they are influenced by prejudices or traditions. What is more, they are deeply influenced by power. In his critique of an approach to ethics consultation based on discourse ethics, Christopher Meyers puts it this way:

> (…) there is still insufficient attention paid to the impact of power within discourse. Those who hold power, especially power historically established within a hierarchical institution like medicine, characteristically dominate conversations. They control the tone, they control the content, and they usually control the outcome. (Meyers 2007: 19)

I agree with Meyers' view. I think that it is just not true that everyone will be heard or can express their views within a practical discourse or an ethics consultation. What is true for ethics consultation is also true for the practical discourse in general. Take as an example the development of guidelines in Germany. As I said before, these guidelines are developed in small expert groups and implemented by a large medical organization such as the German Medical Association (*Bundesärztekammer*). Normally the patients or their interest groups were not heard in this process and the persons mostly affected by such regulations – future patients – are not able to see the relevance of such guidelines for them personally.

I admit that real practical discourses and ethics consultations are power games. Reading articles about ethics consultation makes it clear that most clinical ethicists ignore these aspects of consultations. Christopher Meyers is an exception to this general rule. Nonetheless he misses the central idea of discourse ethics if he wants the reader to believe that in discourse ethics it is the ethicist who should be the one who can alter these power dynamics. Indeed this belief would be simply naive (Meyers 2007: 20) and a discourse-based consensus would be simply unrealistic (ibid.). However, what I think is that Habermas in his essay points to another idea.

Habermas is quite aware that discourses:

> take place in particular social contexts and are subject to the limitations of time and space. Their participants are (...) real human beings driven by other motives in addition to the one permitted motive of the search for truth. Topics and contributions have to be organized. (...) Because of all these factors, institutional measures are needed to sufficiently neutralize empirical limitations and avoidable internal and external interference so that the idealized conditions always already presupposed by participants in argumentation can at least be adequately approximated. (Habermas 1992: 92)

He differentiates between 'rules of discourse and conventions serving the institutionalization of discourses' (ibid.).

Habermas points out that the idealized presuppositions of discourses are implicit in argumentation. Nonetheless they have to be brought to potency in the institutionalization of discourses. My claim is that the same is true for ethics consultation and for practical discourses regarding problems of medical ethics. We do not need more normative ethics of 'experts' in moral judging. What we need is the institutionalization of discourses according to the normative presuppositions that are implied in the argumentative activity of the communication community.

Conclusion

I started with the intention of giving a description of what is 'ethics' in ethics consultation. There are difficult theoretical problems at the beginning of such a description, because it is not possible without precondition. However I adopted the theory that we can only describe the phenomenon of morality adequately if we take the so-called performative attitude. Taking this attitude we learn to see that the uneasiness, the perplexity or conflict among the persons affected is a starting point of ethical thinking and deliberation. It is an ethical deliberation because we search for a valid answer to the question: What shall I do in this concrete situation? In this attitude we see that participants in ethics consultations refer to 'suprapersonal standards'. Ethicists tend to measure such suprapersonal standards of participants and persons affected against their own 'suprapersonal standards'. They tend to believe that these standards are better because they are part of an ethical theory. However, if there is no such thing as 'normative ethics', because every norm has to be justified in the communication community, it will be no longer possible to measure the 'outcome' of ethics consultations with the theories of 'normative ethics'.

I tried to make plausible that we can justify the moral basis of ethics consultation better if we differentiate between ethics consultation, practical discourse and ethical theory. Using the complex justification model of discourse ethics I showed that the main point in establishing ethics consultation and practical discourses is to institutionalize these discourses. If they are established according to contrafactual presuppositions it becomes more probable that agreement upon general norms can be reached. These general rules claim to be valid rules because they are accepted by the communication community, but we will never know if this claim is true. All we can know is that the communication community accepts it now – based on their knowledge, their moral sensitivity, and their morally relevant learning processes.

My argument is that discourse ethics helps us to differentiate our thinking about ethics consultation although we may be sceptical regarding the general justification programme of discourse ethics. To accept practical discourses as the basis for ethics consultation is more adequate and more democratic than to pretend to have found the philosopher's stone.

References

ASBH (American Society for Bioethics and Humanities). 2003. Core competencies for health care ethics consultation, in *Ethics Consultation: From Theory to Practice*, edited by M.P. Aulisio, R.M. Arnold and S.J. Youngner. Baltimore, Maryland: The John Hopkins University Press, 165–209.

Aulisio, M.P., Arnold, R.M. and Youngner, S.J. (eds) 2003. *Ethics Consultation: From Theory to Practice*. Baltimore, Maryland: The John Hopkins University Press.

Fahr, U. 2007. Medizinethische Fallberichte und das Privileg des Erzählers, in *Gekauftes Gewissen? Zur Rolle der Bioethik in Institutionen*, edited by R. Porz, C. Rehmann-Sutter and J. Scully. Paderborn: Mentis-Verlag, 199–220.

Fahr, U. 2008a. Die Aufgaben des Klinischen Ethikberaters aus erwachsenenpädagogischer Sicht, in *Klinische Ethikberatung an Universitätskliniken*, edited by D. Groß, A.T. May and A. Simon. Münster: Lit-Verlag, 69–79.

Fahr, U. 2008b. Die Entwicklung emotionaler Kompetenz in einzelfallbezogenen Lernarrangements. *Ethik in der Medizin*, 20, 26–39.

Habermas, J. 1992. *Moral Consciousness and Communicative Action*. Cambridge: Polity Press.

Meyers, C. 2007. *A Practical Guide to Clinical Ethics Consulting: Expertise, Ethos, and Power.* Plymouth: Rowman & Littlefield Publishers.

Simon, A. 2008. Qualitätssicherung und Evaluation von Ethikberatung, in *Klinische Ethikberatung. Ein Praxisbuch*, edited by A. Dörries, G. Neiztke, A. Simon and J. Vollmann. Stuttgart: W. Kohlhammer, 167–81.

Steinkamp, N. and Gordijn, B. 2003. Ethical case deliberation on the ward: A comparison of four methods. *Medicine, Health Care and Philosophy*, 6, 235–46.

Chapter 6
Implementation of Clinical Ethics Consultation in Conflict with Professional Conscience? Suggestions for Reconciliation

László Kovács

Professional Conscience

Implementing structures of clinical ethics consultation (CEC) is a challenge to traditional ethical standards in clinical decision-making. The Universal Declaration on Bioethics and Human Rights (UNESCO 2005, Art 19b) urges the establishment of independent, multidisciplinary and pluralist clinical ethics committees. This request seems to contradict with another ethical standard expressed in, e.g., in The Universal Declaration of Human Rights (UNO 1948, Art. 18), which ensures the right to freedom of conscience to every human being. Especially physicians are more than only free to make use of their conscience but they are obliged to do so. 'I will practise my profession with conscience and dignity' (WMA 2006a). This sentence of the Declaration of Geneva requires a strong dedication to the use of conscience as a source of professional duties. The International Code of Medical Ethics formulated by the WMA gives a more precise formulation: 'A physician shall be dedicated to providing competent medical service in full professional and moral independence, with compassion and respect for human dignity' (WMA 2006b).[1] For physicians the presented two ethical standards may cause conflicts. Some recent publications argue that CEC services are sources of a more appropriate moral justification in our pluralist culture (e.g. Kettner 2005). Does the commitment to professional conscience still play a morally justified role in clinical decision-making? If yes, what kind of role is this?

Contrary to the systematic reflections about CEC the international agreements of the WMA and the UNO do not explain the term 'conscience', but use it as a black box. Because of repeated misunderstandings there is a need to clarify the idea of a professional conscience and its relation to clinical ethics consultations. For this purpose I am going to discuss:

---

1 That conscience must be seen as independent from law has been clearly expressed in a previous version of the International Code of Medical Ethics of the WMA: 'Therapeutic abortion may only be performed if the conscience of the doctors and the national laws permit'. Both are required, and having legal permission does not commit the physician to perform abortion on request (Conscience Laws 1996).

1. What an appropriate concept of conscience might be.
2. The dynamic of conscience.
3. What professional conscience covers; and
4. What kind of a relation it has to other types of moral justification.

After this introduction I shall analyse possible conflicts of conscience with clinical ethics consultation (CEC) and make suggestions for the right implementation goals of CEC respecting professional conscience.

An Appropriate Concept of Conscience

Since the thirteenth century theologian St Bonaventure, conscience has been interpreted as a mysterious, suprarational, intuitive recognition of good and evil, imposing strong obligations upon the person (John Paul PP 1993). According to this approach, one had to obey conscience in every situation and not doing so had been considered as a major sin. This black-box view was however challenged by philosophers and psychologists who reflected upon the idea of conscience, and succeeded in demystifying it in the twentieth century. Erich Fromm's concept is best applicable here, since he described a relationship between conscience and ethics on the basis of socio-psychology (Fromm 1985). Fromm suggested viewing the early 'authoritative' conscience as a product of internalized rules of external authorities. He said that if one internalized the rules and laws set by such authorities, these rules become personal norms providing a basis of which good and evil can be judged. Accordingly, the feeling of guilt as a product of bad conscience is the internalized fear of this authority. Conscience is more effective in regulating the moral behaviour than any external laws or rules since it is always present. The authoritative conscience claims subjugation not because of physical power but because of moral superiority. Thus one feels that one is not allowed to criticize it. Within this kind of conscience there is no place for personal value judgements but only for rules from external authorities. Fromm, nevertheless, recognized the need to add a second, more developed, kind of conscience, the humanistic conscience, to his theory. Humanistic conscience enables the person to judge whether he or she functions as a good human being from a comprehensive perspective. It helps one become the person that one reckons one should be. On this level, one defines individual values and commitments. A well-developed person possesses both kinds of conscience.

The Dynamics of Conscience

Conscience, in this sense, is an individual, internal moral authority. It plays a role in one's judgements independent from external moral authorities, although the norms applied in conscience are not genuinely new. They are derived from norms of external authorities and reflected within the frameworks of one's individual or professional self-understanding. The normative content of conscience is not innate but is taken from social relations and self-reflection. Hence the content of conscience is individually different but its dynamics and its way of functioning is quite the same in all persons.

Immanuel Kant described function of conscience using the metaphor of a tribunal in man (Kant 1983). He said there was an inner judge who observes everything one does. It is not the norms of the judge but the judge himself that is inborn and it is not possible to escape his judgement. One feels a moral duty to perform the actions claimed by this judge. This metaphor helps distinguish between the sources of the (fallible) norms of conscience and the proceedings of it. Accordingly, the judge might follow morally good or wrong norms, his judgement is binding anyway.

Auer differentiates between two theories of how conscience influences decision-making: voluntaristic theories claim that conscience uses the tools of will, cognitive ambitions and mental drives to fulfil recognized duties; emotivistic theories describe emotional impulses as an instrument of conscience to make us experience the good and the bad of a particular situation with strong feelings (Auer 1962). Both theories seem to show important aspects of the phenomenon of conscience. The judgement of conscience has an imperative character: one must act in accordance with it. The sincerity and the power of professional conscience is proven by physicians or other health professionals who sacrifice personal benefits or even their lives for their conscientious commitments.[2] This is not a rare phenomenon but rather an element of their daily job (Beck 1960, Gillon 1985). Professional conscience formulates the moral obligation to do what they consider to be good, what they are called to do here and now, i.e., to apply the general law to a particular case. Conscience takes all circumstances into account and makes an absolute individual judgement. Conscience cannot be transferred to others, not to the state nor to a church nor to a political party. Professional conscience is like a vital organ which operates with moral sense (Frankl 1959). It has an important role, because it not only has to give an answer to what is good, but it also forces a physician to act accordingly.

The Content of Professional Conscience

One of the most important sources of professional conscience (both authoritative and humanistic), since the very beginning of professional medicine, has been the Hippocratic Oath. The Hippocratic Corpus may be obsolete but the guiding values and commitments set by Hippocrates remain contemporary – to serve the well-being of people who suffer from a disease. From this professional commitment,

---

2   Examples are several physicians and other health care professionals serving in Third World countries and in poor districts or others who risk their health by treating patients with dangerous infections.

physicians deduce many concrete, applicable and effective moral obligations for their professional and private lives. Some obligations are of such fundamental nature that they cannot be changed without losing the commitment itself; the obligation to help, respect for human life, confidentiality, etc. Others, such as telling the diagnosis to the patient or to the family, being paid for teaching medicine, etc., can change over time (Sass 1994). In spite of the controversial discussions about timeless and obsolete parts of the oath, most physicians regard it as fundamental to their professional conscience. They use it first as internalized moral authority and reflect on moral problems in their profession according to it. They also define themselves as physicians through the actual interpretation of the oath. A specific professional moral commitment is, hence, an important part of a physician's professional identity. Similarly to scientific knowledge and technical skills, humanistic conscience is an essential element of the medical profession. Only this triad makes a physician into a trustworthy person. Conscience enables the physician to recognize and do the morally good and avoid evil. This is why international declarations insist upon the term 'conscience'.

Professional Conscience in Relation to Other Moral Authorities

According to the previous description, judgements of professional conscience are not necessarily congruent with the general legal or professional norms of a particular state or culture. The differences are in most cases rather marginal, but sometimes they are considerable. Authors with communitarian preferences demand the priority of legal rules (LaFollette and LaFollette 2007). The international declarations cited, and ethicists with a more individualistic position, claim priority for professional conscience against the law (Smith 2006, WMA 2006a).

LaFollette and LaFollette point out the conflict between widely accepted, legally justified services in health care and the freedom of individual conscience to refuse to provide such services (LaFollette and LaFollette 2007). The authors claim that such services cannot be made dependent on the individual conscience of doctors, because in that case patients would be treated unequally. If society agrees on certain medical practices with morally relevant dimensions, professionals should be required to provide all members of society with them. The best-known paradigm for such a moral conflict is the health professional refusing to terminate a pregnancy based on his or her right of conscientious objection to abortion. LaFollette and LaFollette argue that those who conscientiously object to some of the legally permitted practices of a profession should not choose to follow that particular profession.[3] Savulescu makes another suggestion: Conscientious objection to a legally acceptable service shall only be permitted if a sufficient number of other

---

3 The argument has some limitations, since the legal norms of a profession change over time and professionals cannot anticipate the development of medicine and legal rules. Many gynaecologists who objected to performing abortions in the 1960s were challenged

professionals are willing to provide it. Even physicians who conscientiously object to certain treatment options have to tell patients that these options are available and have to refer them to colleagues who do not object to the treatment sought (Savulescu 2006). Savulescu's proposal might be a step towards a more liberal way of handling the conflict, but it provides no final solution either. Despite the logical persuasiveness of his concept, I question how much he understood the dynamic of conscience. A health professional who is really committed to values that forbid him or her to end unborn life will have conscientious problems about referring a patient to colleagues who are willing to terminate the pregnancy.

Authors emphasizing the priority of conscience argue with the fallibility of general rules and laws with respect to particular cases. Furthermore they stress the general fallibility of laws by referring to the experiments in the Nazi Germany, where several physicians refused to perform painful and lethal human experiments on conscientious grounds. Such a refusal had a heroic character and was often punished with death. In such cases professional conscience has been proven as a stronger guide for moral action than laws. Physicians who collaborated with the Nazi regime have been demonstrated to have been persons with serious personality disorders (Fonk 2004, Mitscherlich and Mielke 1960). To what extent these persons had psychological disorders and to what extent they had erroneous consciences is questionable (Ley 2006), but actually it is less important than the conclusion that the judgements of conscience of majorities are as fallible as those of minorities. In the Third Reich, the majority agreed conscientiously that sterilization of people with inherited diseases is a moral obligation owed to future generations. Many of the 'people with fit genes' were at war and thus at a high risk of dying before they had children. By contrast, 'people with diseased genes', who were not fit for military service, were staying at home and reproducing themselves, thereby creating a 'generation with accumulated diseased genes'. On this ground, the majority accepted the norm of protection of future generations by compulsory sterilization. They integrated this norm into their conscience and acted accordingly. Only a minority rejected orders to carry out sterilization on grounds of conscientious objection, and hazarded the consequences of professional disqualification or even execution.

Ethicists as well as several health care professionals emphasizing the individual moral competency suggest that conscience is more reliable than external moral authorities. The more communitarian view stresses that conscience is not reliable enough for clinical practice. Following the arguments of LaFollette and LaFollette or those of Savulescu, it would be beneficial to have a standardized service even at the price of compromising professional conscience, and to respect conscience only for private issues. I argue that this would have fatal consequences for the clinical practice, not because individuality is compromised, but rather for reasons of the dynamic of conscience. For clinicians it is important to experience the strong

---

after abortion became legally permitted. Because of conscientious objection they lost their jobs and suffered professional marginalization (Walley 1976).

personal moral commitment of conscience. Conscience promotes the internal self-esteem giving professional identity and starting a beneficial circle. As such, it protects from burnout in a profession, too.

One who is aware of the fact that he or she faces a moral challenge is more encouraged to use reason to resolve moral problems. Exercising conscience improves the ability to reflect on decisions and to recognize undue prejudices of external moral authorities. Physicians taking special moral responsibility are more ambitious to achieve a 'good' solution than those who 'delegate' moral problems to external moral authorities.[4] It is not beneficial for everyday clinical activities, that a member of the clinical staff perceives professional competence as a purely technical requirement and views moral decision-making as a competence of a separate profession. Moreover, conscience is a booster for innovative thinking for everyday moral problems. It also highlights matters that are not expressed in discussions in the ward or with the management. And conscience is a permanently present quality control in decision-making which cannot be replaced by controlling institutions. Therefore it makes sense to enhance it rather than to replace it.

Clinical Ethics Consultation as an External Moral Authority

Nevertheless, facing the overwhelming complexity of a moral conflict, it is quite appropriate to call for some help. A physician does not blame him- or herself or the profession if he or she needs support in situations where too much is asked of his or her conscience. Such matters are quite regular in clinical settings in recent times. During the last few decades, the conditions of professional conscience have changed for several reasons. Firstly, new technical equipment and growing scientific rationality have resulted in solutions with morally ambivalent value. Secondly, patients and society have become more ambitious and sophisticated about health and medical interventions. Thirdly, the focus of medicine has changed since issues of prevention, prediction and risks have become more relevant. The moral background of decision-making has become obscure, and deliberation with patients about values and life concepts has become essential for a 'best possible' decision. The certainty of the individual professional moral conscience is diminished also by the plurality of possible values. Under such circumstances ethicists ask the following question more often than ever before: Is it still timely to refer to conscience and what is the appropriate status of conscientious judgements in clinical decision-making?

In order to solve difficult moral problems, Western medicine invented a new institution: the CEC. This institution is practice-oriented: it settles moral

---

4 Of course it is not necessary that by making use of conscience clinicians achieve a morally better solution than external moral authorities, such as a judge or a clinical ethicist, but they are more attached to the results of their own moral deliberation than to any other external moral opinions.

conflicts on the middle level between individual conscience and legal rules of a country. The court is too far from the clinical reality and too static and slow for clinical applications. Conscience, on the other hand, appears not to be transparent enough. It eludes deliberation and is not controllable by reasons of justice and autonomy of the patient. Therefore the CEC has been interpreted as the golden middle between the two extremes. It has the advantage of being sensitive for many aspects of the clinical situation (interdisciplinary setting), fast enough in its reaction and transparent both in the decision-making process and its argumentation. It may, however, be criticized from both sides. From a legal perspective, decisions of a CEC can never be so powerful as a democratically defined moral norm. The legitimation of a CEC advice is questionable by a court. It is still less questionable than a decision based on conscience, because it provides a transparent argumentation and the possibility of interpersonal correction after deliberation. From the perspective of conscience, the CEC is an external moral authority and its use contravenes the use of conscience and its recommendation expresses a loss of confidence in conscience. Physicians with strong conscience and less competence in argumentation may find CEC a burden and a waste of time. As soon as a clinician has to delegate moral responsibility, he or she perceives that the power of his or her internal moral authority diminishes. Delegating the moral dimension of the medical decision-making to ethics consultation as a professional service means that the physician only needs to concentrate on a purely medical problem and is less involved in the whole case (both cognitively and emotionally), saying: 'The ethicist will solve this problem!' Physicians who are left alone with moral problems develop a more sensitive and more powerful conscience and, accordingly, object to the delegation of their conscientious decisions to a committee or even to professional ethicists. An aversion against any external moral authority has not to be interpreted as suspicious morality but can also be a sign of a strong moral opinion. This opinion is probably not sensitive to all kinds of problems and it does not recognize many moral discrepancies,[5] but it is a strong internal power that motivates a person to do his or her best. Thus, it would be a mistake to force an institutionalized ethics consultation against the will of the professionals, because it would be against a very fundamental source of a physician's acting and reflecting power, i.e., his or her professional conscience. Therefore, institutionalization of ethics consultation is a very sensitive issue in hospitals.

Implementation of CEC

Implementation of CEC is the institutionalization of reflections that have been performed before by an internal moral authority. Nevertheless, CEC is more than an

---

5 Empirical studies show that the majority of physicians recognize ethical problems only if and when a conflict arises with colleagues or patients and their representatives. Certain types of normative decisions, however, they do not recognize as such (Hurst et al. 2005).

externalized conscience of the participants. Facing the whole complexity there are at least six aspects to pay attention to in dependence on theories of organizational ethics (e.g., Lozano 2003):

1. CEC is an organizational service that is not intended to replace the conscience of health care professionals but complete it. Therefore CEC must not cause competition, but rather should promote professional conscience. This conscience is a necessary personal component of CEC services. Therefore ethics counsellors may use the conscience of health care professionals as a main source of values and shall reconstruct and highlight them and use them as a basis of reference during consultation.
2. A further dimension of CEC is the relational component: relationships shall not be reduced to merely information-gathering and managing between the values of participating individuals but counselling shall form a convergence respecting the status and the special perspective of the conscience of each participant.
3. The institutional component is the third dimension to keep in mind: CEC shall respect the values of the hospital. Before starting ethics consultation such institutional values have to be expressed in a very concrete manner. The management of the hospital might be interested in that, too, otherwise decisions would not fit to the institutional identity. Making such institutional values applicable is an important condition of successful case consultation. And vice versa it is to be ensured that individual case consultations may also challenge the organizational culture of the hospital.
4. The procedural dimension includes the arrangement of the decision-making process as well as the management of tensions, conflicts and differences in value judgements. Anticipating some of the differences can provide consultants with strategies of how to overcome conflicts. The time frame of CEC shall also be discussed in this dimension.
5. Planning CEC services must include the normative dimension of the work of ethics consultation, i.e., the normative status of the outcome of consultations must be clear for all participants: how far are decisions binding on all parties? Within this dimension also the consistency of the legal environment of CEC decisions has to be respected.
6. Sustainability is the last substantial dimension that deserves attention by implementing CEC services. It includes the establishment of evaluation and success criteria for consultations as well as the future perspective of the service, i.e., how it is possible to make sure that clinicians will ask for ethics consultation also in future. Enthusiasm and charismatic leadership are valuable starting power but do not guarantee sustainability of CEC services in hospitals.

Conceiving all the complexity it makes a difference how much emphasis is placed on the recognition of the professional conscience. In the starting phase ethics counsellors might consider beneficial to emphasize a precise bunch of knowledge of ethics and probably to impress health care professionals or to introduce categories in order to arrange the ethical discussion in a philosophically proper order: which values, which norms, which principles. However, this strategy fails to recognize that ethics consultation does not start from nothing but from having professional conscience based on clinical practice. Giving names to values, norms and principles might be a good retrospective summary of experiences and reflections but introducing them is channelling the discussion into a predetermined direction without having sensitivity to problems besides the predetermined categories. Operating in this way CEC will be perceived as an additional policy with possible strategic advantages for the clinics as an institution but with new burden for the clinical staff. Since CEC is a new type of the clinical organization with little comparable implementation experience there is a need of further systematic research on implementation, especially in those clinical cultures where external moral authorities have been perceived negatively.

The main possibilities of implementation of CEC are: top-down, where CEC is prescribed by the management of the institution for higher organizational, political or financial interests; or bottom-up, institutionalizing the everyday moral exchange of the clinical staff in a transparent form. It is obvious that both strategies have advantages and disadvantages. A one-sided implementation strategy is possible but only up to a certain stage of development. After having taken some initial steps, both strategies are required. Here, I will give a short overview about these aspects and point out their relation to professional conscience.

The Top-Down Model

The top-down implementation of CEC is ethically justified mainly by the need for transparency. Ethical theories suggest that a transparent decision is more suitable for a moral dilemma than a conscientious one. Some legal frameworks or hospital rules make CEC obligatory for certain types of cases especially for cases with specific social dimensions such as organ transplantation. These cases require an ethical reflection on a higher level than professional conscience ever can achieve. The clinical staff may be obliged to follow or at least to take notice of the recommendations of the CEC. A further benefit is that the top-down model makes transparent the influence of institutional interests. Structural conditions for the activities of a consultation service can also be promoted by embedding CEC into the range of institutional interests. Members of a top-down-implemented CEC are regularly exempted from other duties for the time of case consultations, they can be paid for further education in ethics, etc. These conditions confirm the importance of the engagement into ethics consultation and promote the integration of such activities into the individual professional conscience.

Many of the top-down-implemented CEC services start, however, with prescribed norms and values which do not come from the experience of health professionals but from the initiator (the management or a legal framework). Social or political interests, and the mission of the hospital, are introduced as prior to professional conscience. The initiator claims to respect the norms and values in the ethics consultation even if they conflict with professional conscience of one single physician or the majority of them. A discussion about possible inconsistencies between professional conscience and the prescribed guidelines is not foreseen within a case consultation. Sometimes the initiator proposes, e.g., a schematic diagram model for the consultation process, which merely translates prescribed principles and values into concrete actions regardless of personal convictions (Steinkamp and Gordijn 2003). Members of such consultations have to suppress their own conscience with their individual moral experience. Consequently, they will lose motivation and personal commitment in moral questions. The outcome can be a formally functioning consultation forum with professionals discussing prescribed principles and values without seeking conviction for the solution of moral problems of their practice. Convinced value judgements are done on another platform that cannot achieve this abstract level of consultation. The existence of such top-down-implemented and, in fact, ineffective CEC services will hardly be questioned because their functioning as external moral authorities is justified by the underlying theory – i.e., more transparent decision-making is better than less transparency – and by the initiator.

The Bottom-Up Model

The starting point of the model is the 'moral conflict at the bedside' or, more precisely, the need of support in a situation where too much is asked of the individual conscience of a stakeholder. The bottom-up model starts with an individual solution-oriented approach instead of a norm-based approach. In this respect a bottom-up-implemented CEC is not very systematic: patients, physicians or other health workers initiate a discussion about the moral difficulties they face in relation to a concrete moral problem. A CEC – initially without any further formal requirement – is done according to the needs of the stakeholders directly involved. It gives the impression of trustfulness and professional integrity in the ward without foreign influence. This concept fits very much in the tradition of medical professions. It does not have to be 'invented' but only to be advanced. A good doctor recognizes the capabilities, feelings and fears of the patient and integrates them into communication and therapeutic decisions. An important point is that, in the bottom-up model, nobody has the impression that an external moral authority is placed above the conscience of professionals. The model appreciates and enhances the moral conscience of professionals.

The disadvantage of a mere bottom-up implementation is that it does not use external experiences of moral deliberation but is left to the recognition of health care professionals alone. In this sense, it is blind to the shortcomings of the participants' own practice (cf. Hurst et al. 2005). The procedural quality of a consultation based on professional intuition can vary across individual cases and the decision is more fallible than decisions shared with a broader circle of professionals. Moreover, the awareness of moral difficulties is reduced to the perspective of the direct stakeholders; however, not all problematic cases are problematic from their perspective. Due to insufficient institutionalization of CEC, its relation to the hospital and the institutional status of its decisions may be ambiguous (Steinkamp and Gordijn 2003). Decisions seem to have only to do with personal moral views and not with the institutional background. With respect to progressive rationing in hospitals, voluntary bottom-up consultations are only possible under time pressure, which may compromise the quality of the deliberation. If a team tries to find time for discussions about moral difficulties with the bottom-up strategy alone, consultation will soon reach its limits.

A Suggestion to Reconcile CEC with Professional Conscience

Analysing the presented two implementation strategies of CEC, we see that both strategies applied alone cause difficulties. I have identified CEC as an external moral authority that must be sensitive to the internal moral authorities. To be an external moral authority means to operate with expressed values and norms unlike the professional conscience of care-givers. Professional conscience may include aspects of the moral decision that professionals cannot express due to their limited competence in moral reasoning. But these aspects should not be excluded from being relevant for the case. Thus before implementing CEC services and before starting consultations it is important to detect the contents of the internal professional conscience and to recognize and to integrate these values into the value system of the organization.

This should be done because of the function of professional conscience. First, I suggested seeing professional conscience as a treasury of norms to which the physician is devoted, and second as an internal power of engagement. CEC operates primarily on the first level. Decisions of the external moral authority may be better reflected than conscious decisions. But it would be a failure to accept the loss of the second dimension of conscience just in favour of the first one. There are possibilities to implement CEC with respect to the professional conscience even if it requires much more sensitivity by prescribing external norms and pointing out neglected dimensions of moral reflections. Offering CEC in this manner focuses on the experience of physicians and promotes their conscious reflection by uncovering forgotten details, making clear ideals that physicians strive to follow and anatomizing the moral complexity of the situation. Conscience in this sense can be educated rather than be replaced by an interdisciplinary ethics consultation setting. CEC certainly has to function as a normative corrective for erroneous conscience as well as an affirmation for uncertain conscience. It is also necessary that norms of the management are applied in the moral decision-making of a particular case. But ethics consultation services should not play the guardian of new moral norms or a new kind of moral reasoning but rather be a new platform for dealing with values of different moral authorities. On this platform institutional values are reflected on the same level as values of professional conscience. Respecting the judgements of professional conscience is beneficial for the CEC service since professionals do also judge about such services according to their conscience.

International declarations are still very up to date, stressing the importance of conscience even in the face of CEC. In the face of external moral authorities, professional conscience as a source for personal moral commitments needs institutional support. One important task of CEC, therefore, is to achieve a well-developed conscience, which has more value than having a counsellor in everyday moral decision-making.

Recommending this troublesome strategy, I shall finally refer to a saying of Antoine de Saint-Exupery: 'If you want to build a ship, don't drum up people to collect wood and don't assign them tasks and work, but rather teach them to long for the endless immensity of the sea' (Saint-Exupery 2006).

References

Auer, A. 1962. Das Gewissen als Mitte der personalen Existenz, in *Das Gewissen als freiheitliches Ordnungsprinzip*, edited by Karl Forster. Würzburg: Echter Verlag, 37–59.

Beauchamp, T.L. and Childress, J.F. 2001. *Principles of Biomedical Ethics*. 5th edition. New York: Oxford University Press.

Beck, J. 1960. Arzt und Gewissen, in *Das Gewissen als freiheitliches Ordnungsprinzip*, edited by Karl Forster. Würzburg: Echter Verlag, 61–80.

Conscience Laws. 1996. *The Protection of Conscience Project*. [Online]. Available at: http://www.consciencelaws.org/Conscience-Policies-Papers/pppinternational01.html#International%20Code%20of%20Medical%20Ethics [accessed 11 November 2008].

Fonk, P. 2004. *Das Gewissen: Was es ist – wie es wirkt – wie es bindet*. Kevelaer: Topos Plus.

Frankl, V.E. 1959. *Das Menschenbild der Seelenheilkunde*. Stuttgart: Hippokrates Verlag.

Fromm, E. 1985. *Psychoanalyse und Ethik: Bausteine zu einer humanistischen Charakterologie*. Munich: dtv.

Gillon, R. 1985. Conscience, good character, integrity, and to hell with philosophical medical ethics? *British Medical Journal*, 209, 1497–8.

Hurst, S., Chandros Hull, S., DuVal, G. and Danis, M. 2005. How physicians face ethical difficulties: A qualitative analysis. *Journal of Medical Ethics*, 31, 7–14.

John Paul PP. 1993. *Veritatis Splendor*. [Online]. Available at: http://www.vatican.va/holy_father/john_paul_ii/encyclicals/documents/hf_jp-ii_enc_06081993_veritatis-splendor_en.html [accessed 14 November 2008].

Kant, I. 1983. Die Metaphysik der Sitten, in *Werke in zehn Bänden*, Bd. 7, edited by W. Weischedel. Darmstadt: Wissenschaftliche Buchgesellschaft.

Kettner, M. 2005. Ethik-Komitees. Ihre Organisationsformen und ihr moralischer Anspruch. *Erwägen, Wissen, Ethik*, 16, 3–16.

LaFollette, E. and LaFollette, H. 2007. Private conscience, public acts. *Journal of Medical Ethics*, 33, 249–54.

Ley, A. 2006. Wissenschaftlicher Fortschritt, äußerer Druck und innere Bereitschaft: Zu den Bedingungen verbrecherischer Menschenversuche in der NS-Zeit, in *GEWISSENlos – GEWISSENhaft: Menschenversuche im Konzentrationslager*, edited by A. Ley and M.M. Ruisinger. Erlangen: Specht Verlag, 35–51.

Lozano, J.M. 2003. An approach to organisational ethics. *Ethical Perspectives*, 10, 46–65.

Mitscherlich, A. and Mielke, F. 1960. *Medizin ohne Menschlichkeit. Dokumente des Nürnberger Ärzteprozesses*. Frankfurt am Main: Fischer Bücherei.

Saint-Exupery, A. de. 2006. [Online]. Available at: http://thinkexist.com/quotes/antoine_de_saint-exupery/2.html [accessed 22 November 2008].

Sass, H.-M. 1994. *Hippokratisches Ethos und nachhippokratische Ethik*. Bochum: Zentrum für Medizinische Ethik, Medizinethische Materialien, 92.

Savulescu, J. 2006. Conscientious objection in medicine. *British Medical Journal*, 332, 294–7.

Smith, V.P. 2006. Conscientious objection in medicine: Doctors' freedom of conscience. *British Medical Journal*, 332, 425.

Steinkamp, N. and Gordijn, B. 2003. *Ethik in der Klinik – ein Arbeitsbuch, Zwischen Leitbild und Stationsalltag*. Cologne: Luchterhand.

UNESCO. 2005. *Universal Declaration on Bioethics and Human Rights*. [Online]. Available at: http://unesdoc.unesco.org/images/0014/001428/142825e.pdf#page=80 [accessed 11 November 2008].

UNO. 1948. *The Universal Declaration of Human Rights*. [Online]. Available at: http://www.un.org/en/documents/udhr/ [accessed 11 November 2008].

Walley, R. 1976. A question of conscience. *British Medical Journal*, 6023(1), 1456–8.

WMA. 2006a. World Medical Association, *Declaration of Geneva*. [Online]. Available at: http://www.wma.net/e/policy/c8.htm [accessed 11 November 2008].

WMA. 2006b. World Medical Association, *International Code of Medical Ethics*. [Online]. Available at: http://www.wma.net/e/policy/c8.htm [accessed 11 November 2008].

Chapter 7
Ethics Consultation: Facilitating Reflection on Professional Norms in Medicine

Christiane Stüber

Introduction

At a conference dealing with the changing image and self-understanding of nursing in Germany in 2007, some of the speakers were emphasizing the importance of selfless and compassionate care, while others were arguing against such an 'old-fashioned' and 'idealized' understanding. They endorsed a more realistic picture of nursing, one that would be less of a 'social romance'.[1]

One of the nursing managers provided an example to illustrate the point that nurses were often overwhelmed by a diverse net of professional duties that they could not explicitly describe. One day she was asked by two nurses to see them at their ward in the hospital. Both nurses were stressed and complained to the manager that they could not do their job properly. The manager inspected the ward. Everything seemed to be just fine. When she asked which specific tasks the nurses could not complete, they were unable to provide an answer. The nursing manager explained that those nurses could not make explicit what 'doing one's work properly' consisted of. She assumed that the nurses had an ideal vision of 'holistic patient care' in mind, which they did not feel able to meet. The manager commented that one should let go of such ideals, because 'Finally, that's not what staff are paid for'.[2]

---

1   The *Evangelische Akademie Loccum* conducted the conference I am referring to in November 2007, website link: http://www.loccum.de. The programme of the conference is available at http://www.loccum.de/programm/archiv/p0767a.html#programm. In this chapter, I draw on examples taken from the area of nursing to illustrate some of the normative problems that medical staff currently experience in German hospitals. While some authors distinguish between the contents of an 'ethics of care', generally attributed to nurses, and the 'medical ethics' of physicians, I am mainly concerned with the shared role of both nurses and physicians as patient trustees and as providers of 'good health care'.

2   According to the findings of Daniel F. Chambliss, the concept of 'care' seems to imply the following four meanings for nurses: 'face to face working with patients, dealing with the patient as a whole person, *the comparatively open-ended nature of the nurse's duties*, and the personal commitment of the nurse to her work'. Chambliss also points out that 'caring' describes to a moderate degree 'what nurses actually *do*; to a great degree what nurses believe they *should* do' (Chambliss 1996: 63 ff., my italics).

This remark caused considerable emotional outrage amongst the predominantly Christian nursing audience. However, the provocation had an interesting effect: people realized how hard it actually is to defend intuitions about what it means to provide good care when the challenger does not already take their view for granted. Discussing this example with other nursing staff, I gained the following impressions. First, it is difficult for nurses to voice what duties they specifically have to fulfil in their jobs, other than keeping the patient medicated, clean and fed. However, most nurses are convinced that caring for patients involves something more than the fulfilment of routine maintenance tasks and that this 'additional part' of caring is crucial for the trust that patients place in their carers. Second, because nurses cannot say what their duties are, they also cannot say what their duties are not, resulting in difficulties in setting the boundaries of their obligations. Being open to all kinds of obligations can result in the persistent feeling of overload and burnout. Third, what is needed is some space for reflection about the duties and professional norms that nurses should fulfil in their daily work.

Clinical ethics consultation could provide the appropriate institutional setting for medical staff to reflect on their professional norms and duties in the hospital environment. This reflection is a crucial task because the fulfilment of traditional professional norms is challenged by current developments within the health system such as rationalization, rationing and an increased emphasis on economic incentives. The challenge posed by the process of economization does not mean that traditional norms evaporate. It means that the contents of these norms can change in a way that deserves our attention.

What I aim to accomplish in this chapter is to show where my theoretical considerations about professional ethics in the changing hospital environment might have some practical implications for the area of clinical ethics consultation. In the following two sections, I outline two key theories that are centred on the relation between trust and professional ethics. The first theory ('Concepts of Trust') conceptualizes relations of trust as dependent on a shared normative basis between truster and trustee. The second theory ('Between Extremes: The Concept of the "Decent Agent"') introduces the moral type of the 'decent agent'. This theory seeks to determine the extent to which a moral agent who is confronted with various, and possibly conflicting, obligations can reasonably be expected to follow certain ethical norms.

Concepts of Trust

Trust between patients and medical staff is said to improve the willingness of patients to co-operate with physicians and nurses and to comply with their orders. Trust enhances the patient's willingness to communicate with medical staff and this in turn will help physicians to find the correct diagnosis and to initiate the right therapy for the benefit of the patient. Thus, the quality of health care is likely to rest, at least partly, on the existence of relations of trust between patients and medical staff.

There have been many attempts to theorize about trust. I mainly draw on two theories: a rational-choice approach formulated by Russell Hardin, and a theory by Bernd Lahno which describes trust as a disposition resulting from the normative 'connectedness' between truster and trustee.

Hardin's approach can be rephrased as follows: I can expect another agent to be trustworthy with regard to a certain matter as long as I have reason to think that he has an interest to co-operate with me. Hardin claims:

> I trust you, because I think it is in your interest to take my interests in the relevant matter seriously in the following sense: You value the continuation of our relationship, and you therefore have your own interests in taking my interests into account. (Hardin 2002: 1)

Hardin's trust conception consists of three parts: A trusts B under certain conditions to do X. The conditions do not include moral obligations of the respective agents, but the agents' incentive structure in terms of their personal self-interest. Therefore, trusting someone presupposes knowledge about her self-interested motives. The potential truster needs to know whether the co-operation with another person would be in the interest of that person. If continued co-operation is not in the interest of the potential trustee, co-operation will not be rational for that person. According to Hardin, this person could not be expected to be trustworthy in the sense that they would have reason to take the interests of the truster into account. Trusting them would then be irrational for the truster.

Hardin points out one constellation that could be interesting for our purposes. That would be one in which an agent – let us call him Bob – is not directly interested in the continued interaction with another agent, named Alex. However, he is interested in co-operating with two other persons, Clare and Donald, who are able to learn about Bob's behaviour towards Alex. If Bob wants to develop a reputation for being trustworthy in order to secure co-operational advantages with Clare and Donald, it will be rational for him to co-operate with Alex.[3] Equally, even though a physician might not be directly interested in further co-operation with a particular patient, they might well be interested in creating or maintaining a good reputation as a physician. Otherwise they would most likely lose their job.

However, do we really say that someone is trustworthy when they act only according to their self-interest? I do not think so. We can rely on this person as long as acting co-operatively is in their best interest. We can, for instance, rely on the fact that they will do their best, because that will earn them professional respect. We would not trust someone, however, if we knew that they would let us down as soon as those incentives were lacking. On the contrary, we need some certainty

---

3 Hardin explains: 'Reputational effects give me an incentive to take your interests into account even if I do not value my relationship with you merely in its own right. They do that indirectly because I value relationships with others who might react negatively to my violation of your trust' (Hardin 2002: 22).

that the one we trust will continue to be trustworthy even if their trustworthiness does not maximize their personal gain.

Although Hardin's approach does not seem to be fully applicable to reconstruct the relations of trust between medical staff and patients, it contains some aspects that are worth considering. I agree with Hardin that trusting depends to a certain extent on the knowledge a potential truster has about the trustworthiness of other agents. If there were relevant evidence that another person is not trustworthy, trusting would indeed be unreasonable. To remain receptive to evidence that casts doubt upon the trustworthiness of other people is therefore justified. However, I deny that an inquiry into the trustworthiness of agents should only take the self-interested motives of these agents into account. Human beings are not only motivated by such interests; they are – among other things – normative beings with the capacity to act according to certain moral standards. In opposition to Hardin, I claim that such moral standards can provide good reasons to act trustworthily – and to expect trustworthy behaviour from others.

Bernd Lahno has a different conception of the nature of trust. According to him, the trust that person A feels towards person B completely changes the situation in which A and B interact. A starts perceiving B differently from how she did before the trust relationship developed – as a trustworthy person. Lahno stresses that a trust relationship that has evolved for whatever reasons becomes valuable in itself, not just because the agents involved appreciate certain co-operative advantages.

Lahno points out one central type of trust that is grounded in the normative connectedness between truster and trustee. According to him, the perception of the normative connectedness with other agents enables a person to put trust into these agents. Lahno explains:

> [The truster perceives] her partner as a person who acts responsibly, as someone she is connected with by a set of shared norms and values. From this perception of the situation and of the partner an expectation of trustworthiness arises and causes her to trust. (Lahno 2002: 221, author's translation)

In situations in which A has not yet experienced the trustworthiness of B personally, his decision to enter into a trust relationship with B will depend on his expectation that B acts according to normative standards which are directed at his (A's) benefit. Following Lahno's approach, I assume that the application of professional norms that have been institutionalized in medicine provide such a foundation to expect trustworthy behaviour from medical staff. They are associated with the roles of physicians and nurses as providers of beneficial care.

However, the positive expectations of patients with regard to the trustworthiness of these physicians and nurses presupposes some certainty that the medical staff working for the institution will indeed be able to fulfil their roles properly. If the institutional environment of a hospital changes in a way that makes it increasingly difficult for medical staff to act in accordance with their professional norms, the trust-enhancing effect of these norms can be severely diminished. That will happen when patients experience medical staff no longer being able to live up to their professional ideals, due to financial and staff shortages, for instance. Under such circumstances, the continued stress on professional norms by the hospital management will not win patients' trust. Rather it will arouse both patients' distrust and cynical reactions from medical staff.

The professional ethics of medical staff are also likely to deteriorate if individual nurses and physicians lose confidence in the fact that most of their colleagues will adhere to professional norms. Hardly anybody wants to be the 'odd one out' who continues to act according to norms not followed by others. If nurses and physicians themselves lose trust in their capacity to live up to their professional norms, those norms cannot be expected to allow anyone to place trust in medical staff.

Between Extremes: The Concept of the 'Decent Agent'

In order to determine the extent to which a moral agent can reasonably be expected to follow ethical norms, I am introducing the model of the 'decent agent'. This type can be distinguished from the classic *homo œconomicus*, who only follows norms as long as this helps them to maximize their personal benefit in the long run. A *homo œconomicus* can maximize their personal benefits by securing advantageous interactions with others. This might require them to display some commitment to co-operative norms, because potential partners will be more likely to co-operate with them if they are known generally to adhere to such norms. To my mind, this approach is as unconvincing as Hardin's approach to trustworthiness. If someone stops adhering to certain norms as soon as norm compliance does not continue to maximize their personal gain, it does not make sense at all to speak about norm commitment.

I also distinguish between the 'decent agent' and the 'moral rigorist'. The rigorist follows ethical norms under all circumstances. Such people do exist, but they are rare. In contrast to the 'moral rigorist', the 'decent agent' does not display heroic or exceptional behaviour. A 'decent agent' does feel committed to ethical norms, but they do not follow these norms independently of the consequences this will have on their life and on the lives of the people around them. Firstly, they will be interested in the effectiveness of their norm compliance, especially when they feel alone in their norm-following attempts.[4] Secondly, the agent's willingness to comply with

---

4   To illustrate this point, one can consider the following example: Germans like to consider themselves as people who act responsibly when it comes to environmental matters. For instance, we follow the norm of waste separation. Following this norm demands, among other things, to separate the tin-foil lid of a yoghurt container from its plastic component. While this would certainly be effective if everyone separated aluminium from plastic, the practice ceases to have a positive effect on the environment if some people follow it and some do not.

a certain ethical norm is not independent of the question whether regular norm compliance might actually harm them in a substantial way. I believe that it makes a big difference whether I do not follow a norm because that does not maximize my personal benefit or whether I am hesitant about norm compliance because I have reason to fear severe harm. Worrying about the latter is not necessarily egoistical. It only demonstrates some reasonable care for myself, not a lack of care for others. I would even argue that caring for others presupposes the ability to care for oneself.

Nevertheless, it is difficult to determine at what point the costs of norm compliance become unacceptable. That depends on the individual person, their physical and psychological constitution. It also depends on the particular situation and on the content of the norm that is to be followed. Many people would admit that it is acceptable to risk pneumonia by jumping into a cold lake to save the life of a drowning child. The situations I am examining are different. Professional norms, such as the provision of compassionate care, are usually meant to be followed on a routine basis.

An example may illustrate what I mean. During one of my hospital internships I had the opportunity to work with a nurse on nightshift. She was responsible for 36 patients, among them many who needed extensive care. The nurse was able to call upon one physician for support who was exhausted after having already worked during the day. The nurse had to conduct two patient admissions and she also had to care for an elderly patient who had taken a laxative and needed to be put on the bedpan every 30 minutes. The nurse had to oversee all 36 patients (taking rounds and making sure that everyone was still breathing). Furthermore, she documented everything she did. She organized medication and prepared breakfast. Also, the nursing staff on the ward were generally afraid of unemployment. Members of a consultancy company had been inspecting the hospital for weeks and rumours were spreading that the ward was likely to be closed. Additionally, there had always been some tensions among the nursing team. Due to the fear of closure, the lack of staff and a reduced length of patient hospital stay, the stress on everyone had increased making the tension within the team even worse.

The nurse did her work as well as she could. The immediate physical needs of her patients were met. At the end of her shift, she felt pleased that she had done everything and that she had not left any work for the dayshift. However, she also admitted that she was frustrated, because she thought that she could not do her job properly anymore. She said that she had to conduct nursing like assembly-line work, not having enough time to care sufficiently for the individual patient. For example, she felt guilty about not having consoled the elderly lady who had been ashamed of using the bedpan so often. The nurse realized that she was overworked, that she suffered from constant tiredness and burnout. She found herself in a network of different obligations that she felt unable to meet properly; obligations towards her patients, her colleagues, the hospital and, finally, obligations towards herself and her family. She knew that she was able to fulfil the basic tasks of patient maintenance, but she said that under the current circumstances she was not able to be the 'good nurse' that she wanted to be.

Why Reflect on Professional Norms?

The experience of this nurse is not unique. Especially when people gain a great deal of their self-esteem from doing 'good work', the feeling that they cannot deliver that kind of work anymore often results in severe psychological problems. The traditional picture of nursing, which was dominated by the ideal of the loving and self-sacrificing nurse who does everything for her patients while neglecting her own needs, is probably part of the problem.

The professional ethics of nurses and physicians respectively comprise some kind of traditional knowledge of what it means to be a good nurse or a good doctor. A lot of this knowledge has been transmitted by example and has been part of the daily practice of medicine. Usually, however, people have not reflected on the norms that are commonly taken to constitute part of their professional competence. If work conditions change in a way that makes it increasingly difficult to meet certain professional standards, simply referring to the authority of tradition does not help. Instead, one is forced to reconsider what it means to do one's work properly. One needs to reflect on the contents of the professional ethics that have been taken for granted for a long time. That is not easy, because this reflection touches upon identity issues and opens something to doubt that was taken to be certain.

A consequence of my concept of the 'decent agent' is that a moral agent cannot be expected to follow professional norms independent of all external circumstances. That does not mean, however, that an agent would automatically get rid of the respective normative burden. He or she needs to reflect on whether the professional norms in question – and the common ways of following these norms – are really essential to provide good patient care. It is crucial to note that this reflection is not a private enterprise. It cannot be successfully conducted by just one profession and certainly not without consulting the expectations of the public. However, if the answer to this question is yes, but norm compliance has become unacceptable for medical staff, the personal commitment to a norm will have to express itself differently. It can manifest itself in an open criticism of those circumstances that prevent people from continuing to comply with norms. This criticism can, depending on the situation, be directed at nursing managers, at the chief physician of a clinic, at the hospital management and even, if necessary, at the government of a country. If these institutional players have an interest in the retention of traditional professional norms as part of the particular competence of medical staff, they are also responsible for providing or at least enabling work conditions that allow medical staff to follow these norms. In other words these institutional players, and not just the doctors and nurses working in hospitals, become addressees of the respective professional norms.

Admittedly, it might emerge that these traditional norms are not in demand anymore, or that it is simply impossible to improve the existing work conditions sufficiently to disburden norm compliance. If that were the case, it should be made clear that traditional professional standards will not be met anymore – and therefore they can no longer serve as the basis for patients' trust in medicine in the same way. That would be a fairer solution than leaving it up to doctors and nurses to find the balance between highly humane ideals and the opposing realities of daily hospital life. Medical staff could openly reject demands that they cannot possibly meet, and patients would have the chance to establish new and informed trust relations with doctors and nurses, even though those might have to rest on different and even lower normative expectations.

To be sure, it might be argued that professionals such as nurses will resist the adoption of lowered professional standards. Even if their employers did not put any pressure on them to comply with traditional norms, nurses could still experience these norms as essential for their work and therefore as binding. Also, if patients react with gratitude and praise to nurses' attempts to do everything possible, this is likely to confirm them in their compliance with traditional standards. Here we touch upon identity issues and questions of a positive self-perception that cannot be developed further in this chapter.

Implications for Clinical Ethics Consultation

Clinical ethics consultation can help medical staff to express their conflicts and problems more clearly. In the example of the nursing manager and the two nurses that I gave in the beginning, the involvement of an ethics consultant might have been useful. In such cases, the consultant can help to uncover the conflicts that lie at the heart of the bad gut feelings that people have. If there are normative issues involved that concern the professional ethics and self-understanding of individual nurses or doctors, the consultant can help to formulate these norms. She can help to differentiate between general moral principles and more context-specific norms, between norm compliance, overcompliance[5] and non-compliance, and between medical, ethical and economic expectations and arguments. Understanding these distinctions by applying them to problematic cases would enable medical staff to determine their duties more clearly and to recognize which obstacles stand in the way of fulfilling these duties. It would also provide nurses and doctors with a common language with which to express conflicts between different obligations, both amongst each other and towards non-medical managers and superiors. These factors combined would constitute a specific ethical competence that could help medical staff to reflect on ethical norms and to clarify and advocate the professional ethics they have reason to follow.[6]

---

5   In ethical theory, the point of overcompliance could be discussed under the headline of *supererogation*. Acts of supererogation are usually defined as optional and non-obligatory. According to David Heyd: '[…] they are beyond duty, fulfil more than is required, over and above what the agent is supposed or expected to do' (Heyd 1982: 1).

6   As suggested in 'Why Reflect on Professional Norms?', clinical ethics consultation can also serve as a platform to make contact with responsible groups outside the hospital. It could, for instance, help to communicate the ethical conflicts perceived at the hospital level to politicians.

An ethics consultant should have the competence to discuss where ethical, medical and economic goals of an institution are in conflict, and where not.[7] Working in the hospital environment, they will often be confronted with angry and frustrated medical staff who resent management for all the constraints they face in their daily work. Such an unreflected hostility towards economically grounded limitations is likely to have a paralysing effect. It prevents people from developing good arguments that can compete with and perhaps override purely economic considerations. It might, for instance, be helpful to discuss how scarce resources can actually force managers to implement certain measures for the benefit of patient care – rather than just for the financial benefit of the hospital owner. Likewise, the consultant might have to remind management staff that human beings cannot be controlled by economic incentives alone, but that they are normative beings, able to differentiate between right and wrong, just and unjust, and not only between more or less efficient.

As pointed out earlier, following professional norms is part of the specific competence of professionals. If professionals themselves lack the confidence that they, as a group, can follow a common set of professional ethics, the trust of patients and society can hardly continue to rest on these professional ethics. Thus, one important basis for trusting the institution of medicine and its individual members would, at least temporarily, collapse. I presume that the lack of this basis would mean a severe loss for the institution of medicine. To be sure, one could argue that patients could still rely on the law to secure certain norms and standards in medicine, independently of any moral commitment to professional ethics. Even though that might be true, this kind of confidence would significantly differ from the kind of trust described thus far. Just like economic incentives, the law steers and controls human conduct from outside and works through people's fear of punishment. Unlike legal texts, the obligation that shows itself in the adherence to professional norms motivates people to a large extent independently of continual and costly external interventions. It is part of the identity and the specific competence of medical staff, and it accounts for a professional integrity of which nurses and doctors are proud. The substitution of this potential by the placement of external incentives would mean a waste of a proven remedy to orientate the behaviour of hospital workers towards good patient care. Furthermore, the orientation of hospital workers towards good patient care may even be weakened by imposing external constraints. Research conducted by Bruno S. Frey and the Institute of Empirical Research in Economics at the University of Zurich seems to confirm that external constraints such as legal rules and monetary incentives can, under certain conditions, have a 'crowding out' effect on the internal motivation of persons to act 'morally' and trustworthily.[8]

---

7   For a detailed account on the core competencies of an ethics consultant, see the chapter by Beate Hermann in this volume.
8   For a more detailed account, see Frey (1997) and Bohnet et al. (2000).

Avoiding this waste demands some joint investment into the professional ethics of medical staff, not through the stubborn insistence on tradition, but through an open-minded and informed reflection on the essentials of good medical care. This must take into account the needs and capacities of patients and hospital staff alike. At the hospital level, ethics consultation can support this process by providing the space and tools necessary for conducting this enterprise.

References

Bohnet, I., Frey, B. and Huck, S. 2000. *More Order with Less Law: On Contract Enforcement, Trust, and Crowding*. Working Paper No. 52, Institute of Empirical Research in Economics, University of Zurich.

Chambliss, D. 1996. *Beyond Caring*. Chicago: University of Chicago Press.

Frey, B. 1997. Moral und ökonomische Anreize: Der Verdrängungseffekt [Morality and economic incentives: The crowding out effect], in *Moral und Interesse*, edited by R. Hegselmann and H. Kliemt. Munich: Oldenbourg, 111–32.

Hardin, R. 2002. *Trust and trustworthiness*. New York: Russell Sage Foundation.

Heyd, D. 1982. *Supererogation*. Cambridge: Cambridge University Press.

Lahno, B. 2002. *Der Begriff des Vertrauens* [The Concept of Trust]. Paderborn: Mentis.

PART II
Implementation

Setting up CEC structures is not an easy task. Next to the reports on successful implementation of CEC services there are many stories about CEC structures which either do not exist any longer or which have never been more than a 'paper tiger' – possibly developed as part of a so-called 'quality assurance initiative'. One of the important questions regarding the implementation of CEC refers to factors which positively support the process of implementation. At the macro- and meso level, analyses of the political and legal framework as well as institutional characteristics are important in order to understand the potential resources and limits for implementing CEC structures. At the micro level the identification of needs and preferences of those who are confronted with ethical conflicts as a part of their clinical practice is an important prerequisite for developing services which meet the demands of physicians, nurses and other health care professionals.

Chapter 8
The Implementation Process of Clinical Ethics Consultation: Concepts, Resistance, Recommendations

Jochen Vollmann

Introduction

The work of clinical ethics committees and clinical ethics consultation begins with implementing these new ethics structures in hospitals and other health care institutions (Dörries 2008, Dougherty 1995, Kanoti and Youngner 1995, Neitzke 2008, Singer et al. 1990). Compared with the introduction of other innovations in the hospital setting, implementing clinical ethics consultation tends to be more difficult. In practice it is often a complex and long, drawn-out process fraught with information deficits, communication difficulties, conflicts of interest, resistance to change and opposition (Dörries 2003, Dörries and Hespe-Jungesblut 2007, Fletcher and Spencer 1997, Lo 1987, Piette et al. 2002, Scheffold et al. 2006, Vollmann 2001). These problems are often underestimated by the initiators of clinical ethics consultation, so that projects launched in a committed and idealistic spirit are sometimes doomed to fail in hospital practice (Gefenas 2001, Mills et al. 2006). For this reason, the following chapter explores the problems involved in implementing clinical ethics committees and clinical ethics consultation.

The chapter is based on international scientific literature found in a search of the PubMed database as of 9 June 2008 (search keywords: 'ethics consultation' [MeSH = Medical Subject Heading] OR 'ethics committees, clinical' [MeSH] AND 'implementation') and of other relevant reference literature. In addition, data was used from the European Clinical Ethics Network (Molewijk and Widdershoven 2007) as well as my own experience from practice, as one of the implementers of a clinical ethics committee at a university hospital in Germany (Vollmann and Weidtmann 2003, Wernstedt and Vollmann 2005). To date, I have advised approximately 30 hospitals on the implementation and further development of clinical-ethical structures and trained approximately 300 clinical staff members in a qualification programme (Dörries et al. 2005) in clinical ethics consultation.

After analysing the implementation concept and process, the chapter explores the most common objections to implementing ethics consultation. Finally, the chapter presents six concrete steps to achieve an ideal implementation.

Framework Conditions

In practice, the structures of clinical ethics consultation are commonly implemented upon the initiative of the management within the framework of certification processes in order to obtain a positive evaluation for a hospital or health care institution (Piette et al. 2002, Vollmann 2008a). This strategic top-down initiative has the advantage that structural decisions are made by those in responsible positions and can be implemented in a goal-oriented manner (Molewijk et al. 2008). In other instances the impetus comes from dedicated staff members who see a need for a regular discussion of ethical issues which arise in their everyday work (the bottom-up model). This approach has the advantage that commitment and competence are already present in the work environment where ethical decisions must be made. This is of crucial significance for the acceptance and vitality of clinical ethics consultation.

Both aspects must converge in order to implement clinical ethics consultation: without management support it cannot succeed, and without dedicated staff members who identify with its objectives, clinical ethics consultation will not be able to unfold its potential in the day-to-day work of the hospital. But why is this combination – so important to implementing clinical ethics consultation – so difficult to achieve?

From the perspective of the health care professions the focus of clinical ethics consultation is on advising in individual cases. In a difficult conflict of clinical-ethical decision-making, e.g., whether treatment of a patient in intensive care should be discontinued, an ethical consultation regarding the individual case seeks to support all of those involved. However, this case-specific perspective does not sufficiently take into consideration that the implementation of ethics consultation is not limited in a hospital to the case-specific level. Implementation of ethics consultation always takes place in a social-institutional context and transforms the organization and culture of a hospital. Therefore it is helpful to differentiate between the organizational level and the case-specific level, which converge in the implementation of clinical ethics consultation.

Organizational Level

- corporate identity
- quality development (certification)
- employee and organizational development.

Case-specific Level

- improved patient care
- support of staff members.

On the *case-specific level* the treatment and care of the individual patient is the main focus. Here it is a matter of ethical conflicts and concrete decisions in the individual case, which must be made by doctors, nurses and other health care professionals in everyday situations in a hospital ward. What staff members expect from the ethical case discussion is concrete support in dealing with the individual patient or the 'difficult case'.

In contrast, on the *organizational level* the implementation of ethical structures is viewed from institutional and strategic perspectives, e.g., with respect to organizational and employee development and economic and legal issues. The organizational level in management is mostly made up of economists and lawyers who do not know the individual patient but who focus on the quality and corporate identity of the hospital as a whole. Their task is to secure the position of the hospital in a changing hospital market. However, decisions on the organizational level in the hospital have an indirect influence on the treatment options of the individual patients. They are therefore ethically relevant and must be sufficiently considered in the complex structure and interaction in an institution (Vollmann 2008a).

The vision, tradition and self-image of hospitals can vary widely, for instance, between church-related hospitals, private hospitals and university hospitals. Social framework conditions, such as different financing modalities, shortages of beds or physicians or different health care systems in the European countries, have an indirect impact on the implementation of ethics consultation structures. For that reason, the implementation models cannot simply be copied from one hospital to another (Dörries 2008, Neitzke 2008); neither can they be exported from one country to another without prior evaluation. This applies both to the transfer from the USA to European countries and to the transfer from one European country to another.

Many Eastern European countries are now in a fundamental social transition process ('transitional societies'), which also affects their health care systems. In the decades of socialist rule, state-controlled bureaucratic health care systems evolved which were politically steered 'from the top'. Accordingly, the hospitals and the physician-patient relationship had a hierarchical and collective character. Due to this political experience many citizens show a pronounced scepticism towards decisions 'from the top', which speaks against a 'top-down' implementation of clinical ethics consultation in Eastern European hospitals (Borovecki et al. 2006) (compare also the chapters by Borovecki and Kovács in this volume). At the same time, the problem is posed how an implementation from the 'bottom-up', that is, via an initiative starting from the basic level, can succeed without the tradition of citizen commitment and democratic participation. In a social and institutional environment in which the protection of human rights and respect for the opinion of others is not very well developed, a 'bottom-up' implementation tends to be more difficult.

Additional factors are the loss of trust in the health care system, unequal provision of medical care in the population, economic problems in the health care system, corruption and lack of information, a low level of education and underdeveloped patients' rights. Indeed, the democratic transformation of society has improved the rights of citizens and thus the rights of patients. These new legal standards are intended to lead to an increase of ethically reflected decisions in the day-to-day work of the hospitals. In Georgia and Croatia, for example, clinical ethics committees are even legally required in some areas of the health care system, but in reality they have not yet been established (compare the chapters by Chikhladze and Pitskhelauri, as well as Borovecki, in this volume). In contrast, empirical studies from Bulgaria show that the majority of the hospital physicians surveyed have a positive attitude towards the establishment of clinical ethics consultation, but in practice continue to solve ethical problems within the medical profession (compare the chapter by Aleksandrova in this volume). These examples illustrate the great importance of social and institutional framework conditions for the implementation of clinical ethics consultation.

Objectives and Tasks

Furthermore, when implementing clinical ethics consultation, the goals and tasks need to be clearly defined. For most professional groups in the health care system, 'ethics' is a diffuse term linked with different and even contradictory and unrealistic expectations.

The scope of duties of clinical ethics consultation encompasses clinical-ethical issues which arise during patient care. In practice in medical-ethical conflict situations, a consultation/liaison psychiatrist is often called in, since as representative of biopsychosocial medicine, a holistic approach to the patient with communicative competence is expected from them. Despite the obvious overlapping, a lack of differentiation between ethical and psychiatric/psychosomatic issues is connected with the risk that a primarily ethical problem will be masked and 'psychiatrized' or that the presence of a treatable psychiatric disorder will be mistaken for an ethical conflict situation.

A consultant psychiatrist, as a specialist physician, has diagnostic, therapeutic and prognostic competence and bears personal medical responsibility for this (the delegation of medical responsibility within a consultation of a specialist physician). In contrast, the task of a clinical ethicist is to identify and analyse ethical issues and conflicts. For this they need professional training in fundamental philosophical and medical-ethical principles and their application in concrete situations, such as communication and moderation competence. Due to the normative character of an ethical conflict situation, responsibility for the decision to be made nevertheless cannot be transferred to the clinical ethicist, but remains with the physician responsible for the treatment (Bauer and Vollmann 2004). Corresponding professional delimitations of clinical ethics consultation exist with respect to palliative-medical advice, psychological consultation, social consultation and pastoral counselling.

Furthermore, a clinical ethics consultation is to be distinguished from team supervision, a Balint group, etc., and cannot take on the tasks of the works council, social consultation services, etc. Conflicts in the field of labour law and mobbing, tension between the management and the works council, aspects of superordinate

Table 8.1 Three Levels of Clinical-ethical Institutionalization

Body	Level of impact
Superordinate ethics committee/ethics forum	Hospital group or association
Clinical ethics committee	Local hospital
Mobile ethics consultation team	Ward or care unit

company development and management, as well as issues of fair distribution on the macro level are not the primary tasks of *clinical* ethics consultation. In the reference literature, *organizational* ethics committees are suggested for this task. They can advise the management on superordinate issues which especially concern the development of the institution as a company and advise those responsible in the institution on ethical matters. For this task the committees have the respective legitimacy, composition and working methods (Zentrale Ethikkommission bei der Bundesärztekammer 2006).

In recent years different structures of clinical ethics consultation, such as clinical ethics committees, superordinate ethics councils, decentralized ethics forums as well as professional clinical ethics consultants, etc., have arisen (Dörries and Hespe-Jungesblut 2007, Vollmann 2008a). The different forms of clinical ethics consultation generally have three task fields in common: ethical consultation with respect to the individual case, development of guidelines as well as the education/training of physicians and other health care professionals and continued, on-the-job training. In particular in hospital groups which have been established through the consolidation of formerly independent hospitals (van der Kloot Meijburg and ter Meulen 2001, Vollmann 2008a) there are often in practice three levels of institutionalization (see Table 8.1). The hospital group usually has a superordinate ethics committee, ethics council or ethics forum, the respective local hospital usually has an (advisory) ethics committee and mobile teams also provide clinical ethics consultation wherever they are needed. For the decentralized inclusion of ethical work in individual wards and specific functional units, the local hospital management or hospital employees can initiate ethics groups moderated by members of the mobile ethics consultation. Through these arrangements, the inhibition threshold for requesting an acute, case-relevant ethics consultation is lowered, and at the same time, for instance, by discussing complex and difficult past cases, the staff members' further training in ethics is promoted.

Objections in Practice

'We don't have time for that!'

'We already have hardly any time' is one of the most common objections to implementing clinical ethics consultation in the everyday work of the hospital. And it is certainly true that the implementation and work of clinical ethics consultation are quite time-intensive. Discussing a case in a clinical ethics consultation usually takes 45–60 minutes and can hardly be done in less time. However, on closer inspection, what really is behind the time argument is a priority conflict: in our work we have time for what we think is important! It is only superficially a question of lack of time. Deep down it is a question of how important reflecting on ethical considerations is for an institution and its staff in their everyday work. In practice such ethical reflection can make unresolved communication problems or subliminal conflicts transparent and can contribute to their resolution. Unexpressed and unresolved moral conflicts in the treatment team often lead to 'friction losses' or even ruptured communication, misunderstandings, errors in treatment, and demotivation with a high number of staff absent due to illness and burnout problems. As these problems cost an unnecessary amount of time and energy, ethics consultation can over the long term be time-efficient and contribute to an improvement of patient care and the work atmosphere among colleagues (Zentrale Ethikkommission bei der Bundesärztekammer 2006). The same applies to the development of guidelines and training modules in ethics, which first appear to be time- and effort-intensive, but over the long term help to prevent ethically questionable treatments, etc.

'That interferes with a trusting doctor-patient relationship!'

Many doctors fear that their personal relationship to the patient and their freedom to choose the therapy would be impaired by the clinical ethics consultation. They are afraid they would have to justify their ethical decisions as physicians in the clinical ethics consultation, although the particularities of the individual case would not be known there (Davies and Hudson 1999, Dörries 2003). However, this widespread fear is unfounded and is often due to insufficient knowledge about the tasks and methods of clinical ethics consultation. In our model each ethics consultation only takes place at the request of those affected, without curtailing the responsibility and decision-making authority of the treating physician (Dörries 2003, Greco and Eisenberg 1993, Lo 1987, Vollmann 2008a). In practice, ethical consultations only take place for a very small percentage of patients (Vollmann 2008a). Usually, a clinical ethics committee does not make a 'round-the-table' vote – it is a misconception to see it as a tribunal. Rather, a few members of the committee go to the ward and take part in the discussion process with the team treating the patient. All participants – including the physicians – are asked to communicate their views based on ethical arguments and make them clear to other professional groups. It does not appear convincing that this interferes with the physician's freedom to make a decision and impairs a trusting physician-patient relationship. Rather, the practice shows that a credible, serious and multidisciplinary consultation regarding difficult ethical decisions can strengthen the trust of patients and family members (Schneiderman et al. 2003).

'Oh no, not more bureaucracy in the hospital/nursing home!'

In recent years, doctors, nurses and others working in the health care system have been increasingly burdened with documentation and administrative tasks, which involve bureaucracy, meetings, on-the-job training, etc. It is therefore understandable that there is a general aversion towards additional bureaucratic activities. While it is true that clinical ethics consultation also involves some 'paperwork', for instance, in the form of developing guidelines and statutes and writing consultation reports, it is mainly a matter of fundamental ethical principles, a – often neglected – core area of activity of a doctor or health care professional. That is why the focus of clinical ethics consultation must always be on the ethical issues and needs of the patient and of the affected health care professionals and not on formal aspects. Clinical ethics consultation is not a bureaucratic control instrument, but a modern and voluntary consultation service in the hospital and nursing home.

'This is just something the administration wants!'

If the hospital staff gain the impression that a clinical ethics consultation has been ordered 'from the top', there is usually a discrepancy between the initiative of the administration (top-down model) and the need, acceptance and credibility on the side of the staff (bottom-up model). In such a situation each case must be investigated individually as to why the staff members do not feel included and why they have negative feelings about clinical ethics consultation. Experiences from practice have shown that a clinical ethics consultation which was quickly established by the management in the context of a certification process frequently did not develop any practical impact. Instead, this 'deceptive marketing on glossy paper' arouses staff scepticism and detracts from the credibility of ethics consultation and of the hospital or nursing home management. On the other hand, there are positive examples of clinical ethics consultation which, although initiated in the process of certification by the management, was so filled with life by the staff members that the needs 'at the bottom' were taken into consideration. Credibility, acceptance, competence and independence are indispensable for the success of any clinical ethics consultation.

Six Implementation Steps

Each clinical ethics consultation in a hospital or nursing home has its own developmental history, identity, structure and working method, which are shaped by the members and reflect the special characteristics of the respective institution (Dörries 2008, Neitzke 2008, Simon 2000, Vollmann and Weidtmann 2003, Wernstedt and Vollmann 2005). The implementation steps in Table 8.2 are therefore meant to serve as an orientation aid in founding a clinical ethics consultation using the example of clinical ethics committees and must be dealt

Table 8.2 Steps to Implement Clinical Ethics Consultation

Step 1	Hospital management: • commissioned task • definition of objective • appointment of a coordinator • regulation of staff working hours • material resources
Step 2	Coordinator: • informal conversations • in-house hospital announcement • inclusion of existing structures • first meeting
Step 3	Working group 'Ethics in the Hospital': • open working group • process of gaining members • fixed dates for meetings, e.g., monthly, in the afternoon, 90 minutes • 'example ethics consultations' • development of own work style
Step 4	Clinical ethics committee: • founding • 7–20 members • appointment by hospital management • 2–3-year term • election of a committee chairperson and if necessary vice-chairperson • rules of procedure/statutes • fixed monthly meetings • material resources
Step 5	Clinical ethics committee: • working groups • ethics day • development of guidelines • further training
Step 6	Clinical ethics committee: • development of consultation services for clinical specialities • networking with other committees • quality assurance • scientific research • international cooperation

with individually in each single instance. Here modifications, deletions or extensions may seem reasonable.

Step 1

Hospital management:

- commissioned task
- definition of objective

- appointment of a coordinator
- regulation of staff working hours
- material resources (photocopies, reference literature, external consultation)

When implementing the structure of clinical ethics consultation, here using the example of a clinical ethics committee, the active support of the hospital management is needed. The management must commission the task and issue an authorization with clearly defined goals, appoint a coordinator or contact person, and establish the task of future committee members through clear regulations. This also includes ensuring the independence of the clinical ethics committee as far as its work is concerned. In practice it has proved beneficial to make it possible for this work to be carried out during the staff members' working hours, so that the burden on the staff is fair. Furthermore, the hospital management must provide the necessary space and communication and financial requirements for a professional development of clinical ethics consultation. The funds necessary, e.g., for specialist reference literature, photocopies and training events, are small and can be allocated from the budgets even of smaller hospitals. However, in practice there are a multitude of difficulties in this respect which can unnecessarily demotivate and discourage the staff. This often reveals just how seriously the hospital management is interested in the establishment of a clinical ethics committee.

Step 2

Coordinator:

- informal conversations
- in-house hospital announcement
- inclusion of existing structures
- first meeting

In the next step the coordinator initiates the founding of a working group on 'Ethics in the Hospital' by means of informal conversations and internal announcements, e.g., in the in-house newspaper or intranet newsletter. Good internal PR work is of central significance, because all staff members must be informed in good time and have the opportunity to participate. Furthermore, already existing ethical structures and initiatives must be taken into consideration, for example working groups and pastoral counselling, and must be included in the founding process. In many hospitals, cooperating with the quality assurance department has proven to be beneficial, because it can support the process of implementation structurally and through communication. As quality assurance is not possible without a reflection on values and on the overall concept of an institution and the people who work there, there is considerable congruence as far as content is concerned.

This must occur in a transparent and trust-inspiring atmosphere in order not to provoke unnecessary resistance and blocking. It is important to remember that in every founding process of a clinical ethics committee, scepticism, reservations and resistance arise. It is particularly difficult to deal with concealed rejection, frequently from head physicians, who feel restricted in their decision-making authority as physicians or who feel they are being monitored. That is why it is so important to proceed in a transparent manner, pursuing the goals that the management has specified. In the founding process one cannot wait until the last person in the hospital has been convinced.

Step 3

Working group 'Ethics in the Hospital':

- open working group
- process of gaining members
- fixed dates for meetings, e.g., monthly, in the afternoon, 90 minutes
- 'example ethics consultations'
- development of own work style

After the coordinator has approached potential members from the different professional groups of the hospital and, if necessary, has also approached potential external members, a first meeting takes place. In this founding phase the form is an open working group; interested staff members or individuals from outside the hospital can also attend the following meetings or decide not to attend. While the working group shall be open to all interested staff members, even during the founding phase the later size and interdisciplinary composition of the clinical ethics committee should be kept in mind. This means that the coordinator, in cooperation with the hospital management, has the difficult diplomatic task of including as many employees in the founding process as possible while at the same time shaping a viable and competent clinical ethics committee. In practice this task is often facilitated by the fact that only a limited number of staff members volunteer to work in clinical ethics consultation.

At the earliest possible time, fixed meeting dates should be introduced (e.g., monthly on a fixed day of the week, in the afternoon, lasting no more than 90 minutes) in order to establish a set rhythm for meetings from the very beginning. The first steps with respect to content are to establish or update the task commissioned by the management (see *Step 1*), providing information about clinical ethics committees and clinical ethics consultation and deciding on the topics of the on-the-job training modules. Working group members can prepare proposals for these or an external specialist can be called in. If there is already a clinical ethics committee at another hospital in the region, it may be helpful to make contact at an early stage to exchange experiences.

It is a good idea to begin with the actual ethics work already in the founding phase so as not to demotivate the members with exclusively bureaucratic and organizational tasks. In practice 'example consultations' have proven to be useful, in which either a real case from the hospital is discussed retrospectively or, alternatively, case examples from the medical-ethical reference literature are discussed in the working group. Beginning with practice-oriented ethics consultation at an early stage has the important advantage that the members quickly get a work-relevant impression of the issues the clinical ethics consultation faces and the work methods involved. In doing so, the need for further training in the area of clinical ethics and moderation techniques will soon become apparent and can be met at an early stage. By discussing difficult ethical decisions together, an open discussion style and mutual trust can be fostered, which can positively contribute to the early development of the committee's own work style.

Step 4

Clinical ethics committee:

- founding
- 7–20 members
- appointment by the hospital management
- 2–3-year term
- election of a committee chairperson and if necessary vice-chairperson
- rules of procedure/statutes
- fixed monthly meetings
- material resources

After this preparatory phase in an open working group, which usually takes about a year, the hospital management should officially found the clinical ethics committee and appoint its members. An appointment for a term of two to three years appears to be the best option, since shorter terms are not sufficient for thorough, well-founded work, and since many employees are often not available for longer terms. It is possible to appoint members for a further term. Due to the personnel carrousel in the hospital, it may be necessary to nominate new members to replace those who are leaving. Furthermore, a regulation must be made regarding working hours. Committee members should elect the committee chairperson and vice-chairperson.

With respect to the composition of the clinical ethics committee, care should be taken that it reflects the diversity of work areas and professional groups of the institution. However, the clinical ethics committee should not be too big in order not to inhibit its ability to work. In practice a size of 7–20 members has proved to work well. The members should represent the broadest possible spectrum of work fields and professional groups, but they should not see themselves as 'lobbyists' of a particular interest group. Besides doctors and nurses, the committee should include members of other health professions in the hospital such as medical-technical assistants, physiotherapists, speech therapists, psychologists and social workers, pastoral counsellors, employees in the hospital administration, etc. Within the individual professional groups the different hierarchical levels and activity characteristics should be considered. For additional expertise, it may be useful to appoint an external member to the committee, such as a lawyer or citizen representative. The clinical ethics committee must be compatible in its composition with the corporate identity and overall concept of the hospital. If head physicians and heads of the nursing staff are members, the status and networking opportunities of the committee increase within the hospital. On the other hand, it must be ensured that nurses, interns and residents can express their opinion on equal footing and without fear of detriment to their careers. This is crucial for the credibility and acceptance of the clinical ethics committee in the everyday life of the hospital. In practice, achieving a successful balance is not always easy. It often takes a certain time, since the normal ways of communicating within the committee are usually quite different from the, in general, hierarchically structured, medical-specialty-specific work routines in the hospital.

It has been shown to be useful to launch the clinical ethics committee in connection with a kick-off event held within the hospital. During this event the hospital management can present the members of the clinical ethics committee and schedule lectures on an ethical topic with sufficient discussion time. It is up to the individual hospital whether to invite the general public and the press at this time (external PR work). Other hospitals have combined the founding of the clinical ethics committee with a series of public lectures on practice-relevant ethical topics such as limitation of life-sustaining treatment, advance directives, self-determination of the patients or tube feeding.

Besides the official appointment of the clinical ethics committee by the hospital management, characteristic attributes of a professional, established clinical ethics committee include the following: an authorization defining the task it is to perform, regular meetings, records of the meetings and a set of procedural rules and/or statutes. Statutes should be developed by the committee in cooperation with the hospital management and should not regulate procedures in too much detail because this may later restrict the everyday work of the clinical ethics committee unnecessarily.

Step 5

Clinical ethics committee:

- working groups (teams)
- ethics day
- development of guidelines
- further training

After its successful founding, the crucial test for the new clinical ethics committee in everyday clinical practice still lies ahead. Can the committee develop its own style of working, to which all of the members can contribute? Is the conceptual and communicative work developing in such a way that the committee members have the feeling they are doing a good job? This aspect can hardly be overestimated in practice, since although health care professionals intuitively carry out ethical analysis and argumentation and reach decisions every day, ethical reflection and argumentation is neither part of the medical training curriculum of physicians and other health care professionals nor is it part of their everyday work routine. Traditionally, the reasoning behind ethical decisions is not made transparent. Instead, decision-making occurs within the trusted confines of one's own professional group, where often professional experience and hierarchical position and not ethical arguments determine the decision.

Another important task for the newly formed committee is to establish contact with the individual departments and wards of the hospital. This is possible because the members come from different professional groups and medical fields of the hospital and can act as information multipliers there. In addition, the clinical ethics committee can draw attention to its activities by providing information leaflets and ethics folders on every ward, which contain, for instance, ethics guidelines, forms for advance directives, texts and further training materials. What is important is that an exchange of ideas takes place between the committee and the staff of the hospital. In practice this exchange can be improved and deepened through informal contacts and short training modules which take place in the individual wards.

Due to the heavy workload and the extreme time pressure in the hospital, staff members will only take advantage of the services of the clinical ethics committee if they expect a personal benefit for their daily work. This can occur prospectively through ethical case discussions about current cases for which decisions must be made, or it can take place retrospectively within the framework of a training module. According to our data, several months can go by before the first requests for prospective ethical case consultations are made (Wernstedt and Vollmann 2005). This 'dry spell' can be shortened in practice if the members of the clinical ethics committee initiate ethical case discussions in their own medical areas (Vollmann 2008b) or present retrospective cases, in which an ethics consultation might have been meaningful, within the framework of on-the-job training sessions in their respective wards. Here it is highly recommended to choose real cases from the work environment of the respective employees.

To carry out more extensive, specialized work, such as developing guidelines or a concept for further training, it is recommended to create teams for this purpose. Here employees who are not members of the ethics committee can make a significant contribution and at the same time promote networking between the clinical ethics committee and the staff in general. Examples of this are the development of ethical guidelines for practice-relevant issues in the hospital such as refraining from resuscitation, limitation of life-sustaining treatment in the intensive ward, terminal care, advance directives or the use of tube feeding. As the quality of the work of the clinical ethics committee depends on its members, their advanced training in the field of clinical medical ethics is of central importance. In practice, unfortunately, hospitals do not always provide enough resources for this. Generally, the committee members benefit from the practice-related advanced training sessions in clinical ethics and moderation techniques.

Training courses in clinical ethics consultation which are conceptualized in the hospital are preferable to courses which are not as specific (Dörries et al. 2005). General moderation training or general ethics lectures can provide basic knowledge, but they are often quite far removed from what the practice-oriented committee members experience and need. In addition, the implementation and work process of a clinical ethics committee can be facilitated by consulting a professional clinical ethicist.

Step 6

Clinical ethics committee:

- development of consultation services for clinical specialities (e.g., psychiatry, paediatrics, etc.)
- networking with other committees
- quality assurance
- scientific research
- international cooperation

Practice has shown that the issues and problems in clinical ethics consultations can vary greatly from one specialized area to another. For that reason, it can be helpful to adapt the setting and the procedure of clinical ethics consultation to the particular situation, e.g., in psychiatry, paediatrics, intensive medicine, nursing home or in late terminations of pregnancy.

Exchanging experiences and networking with other clinical ethics committees can be the next step. On the European level, in 2005 clinical ethicists and research institutions in the field of clinical ethics consultation founded the European Clinical Ethics Network (ECEN), which is devoted to promoting the international exchange of experience and the accompanying scientific research (Molewijk and Widdershoven 2007). The efficiency and effectiveness of clinical ethics consultation has hardly been scientifically investigated until now (compare the chapter by Schildmann and Vollmann in this volume and see Schneiderman et al. 2003). In addition, we know too little about the optimal implementation process, the acceptance and effectiveness of ethical guidelines in practice. Despite the methodical problems in studying these complex relationships, these research questions should be pursued, for instance, within the framework of European research collaborations.

References

Bauer, A. and Vollmann, J. 2004. Ethische Fragen in der Konsiliar- und Liaisonpsychiatrie, in *Psychiatrie in der klinischen Medizin.*

Konsiliarpsychiatrie, -psychomatik und -psychotherapie, edited by V. Arolt and A. Diefenbacher. Darmstadt: Steinkopff, 211–22.
Borovecki, A., ten Have, H. and Oreskovic, S. 2006. Ethics committees in Croatia in the healthcare institutions: The first study about their structure and functions, and some reflections on the major issues and problems. *Health Care Ethics Committees Forum*, 18(1), 49–60.
Davies, L. and Hudson, L.D. 1999. Why don't physicians use ethics consultation? *Journal of Clinical Ethics*, 10(2), 116–25.
Dörries, A. 2003. Mixed feelings: Physicians' concerns about clinical ethics committees in Germany. *Health Care Ethics Committees Forum*, 15(3), 245–57.
Dörries, A. 2008. Beispiel einer Implementierung (Diakonische Einrichtung), in *Klinische Ethikberatung: Ein Praxisbuch*, edited by A. Dörries, G. Neitzke, A. Simon and J. Vollmann. Stuttgart: Kohlhammer, 129–36.
Dörries, A. and Hespe-Jungesblut, K. 2007. Die Implementierung Klinischer Ethikberatung in Deutschland. *Ethik in der Medizin*, 19(2), 148–56.
Dörries, A., Simon, A., Neitzke, G. and Vollmann, J. 2005. Ethikberatung im Krankenhaus: Qualifizierungsprogramm Hannover. *Ethik in der Medizin*, 17(4), 327–31.
Dougherty, C.J. 1995. Institutional ethics committees, in *Encyclopedia of Bioethics*, edited by W.T. Reich. New York: Macmillan, 409–12.
Fletcher, J.C. and Spencer, E.M. 1997. Ethics services in healthcare organizations, in *Introduction to Clinical Ethics*, edited by J.C. Fletcher, P.A. Lombardo, M.F. Marshall and F.G. Miller. Hagerstown, MD: University Publishing Group, 257–85.
Gefenas, E. 2001. Is 'failure to thrive' syndrome relevant to Lithuanian healthcare ethics committees? *Health Care Ethics Committees Forum*, 13(4), 381–92.
Greco, P.J. and Eisenberg, J.M. 1993. Changing physicians' practices. *New England Journal of Medicine*, 329(17), 1271–3.
Kanoti, G.A. and Youngner, S. 1995. Clinical Ethics Consultation, in *Encyclopedia of Bioethics*, edited by W.T. Reich. New York: Macmillan, 404–9.
Lo, B. 1987. Behind closed doors: Promises and pitfalls of ethics committees. *New England Journal of Medicine*, 317(1), 46–50.
Mills, A.E., Rorty, M.V. and Spencer, E.M. 2006. Introduction: Ethics committees and failure to thrive. *Health Care Ethics Committees Forum*, 18(4), 279–86.
Molewijk, B., Verkerk, M., Milius, H. and Widdershoven, G.A.M. 2008. Implementing moral case deliberation in a psychiatric hospital: Process and outcome. *Medicine, Health Care and Philosophy*, 11(1), 43–56.
Molewijk, B. and Widdershoven, G.A.M. 2007. Report of the Maastricht meeting of the European Clinical Ethics Network. *Clinical Ethics*, 2(1), 45.
Neitzke, G. 2008. Beispiel einer Implementierung (Universitätsklinikum), in *Klinische Ethikberatung: Ein Praxisbuch*, edited by A. Dörries, G. Neitzke, A. Simon and J. Vollmann. Stuttgart: Kohlhammer, 137–44.

Piette, M., Ellis, J.L., St Denis, P. and Sarauer, J. 2002. Integrating ethics and quality improvement: Practical implementation in the transitional/extended care setting. *Journal of Nursing Care Quality*, 17(1), 35–42.

Scheffold, N., Paoli, A., Kern, M., Bohringer, S., Berentelg, J. and Cyran, J. 2006. Foundation of a Health Care Ethics Committee (HEC) in a nonconfessional hospital: Initial experiences and prospects of the future. *Medizinische Klinik (München)*, 101(7), 584–9.

Schneiderman, L.J., Gilmer, T., Teetzel, H.D., Dugan, D.O., Blustein, J., Cranford, R., Briggs, K.B., Komatsu, G.I., Goodman-Crews, P., Cohn, F. and Young, E.W. 2003. Effect of ethics consultations on nonbeneficial life-sustaining treatments in the intensive care setting: A randomized controlled trial. *Journal of the American Medical Association*, 290(9), 1166–72.

Simon, A. 2000. Ethics committees in Germany: An empirical survey of Christian hospitals. *Health Care Ethics Committees Forum*, 13, 225–31.

Singer, P.A., Pellegrino, E.D. and Siegler, M. 1990. Ethics committees and consultants. *Journal of Clincal Ethics*, 1(4), 263–7.

van der Kloot Meijburg, H.H. and ter Meulen, R.H. 2001. Developing standards for institutional ethics committees: Lessons from the Netherlands. *Journal of Medical Ethics*, 27(1), 36–40.

Vollmann, J. 2001. Healthcare ethics committees in Germany: The path ahead. *Health Care Ethics Committees Forum*, 13(3), 255–64.

Vollmann, J. and Weidtmann, A. 2003. Das klinische Ethikkomitee des Erlanger Universitätsklinikums. Institutionalisierung, Arbeitsweise, Perspektiven. *Ethik in der Medizin*, 15(2), 229–38.

Vollmann, J. 2008a. Klinische Ethikkomitees und Ethikberatung in Deutschland: Bisherige Entwicklung und zukünftige Perspektiven. *Bioethica Forum*, 1(1), 33–9.

Vollmann, J. 2008b. Methoden der ethischen Falldiskussion, in *Klinische Ethikberatung: Ein Praxisbuch*, edited by A. Dörries, G. Neitzke, A. Simon and J. Vollmann. Stuttgart: Kohlhammer, 87–101.

Wernstedt, T. and Vollmann, J. 2005. Das Erlanger Klinische Ethikkomitee. Organisationsethik an einem deutschen Universitätsklinikum. *Ethik in der Medizin*, 17(2), 44–51.

Zentrale Ethikkommission bei der Bundesärztekammer. 2006. Ethikberatung in der klinischen Medizin. *Deutsches Ärzteblatt*, 103, A1703–7.

Chapter 9
What Does the Ethical Expertise of a Moral Philosopher Involve in Clinical Ethics Consultancy?

Beate Herrmann

Introduction

This chapter deals with the question of what exactly the ethical expertise of a professional ethicist is in the context of clinical ethics consultancy – whether as a member of a clinical ethics committee or in the capacity of an individual on-ward advisor. Ethics consultancy in day-to-day medicine is required for moral problems, amongst other things, and has to be seen in the context of medical treatment and patient care.

This calls for specific standards for such consultancy; the consultation must be solution-orientated and practice-related. It is a question of deciding upon courses of action. As a rule, recommendations for action must be made under stringent time demands and a consensus should be reached regarding further action. Finally, the opinions, wishes and expertise of different professionals as well as those of other people involved in the treatment of the patient (e.g., family members) must be taken into account and integrated into an overview of the situation. According to widespread opinion, it is the primary task of the consultant to moderate and mediate the communication between different agents – the clinical team, the patients, and their family members – in order to facilitate the discussion and to achieve a consensus among them. Therefore, it is common practice to put the main emphasis on the education and training of the consultants as mediators, as so-called 'facilitators'.[1] In this chapter, however, I will argue that it is not the primary concern of the consultant to achieve a *factual* consensus.

The term 'ethics' in 'ethics consultancy' refers to the fact that it is not simply a question of those involved reaching a general consensus about further action or about one particular course of action. Moreover, this consensus should be 'ethically qualified' in a more closely defined sense because a factual consensus fails to authenticate the normative accuracy or moral validity of the decision.

---

1   Aulisio et al. call this the 'pure facilitation approach'. Its goal is to reach consensus among the involved parties (Aulisio et al. 2008: 60). See also the chapter by Stolper et al. in this volume.

In this sense an ethics consultant should be, as Meyers puts it, an advocate not for the hospital, the physicians or the patients, but for the 'best ethical outcome' (Meyers 2007: 17).

In view of the fact that, amongst ethicists as well as ethical laypersons, people hold different moral perceptions and come to differing and often contrary conclusions when judging concrete problem situations, what does 'ethically qualified' really mean? An analogous problem is presented in the *reasoning* behind moral judgements: predominant factors are the competing varied approaches to ethics and a plurality of criteria which are drawn upon when tackling moral questions in clinical ethics.

In order to characterize more closely what it means to come to an 'ethically qualified' consensus, in the first section, I would like to explore the following question: What can be the specific contribution of a moral philosopher in the capacity of a professional ethicist, when advising about courses of action in cases of moral incertitude? For this purpose, in the second section, I will briefly characterize the role and tasks of an ethicist during the consultation process. Further to this, in the third section, I will outline a typology of competences as well as presenting their usefulness for consultation processes. Against the background of these considerations, in the fourth section I will shed light on the relationship of ethical expertise and moral judgement: should the ethics expert restrict themselves simply to the theory-based analysis of cases during the consultation process, or should they also deal with fundamental moral judgements?

The Role of the Ethicist in the Consultation Process

During the consultation process, what function can an ethicist meaningfully fulfil in their capacity as an ethics expert? It seems clear that they are not required simply to be a comforting layman, an ambassador of public opinion or the advocate of the patient's interests. A representative of any other profession could carry out this task. Dieter Birnbacher puts forward the idea that the term 'ethics expert' itself is even associated with a certain embarrassment which does not occur when legal or theological representation is requested. The expertise of a lawyer is required to offer applicable legal information and to give an opinion on, for example, the legality or constitutional conformity of proposed solutions. In formulating the necessary expertise, theologians can anticipate and articulate possible reflections and objections from the Church because, even in secular and pluralist societies, they represent a moral view that, as ever, has great authority (Birnbacher 1999: 268).

According to Birnbacher, an ethicist is not only in competition with the normative assessment of law and theology but also with the respective morals of different standpoints and professions – those of medicine or of care ethics, for example – which are often not in agreement with general normative principles asserted by philosophical ethicists (Birnbacher 1999: 268).

It is not only practitioners who question the expert capabilities of ethicists, however. The theory that there can be ethical expertise but no ethical experts is also occasionally supported in the ethicist community. Birnbacher cites Arthur Caplan, who claims that the status of an expert should be something exclusive, whereas expertise could be possessed by everyone. In principle, everybody, including enthusiastic laymen, can be accredited with expertise in the sense of expert knowledge (Birnbacher 1999: 269). According to Caplan, there should be no ethical experts who offer exclusive wisdom or considered insight concerning moral questions because they could evade democratic power in their decisions, as these are based only on the 'truth' that is accessible to them (Caplan cited in Birnbacher 1999: 269). Birnbacher is correct in saying that the fact that the term 'expertise' is a derivation of the word 'expert' contradicts Caplan's conceptual differentiation of 'expert' and 'expertise' (Birnbacher 1999: 270). An expert is precisely one who possesses expertise, although what is meant here is that the expert possesses a knowledge that is not possessed by every layman. Irrespective of the conceptual differentiation, it is also indisputable, with regard to this subject, that philosophical ethicists possess specific competencies which make them experts in their field.

The Competencies of a Philosophical Ethicist

In order to characterize the role of a moral philosopher in the context of ethics consultations more closely, two groups of competencies will be established: *key* competencies and *discipline-specific* competencies.[2] *Key competencies* comprise the skills which philosophers possess in large quantity thanks to their training but which are fundamentally possessed by other people and other professionals. *Discipline-specific competencies* are obtained by a professional ethicist in their training either as a moral philosopher or as a moral theologian.[3] They permit ethical expertise in a more precise sense.

Discipline-specific Competencies

Expert knowledge Firstly, expert knowledge in the field of ethics belongs to the grouping of discipline-specific competencies. This includes the awareness of different theories of ethics as well as the knowledge of the relevance of these theories for different problem areas. At least equally as important is the ability

---

2 In this context, compare a distinction made by Aulisio et al., who differentiate the following core competencies required by ethics consultants: 1) Ethical assessment skills, needed to identify and analyse the emerging ethical issues in the consultation process; 2) Process skills, needed for resolving value uncertainty or conflicts; 3) Interpersonal skills, for example, the capability to listen well and to represent the views of involved parties (Aulisio et al. 2008: 61).

3 For the discipline-specific competencies of the clinical ethics counsellor, see, e.g., Engelhardt (2003: 370).

of the consultant to apply the theories as well as basic moral terminology to concrete case examples (cf. Birnbacher 1999: 270). It is therefore not sufficient simply to lecture on the topic of ethics. In a concrete problem situation, an ethics consultant should be in a position to analyse different options of action in view of the underlying norms and values, as well as their theoretical basis. In addition, they must be able to communicate this analysis in a way that is comprehensible for all concerned. Equally essential is the awareness of the moral notions that have developed within a particular profession. Two examples of this are, firstly, medical ethics and, secondly, the norms and values of care ethics as documented in different moral codes.

Analytical and reconstructive competencies A philosophical ethicist also possesses specific analytical and reconstructive competencies. This includes firstly the consistent assessment of possible courses of action: What theoretical implications does one particular option have? Do we accept these implications in comparable cases? What is a comparable case? Secondly, the analysis of central terminology plays an important role. Terms can often have several different meanings and must therefore be clarified in each individual situation.

Ethical expertise includes, thirdly, the ability to empathize with the views of others. This demands a distancing from one's own, theory-based moral convictions. The ethical viewpoint is a theoretical one. Birnbacher is right in saying that an ethicist's typical conclusion, contrary to that of the moral preacher, is not a categorical one but a hypothetical: 'What results from which premises for what situation? What problems, difficulties and contra-intuitive consequences confront the representative of which principles? Which positions are compatible with each other and which not?' (Birnbacher 1999: 270, my translation).

Powers of judgement Finally, power of reason skills are required to judge concrete situations adequately and according to their relevant aspects – with consideration also of non-moral reflections – as well as the norms and values in question and their application.[4] The power of reason is both a discipline-specific competency and a key competency, because, as well as expert knowledge, it demands knowledge and

---

4 Caplan (1982: 13f.) stresses that it is not enough for an ethics consultant to be familiar with moral theory and analysis of different arguments according to their theoretical background. Caplan cites Peter Singer, who grounded ethical expertise in 'theoretical mastery and analytical skills' (Caplan 1982: 7). It is of equal importance to have the capacity of moral judgement:

> Good judgment in ethics is not merely a function of the rapidity with which a principle can be applied to a case. It consists in the sensitivity and thoughtfulness which are brought to bear on the history and circumstances pertaining to any given situation, action or policy. Good judgment about moral matters demand the ability to know how and whether various kinds of relationships alter the duties and rights of various individuals. (Caplan 1982: 16)

experience of the world, awareness of people and situations and much more. In ethics consultancy, one furthermore needs a feeling for which moral problems are perceived by representatives of a particular moral perception and which principles and viewpoints are shown to advantage (cf. Birnbacher 1999: 270). When specific values and standards have been established and checked for consistency, power of reason is essential in judging the concrete moral conflicts in view of the normative bases. The analytical-reconstructive process consists of establishing which implications arise with regard to concrete problems.

Discipline-specific competencies in the practice of consultancy Where do discipline-specific competencies come into operation in the practice of consulting? I will elucidate upon this using the following three competency areas:

1. The organization of ambiguous values and standards that require interpretation into concrete terms, and their application
2. The clarification of terms, for example, the disclosure of implicit judgement
3. The examination of moral convictions with regard to consistency.

Concerning the first point, here is an example from everyday life in the hospital. A while ago I was present when a doctor was explaining to a trainee medical student which patients should be taken onto the ward. Among other things, he commented that admitting young people from nearby hospitals who were suffering from severe septicaemia[5] should be favoured. The reason for this was that, in the nearby hospitals, there were fewer facilities to care for these patients. Then, upon noticing me, the doctor looked concerned and said: 'Oh, Frau Hermann, you really should not have heard that'. When I asked why not, he said that in principle all patients should be treated equally and it was therefore not acceptable simply to take the younger patients.

This gave me the opportunity to comment on the problem, as I perceived it. The principle of treating all patients equally, as the doctor had in mind, includes the obligation of providing the same, and the best possible, treatment for all patients with similar illnesses. Fulfilling this obligation requires there to be sufficient available resources to treat all patients appropriately. It seems that there are not enough intensive-care beds to care for septicaemia patients in the best way possible (whether this view is factually correct remains to be seen). This means that we are structurally in the same situation regarding intensive-care beds as we are regarding organ donations – both are in short supply. If this is the case, then the goal of equal treatment, as it is presented above, cannot be reached. It is rather the case that criteria must be considered which permit the execution of a prioritization. Each of these criteria requires justification. This must also be done for criteria such as the age of the patient and the severity of the illness (in this case it was the diagnosis

---

5   Septicaemia is a potentially life-threatening infection in which large amounts of bacteria are present in the blood. It is commonly referred to as blood poisoning.

of 'severe' septicaemia), the two criteria mentioned by the doctor, as well as for other imaginable prioritization criteria. Two aspects were important for the doctor, which had hitherto not been present: where an absolute equality of treatment is not possible due to limited resources, there cannot be a question of an 'immoral' violation of the principle of equality. Whenever it is necessary to prioritize, this should be done in an explicit way. This means that actions should be based on what is in line with the discussion and justified selection of appropriate criteria.

Concerning the second point, it is often the case that ambiguous terms are used in moral conflicts, terms which require interpretation. This is certainly the case for terms relevant to ethics such as 'human dignity', 'autonomy', 'equality of treatment' and 'distributive justice'. The same is to be said of supposed 'purely medical' terms such as 'medical prognosis' or 'benefits of therapy'. In medicine, one important everyday task for an ethicist involves presenting the implicit normative evaluations of these terms. The term 'medical prognosis', as one example, contains not only objective medical parameters but also normative assumptions (therefore requiring justification) regarding perhaps the patient's expected quality of life or the relevance that the patient's age can have for the prognosis. Another example is the term 'benefits of therapy': it is easy to agree upon the fact that in deciding on a course of therapy, considering the benefit for the patient is a priority. However, what does 'benefit' mean in this context? When asking whether a particular therapy is beneficial for the patient in the above-mentioned sense, judgements based on medical expertise as well as normative judgements are involved. Judging the benefits based on medical expertise predominantly concerns the physiological effectiveness of a therapy. However, not every therapy that is physiologically effective, in the sense that it prolongs the life of the patient for a particular period of time, is actually beneficial to the patient (cf. Marckmann 2004: 380). The concept of the benefits of therapy, in the sense that therapy is beneficial *for* the patient, moreover implies normative suppositions in view, for example, of the judgement of quality of life. Does this therapy offer the patient a *worthwhile* and *desirable* end result? After the therapy can an acceptable quality of life be expected for the patient? What are the chances of success? Is the anticipated benefit *for* the patient greater than the disadvantageous aspects of the therapy?

As an example of the third point, the assessment of consistency, the debate surrounding the moral status of an embryo in stem cell research can be drawn upon. Many people consider the use of the surplus stock of cryogenically frozen embryos for research purposes to be morally justifiable in view of its huge potential benefits (e.g., curing serious illnesses). One of the arguments for this is that the embryos are never going to develop into living human beings (cf. Schönecker 2005: 61f.). However, this belief is not consistent with the deontological notion that human beings should not be used for medical research purposes, even if this were of great benefit to future generations. If a human embryo is a human entity, then it should not be sacrificed to medical research, nor indeed for any other purpose. Whether or not an embryo is a human entity is another question. With the aid of coherent arguments, however, this question can be addressed: a moral philosopher could present to the members of an ethics committee the consequences of the different criteria for the attribution of human status. For example, it could be said that a human embryo is similar to a person in a reversible coma insofar that, in time, both will possess the characteristics and abilities which we ascribe to 'normal' human beings. If, based on the argument of potentiality, we therefore accord one entity the right to not be killed then it would be inconsistent not to grant the same right to the other. Another argument in favour of stem cell research is that it can save human life. Nevertheless, if this is the question, then we must ask whether the investments made in stem cell research, if invested into other areas, could save just as many human lives just as effectively with, for example, investment in the prevention of diseases.

Key Competencies

Ethics consultants in their daily work are only in part – and, in fact, in small part – active in the role of an ethical expert. This is at least my opinion after one year of working as a clinical ethics consultant. Most of the time, consultants perform the role of a skilled, thoughtful and sensitive layman, who possesses certain key competencies. These include the power of judgement, as mentioned above, empathy and linguistic competence.[6] In this capacity, the ethics consultant performs, amongst others, the following tasks:

- The identification of latent and explicit moral problem situations.
- The introduction of problem dimensions that have not been recognized hitherto.
- Mediation between contradictory views and judgements, the balancing of (power) hierarchies in order to enable or facilitate discourse.
- The acknowledgement and representation of unrepresented interests.
- Secular form of clinical pastoral care: caring for patients and relatives in situations of difficult treatments, particularly those where fatality is a factor.

A good ethics consultation requires not only the analytical, conceptual and theoretical capabilities of a philosophical ethicist, but also the already mentioned key competences. As Meyers puts it convincingly, these capacities have to be complemented by an experience-based moral wisdom:

> The ability to listen with care and discernment; the ability to speak and write with clarity and precision; skill at managing egos, emotions, and political environments so as best to facilitate effective communication; sufficient understanding of one's own hierarchy of values and knowledge of one's limitation. (Meyers 2007: 29)

---

6   Engelhardt, for example, points out, 'that the bioethics consultant's role is a collage of roles' and that it is mostly unclear what their specific profession comprises (Engelhardt 2003: 379f.).

Ethics Expertise and Moral Judgement

Should Ethics Consultancy be Morally Neutral?

In view of the varied roles taken on by an ethics consultant in their different competency areas, the question is raised whether their expertise is limited simply to the theory-based analysis and reconstruction of moral problems, or whether they should also act as a moral judge.

Birnbacher is correct in remarking that an ethics expert, by that very name, is not a specialist in fundamental moral judgements: 'Being able, with the use of his or her qualifications, to grasp moral terms, ethical norms and their foundations does not mean that he or she also knows which norms and values are the right ones' (Birnbacher 1999: 271, my translation). For this reason, it is expressed by some writers, such as C.D. Broad and Kai Nielsen (cited in van Willigenburg 1999: 291), that an ethics consultant should act in a 'morally neutral' way, that is to say, he or she should not offer any judgements on morality. I will now outline and comment on three arguments presented by van Willigenburg which support this theory (van Willigenburg 1999: 292).

The moral views of an ethics consultant can threaten the moral autonomy of those who consult them. Here, moral autonomy is meant in the Kantian definition. It refers to the capacity to impose objective moral law on oneself and comprises the ability to define one's own wishes in a well-grounded manner. Van Willigenburg (1999: 294) is correct in objecting that an expert's moral advice is not authorized primarily from the individual receiving consultancy, but from the arguments that underlie this advice. The fact that an *ethics* expert considers a course of action to be morally sound is therefore not important for the morally autonomous person. Important are the arguments that result in this expertise. The consulted individual can examine these arguments in the light of general rationality standards and, therefore, autonomy is maintained.

The second argument is based on the supposition that moral values are often incommensurable (incomparable with each other) or incompatible. Moral judgements are often not based upon arguments that lead to a particular conclusion. The latter can in no way be derived from any ethical theory (or a combination of theories) or their premises. If an ethics expert draws a clear moral conclusion, this would suggest that moral questions permit clear and simple answers. In fact, however, the moral world is full of ambiguity and uncertainty. In my opinion, this argument is less in support of the claim for the moral neutrality of the expert but more of the claim for transparency. An ethics consultant should make it clear by which theoretical considerations and, where applicable, by which reflections on plausibility, they come to a moral judgement. Ambiguities or possible alternative argument strategies should be shared. Van Willigenburg (1999: 296) is correct in asserting that the ambiguity of moral reality does not suggest that the professionals who tackle these questions should not make judgements. I find it to be essential that moral judgement is not presented with the air of apodictic truth, but disclosed along with the accompanying challenges and questions of validity.

The third argument is based on one of Thomas Nagel's distinctions between so-called 'agent-neutral' values and 'agent-relative' values (Nagel 1986: 152). Agent-neutral values present a reason for each individual to comply, that is to say to act in a moral fashion, by adhering to these norms. Agent-relative values provide only the person in question with a reason for an act. They provide no neutral, objective or unbiased background to an act. This means that, from a viewpoint which is not that of the person performing the act, it is not possible to understand (to the same extent) why these norms and values form a moral justification, or reason, to act in a certain way.[7] There can therefore be no morally neutral perspective from which a moral problem can be assessed. The very fact that the persons performing an act are in a categorically different situation from that of those who are simply judging it can lead to each individual forming different judgements. In this way, an ethics consultant, for example, cannot present a judgement about something that demands the morality of a doctor (van Willigenburg 1999: 298). In individual cases, they cannot give the particular obligations the importance they deserve because they are not in the situation of the doctor involved. An ethics consultant should therefore stay within the limits of a moral framework.

It should be objected here that the presence of agent-relative values does not rule out the possibility of a third person being able to suitably appreciate the agent-relative values of another person. After all, one characteristic of moral judgement is that one puts oneself in the position of others, which involves judging *for them* the intentions and duties which are presented to them by particular relationships towards other people. As van Willigenburg (1999: 301) accurately notes: 'A doctor's patients are never the patients of an ethics consultant, although this does not rule out the possibility that the latter may appropriately take into account the norms and values which play a role in the special doctor-patient relationship'.

To summarize, it must be emphasized that an ethics consultant does not have to abstain from every moral judgement. The consultant should, however, not simply pass fundamental moral judgements but should justify these by considering general rationality standards such as transparency, explicitness and logical coherence. Adhering to these is most certainly not the privilege of a professional ethicist; however, an ethicist's training renders them competent in this area to a significant extent. In being careful to pay attention to transparency, consistency and necessary distinctions, an ethicist overcomes the necessary challenges facing a professionally accurate judgement. It is precisely when tackling moral questions that one can tend to a large degree towards the rash polarization, wishful thinking and personal preference of confusing terminology, contradictions and misjudged conclusions.

---

7 It is at least not possible to gauge, from an external perspective, the full weight of these reasons inclusive of their motivational force.

It would nevertheless be wrong to expect an ethicist to decide questions of moral conflict. In their moral judgement, an ethics expert is competing with the moral judgements of others. As Birnbacher accurately puts it, an ethicist can express:

> (...) which arguments do not satisfy the elementary minimum conditions, inherent to the term 'moral', of a moral reasoning. An ethicist cannot, however, organize the arguments which do not pass this test into an objective order. (Birnbacher 1999: 273, my translation)

This is because moral convictions cannot be conclusively proven. For the explanation of these convictions, it is necessary to consider plausibility, and it cannot be assumed that everybody will accept the convictions based on these considerations. Although universal validity is claimed to be inherent in moral judgements, this claim cannot actually be realized in pluralist societies. The debates, brought into both the ethical and public arenas, regarding, for example, life before birth or the moral admissibility of actively assisted suicide, show that it is not possible to achieve a unified consensus in questions of morality, even after intensive discussion.

An ethicist should be able to give reasons explaining why certain principles were favoured in certain areas, and this is a call to ethical theory.[8] One of the proper tasks of an ethicist is the systematization of different judgement criteria and their coherent contextualization. The use of different bases of judgement in different areas requires justification. An ethicist is, therefore, essentially an ethics *expert* because they do not just proclaim morality, but can substantiate these proclamations.

References

Aulisio, M.P., Arnold, R.M. and Youngner, S.J. 2000. Health care ethics consultation: Nature, goals, and competencies. *Annals of Internal Medicine*, 133(1), 59–69.

Birnbacher, D. 1999. Wofür ist der 'Ethik-Experte' Experte?, in *Angewandte Ethik in der pluralistischen Gesellschaft*, edited by K.P. Rippe. Freiburg, Switzerland: Univ.-Verlag, 267–83.

Caplan, A. 1982. Mechanics on duty: The limitations of a technical definition of moral expertise of work in applied ethics. *Canadian Journal of Philosophy*, 8(suppl.), 1–18.

Engelhardt, T. 2003. The bioethics consultant: Giving moral advice in the midst of moral controversy. *HEC Forum*, 15(4), 362–82.

---

[8] For the theoretical foundation and performance of clinical ethics consultation, see, e.g., the contribution by Gordon in this volume.

Marckmann, G. 2004. Lebensverlängerung um jeden Preis? Ethische Entscheidungskonflikte bei der passiven Sterbehilfe. *Ärzteblatt Baden-Württemberg*, 59(9), 379–82.

Meyers, C. 2007. *A Practical Guide to Clinical Ethics Consulting. Expertise, ethos and power*. Lanham, MD: Rowman & Littlefield Publishers.

Nagel, T. 1986. *The View from Nowhere*. Oxford: Oxford University Press.

Schönecker, D. 2005. The role of moral philosophers in ethics committees. *Erwägen, Wissen, Ethik*, 16(1), 60–62.

Van Willigenburg, T. 1999. Soll ethische Fachberatung moralisch neutral sein?, in *Angewandte Ethik in der pluralistischen Gesellschaft*, edited by K.P. Rippe. Freiburg, Switzerland: Univ.-Verlag, 285–305.

Chapter 10
Moving Towards Clinical Ethics Consultation in Italy: Practical Experience, Foundational and Methodological Considerations

Nunziata Comoretto

Introduction

Advances in life-sustaining interventions as well as increased cultural diversity lead to ethical dilemmas which often require advice about ethically permissible activities. In truly complex cases, the personal capacity for discernment might not be enough. Although some physicians are still confident that they have themselves an intuitive grasp of what is right, they should take advantage of adequate methodology to make moral judgements (Childress 2007).

For this purpose, clinical ethics investigation within medical schools, as well as clinical ethics consultation (CEC) in hospitals, has increasingly developed. In Italy, however, CEC is still a new phenomenon. Italian medical practice is deeply rooted in medical ethics and law, while culturally Italian physicians are still considered as having a protective role towards their patients. In general, one can say that not much conflict between physicians and patients or their families can be observed in Italy. However, exceptions exist and they have been increasing recently, requiring support for ethical decision-making.

In recent years few CEC services have emerged in Italian health care institutions. The Institute of Bioethics of the Catholic University of the Sacred Heart is the oldest one within a medical school in Italy. It performs CECs, in addition to teaching and research. CECs are conducted at the *Policlinico Gemelli Hospital*, a tertiary-care academic centre in Rome. In our practice, CEC is usually performed by two physicians with training in clinical ethics.

Since the beginning of our consulting activity, defining a decision-making approach for CEC has been one of the most important problems to solve. The method in clinical ethics is supposed to be a 'procedure' to determine the best course of action in clinical decision-making, which can follow either a pragmatic way or a more systematic reflective methodology (Green 1990). In the following pages I will show the methodology used at the Catholic University of the Sacred Heart-Policlinico Gemelli Hospital, illustrated by a case coming from the activity in CEC. Some major theoretical features grounding the approach, the so-called 'person-centred' approach, are also discussed.

Person-Centred Ethical Theory: Case Report

The methodology here proposed can be labelled as a casuistic approach, supported by a person-centred ethical theory. 'Casuistic' approach must be intended here in the sense that moral rules require modes of interpretation in actual situations (Jonsen 1988). For this purpose, constant attention must be paid to those details that make the case so particular, because any change in the circumstances will also tend to change the specific typology of case. It must be pointed out that in order to determine the right thing to do, the factual dimensions of the case are as important and substantive as is the ethical theory. However, the background theoretical assumptions also intervene when determining what facts are most relevant to the case and how those should be organized to develop ethical considerations. Hence this model has two phases: the first one emphasizes fact-gathering and the second one applies evaluative standards.

Analysing the case, we recognize four areas of concern, into which all factual considerations fall:

1. 'Medical indications' in the case – this criterion also includes the appropriate moral description of the kind of action, for example, killing versus allowing to die.
2. 'Patient's preferences'.
3. 'Proportionality' of medical treatments, that means how medical treatments modify the patient's quality of life.
4. Other relevant factors, external to the immediate physician-patient encounter, including, for example, family wishes, cost issues, societal interests, religious perspectives, etc.

In this methodology the evaluative standard is provided by the person-centred ethical theory (Carrasco 2004). This theory assumes that the medical act must be appropriate to the nature of the patient. This means that the patient is a human being, and at the same time, he is a unique, unrepeatable and irreplaceable individual and, for these reasons, he has an incomparable dignity. In this sense we speak of person-centred care. A person-centred clinical approach also holds that every patient is a suffering subject facing his illness in a unique way – unique because it is referred to that specific patient. At the same time this theory holds that the aim of medical acts is to cure the disease or, if that is not possible, to alleviate symptoms (almost always possible), or at least to comfort the patient (always possible), in order to improve as much as possible his quality of life.

In my contribution, the attention will focus on the ethical problems implicated in the assistance of a patient affected with mucopolysaccharidosis (MPS), a congenital metabolic disease, in its terminal phase. The management of this patient has resulted in the need to have criteria which may guide the decision-making process of the choice of treatment in accordance with the best interests of the patient himself.

The Case

The patient was born in 1989. Diagnosis of MPS type IIIA was made when he was five years old. From school age there was progressive loss of psychomotor and neurological development. Loss of speech occurred at nine years of age. Complete loss of motor functions have been recorded since he was 11, with progression to severe cachexia. Cardiomyopathy and moderately extended valvulopathy with satisfactory residual functionality were diagnosed. Recurrent respiratory infections occurred. His severe bedsores required photocoagulation of exuberance of granulated tissue.

In 2002 the patient was admitted to the hospital for a respiratory infection and he required a gastrostomy tube for feeding. The first CEC was requested to evaluate the significance of percutaneous endoscopic gastrostomy (PEG) and a possible tracheotomy in case of cardio-respiratory arrest during surgery. In March 2003, a new bout of acute respiratory infection occurred requiring the patient's admission to the intensive care unit for positioning of a permanent tracheostomy tube. In April, the worsening of respiratory function required intensive assistance and mechanical ventilation. A second CEC was requested to evaluate the significance of cardio-pulmonary resuscitation (CPR). The tracheostomy tube caused the formation of granulomas, which required photocoagulation.

The problems arising in the assistance of the case are evident: the best choice of feeding mode (most efficient and least invasive), pain management and palliative care, management of respiratory problems (preventive tracheostomy and CPR), and ethical considerations of suitable involvement of the family in the decision-making process and assistance. CEC has been an indispensable tool in this case in the guidance of resolving ethical dilemmas and it has also been relevant to obtain a constant awareness on the part of medical and nursing staff of the ethical aspects of assistance, particularly in the terminal phase. The main issues to solve have been whether to perform a tracheostomy if requested during the surgery for PEG, in opposition to the parents' wishes, and whether to resuscitate the patient in the event of a cardio-respiratory arrest in the advanced stages of the disease.

Medical Indications

The medical indications criterion includes the clinical strategy based on risks and benefits of various courses of treatment, including the uncertainties associated with scientific understanding in medical practice. This is the physician's domain. From the standpoint of person-centred theory, not only the probable effects of actions, but also some inherent features of acts (the object of the action and the intended ends) are relevant to make them right or wrong (Cataldo 2001). Therefore, evaluation of medical indications must be based primarily on an appreciation of the nature of the action itself (e.g., curative treatment versus palliative care). Certainly we have to pay explicit attention to how we morally describe cases and actions. However, the person-centred ethical theory also gives a clear content to identify relevant features of cases and actions.

Regarding the case of our patient, the availability of life-support systems came with a growing need to recognize the limits beyond which the use of such systems was no longer in the interests of the patient. The beginning and suspension of life-support treatments represent one of the most difficult and harrowing decisions for both physicians and patients' relatives, since the use of such systems can sometimes interfere with the process of dying, prolonging and, in a certain sense, obstructing death. Therefore, in certain conditions it could be morally justified to refuse or to suspend such treatments. The criteria of legitimacy in such circumstances are represented by their futility and seriousness seen in terms of efficacy, invasiveness and possible side effects. If the death of a terminal patient is imminent, life-prolonging treatments are generally futile. In this patient the goals of treatment were to sustain the vital functions, temporarily compromised by critical events (e.g., respiratory failure), and to obtain the best possible control of pain and other symptoms.

If one applies a clear ethical theory, no conflicts can emerge about the moral description of actions. However, physicians often face the ethical dilemma of performing an action which has both a good and an evil effect. How does one approach such apparent but not uncommon dilemmas resulting from the need to take action? According to the double-effect reasoning (Moraczewski 2001):

1. The voluntary act must be itself good (evil can never be chosen directly).
2. The good effect and not the bad effect is intended.
3. The good effect is not produced by means of the evil effect.
4. There must be a proportionately grave reason for performing the act and permitting the evil effect (it would be unreasonable to allow a grave evil for a relatively insignificant good).

Patient's Preferences

The patient's preferences criterion includes what the patient thinks (wishes, feelings, etc.) about the proposed medical plan. According to the person-centred ethical theory, respecting the dignity of the patient means respecting his autonomy and therefore his capacity to decide (Carrasco 2004). In that model, autonomy is construed as relational autonomy. A relational understanding of autonomy means to recognize that patients' helplessness, dependence and sickness are expressions of limited freedom and that the networks of social relationships (including the doctor-patient relationship) facilitate autonomous action.

In this model narratives assume a great importance, because they examine the 'true' perspective of the patient and at the same time allow the patient to achieve an autonomous choice in a meaningful sense (Breeur 1999). According to the reported consulting experience, this kind of narrative analysis becomes particularly important in the evaluation of end-of-life issues as well as the withdrawing of life-sustaining treatments.

Another important aspect in evaluation of the patient's preferences is that the autonomy of the patient cannot supersede the autonomy of the doctor. Furthermore, autonomy is at the root of the need for communication between health care workers and patients/relatives. Obviously, there may be patients who understand autonomy in a more individualistic way. However, without neglecting the patient's right to privacy and self-determination, I would recommend physicians to be 'open' to relationship and communication as effective ways to promote patients' autonomy.

In the case that is the subject of this discussion, the consultants suggested a constant and uniform communication between the medical team and family and furthermore that this be given in a coherent way through a complete assistance team and supported by a psychologist. The CEC itself was a useful communicative means in order to clarify to the patient's parents as well as to the medical team some ethical concepts relevant to decision-making.

Proportionality

The proportionality criterion refers to how treatment options and foreseeable benefits and burdens apply to the patient. The burdens here considered are both physical and spiritual, consequently the evaluation of the burden of a means embraces not only clinical aspects (pain, function, consciousness, capacity for relationship, etc.), but rather all the circumstances of the case viewed in its clinical and personal dimensions are relevant.

According to the person-centred ethical theory, even though health is an important goal, it is not the final one in human life; instead it is a vital capacity, with the aim to give to patients the bodily and the mental conditions to fulfil their global good as persons (good of the person as a whole). Therefore, a physically and/or mentally ill person can, in spite of the disease, be more complete than a healthy person (Carrasco 2004).

Proportionality evaluations mostly occur when patients are unable to make judgement or express preferences and, at the same time, medical goals are limited (e.g., cases involving terminal illness). A decision to forego extraordinary means rests on a recognition that the means of preserving life or restoring health are no longer beneficial or useful, or are too burdensome.

With regard to the case of our patient, the issue of artificial feeding and hydration, not only by means of PEG, is surely one of the most argued and controversial of possible treatments for terminally ill patients. The debate revolves, in most cases, around the question of whether these practices should be considered as medical or non-medical treatments (Gleeson 2003). However, the problem could be misleading, in that a misunderstanding at the root of conflicting interpretations may be more apparent than real. The real question is whether the aid given to the patient is proportionate or not, in other words, whether benefits are expected and if these benefits are proportionate to the suffering caused to the patient by the application of medical decisions.

To guarantee a better quality of life in this patient, feeding and hydration by PEG were recommended as well as a personalized palliative treatment including, apart from analgesia, prevention and treatment of bedsores and muscular contractions. Regarding CPR, when it is appropriate (as it was at the time of the first CEC), it becomes an essential means of life support. It could be legitimately refused when excessively onerous, therapeutically futile or non-beneficial for the patient, given his general conditions together with the fact that the use of such treatment could mean only a precarious and painful prolonging of existence. At the time of the second CEC, CPR was considered not obligatory, due to the terminality of the patient.

In the same way, the choice of tracheostomy in the case of this pre-terminally ill patient was made with the aim to relieve suffering, favouring drainage of secretions (thus preventing repeated trauma of the airways resulting from repeated naso-tracheal aspirations with the use of a probe) in the hope of improving pulmonary ventilation, mitigating, as much as possible, the feeling of inevitable progressive loss of respiratory functions. However, to ascertain the appropriateness of treatment, the possible complications of a permanent tracheostomy tube (sores at the site of extreme distal contact of the tube with possible development of granulomas that obstruct airways, haemorrhage, infections) must be carefully considered and monitored.

Contextual Factors

The contextual factors criterion includes the effects of decisions upon others, such as the patient's family, resources, medical teaching needs, legal issues, etc. Because these factors extend beyond the doctor-patient relationship, they are not usually considered worthy of note in ordinary decisions. In the case I have described, no contextual factors relevant to decision-making emerged.

Sometimes, legal aspects have to be taken into account before reaching an ethical decision, but most often the law is satisfied when persons involved in decision-making are careful and systematic about how they make decisions (Childress 2007).

As can be seen, the methodology I have proposed is similar to that described by Albert Jonsen and colleagues in their well-known book, *Clinical Ethics* (2002). However, unlike Jonsen's methodology, in my practice, personalistic theoretical assumptions are operative as well as the explication of factual considerations. In my opinion, connecting the evaluative standards to the factual elements should be regarded as one of the most important steps of a methodology.

Moreover, the person-centred ethical theory delineating the exact content of a moral rule (which are necessarily general in formulation) offers a way to eliminate potential conflicts, particularly in the application of the moral rules themselves (Clouser and Gert 1990). Only by this preventive clarification can moral rules function as concrete action guides (Gert 1990). For instance, the interpretation (as well as the application) of the moral rule affirming the respect for the autonomy of the patient, as we have seen, needs an adequate comprehension of the meaning and value of the personal autonomy of the patient as well as the physician. An adequate interpretation and application of the moral rule that prohibits killing needs a clarification of the meaning of killing, that is, of the taking of innocent human life and of killing as direct action. Clarification of the moral rule is not arbitrary and intuitive because the interpretation of key moral categories (lying, killing, etc.) is included within the ethical theory. In order to avoid moral conflicts, moral rules are also harmonized inside the person-centred ethical theory, providing a rank order of human goods (Carrasco 2004).

Clinical Ethics as Applied Ethics

According to our way of working, as I have shown, methodology represents a necessary mediation between the moral norm and the practical decision. Consequently, clinical ethics could be viewed as a kind of 'applied ethics', that is to say, a reflective activity of applying an ethical theory to the domain of the medical decision (Kopelman 1990). In my experience, I have noticed that in the perspective of applied ethics it is possible to find an effective guide to actions from a certain theory in the field of clinical ethics also.

I am aware that 'deductive' ethics has been often considered to be in contrast with 'practical' decision-making about medical issues, and I am also well aware that many bioethicists generally criticize the method of 'application'. It seems in fact that simple application does not cover all the connections between moral rules or ethical theories and particular judgements about concrete cases, because not all such connections involve a rational deduction (Jonsen and Toulmin 1991).

Without denying the importance of practical experience, against this criticism it can be said that the person-centred ethical theory gives not only the logic of moral reasoning, but also the content for the ethical judgement. Person-centred ethical theory is both a method and a doctrine. It is the content itself (the absolute dignity of the human being) that gives a normative meaning to the ethical judgement, as determined by the ethical method.

From our experience of CEC, there are some major advantages of a proper ethical theory:

- An ethical theory can provide indispensable assistance in making defensible decisions, representing the major evaluative element in clinical ethics decision-making.
- An ethical theory offers principles, moral rules as well as the way to justify those principles and those moral rules and to connect them to concrete cases. The knowledge of an ethical theory is justified by the need to gain a full comprehension of the meaning of the moral rule.
- An ethical theory rarely faces uncertainties about which course of action would satisfy the best interest of the patient. In any case an ethical theory

never faces moral dilemmas created by conflicting principles because it recognizes a hierarchical order of values (principles and rules) within the theory itself.
- The current pluralistic climate has led some to the conclusion that it is not possible to find an agreement about morally right and wrong decisions (MacIntyre 2006). In these cases, it is not necessary to conclude that only negotiation and compromise are possible. Ethical theory gives solid grounds for overcoming radical relativism in order to reach an agreement in most clinical situations.

Relational Ethics

The expectations that would be appropriate in a clinical encounter are to cure as well as to care for the patient (Pellegrino and Thomasma 1988). Therefore the ethical assessment of physicians' conduct should be based on actions as well as relationships. Action ethics focuses on the treatment, and on the reasons for acting in a certain way, while relational ethics focuses on how physicians meet challenges in their relationships with the patient. The specific challenge in medical relationships is to understand the vulnerability, fragility and dependence of the sick human being. It requires a focus on the individual personality of the patient, that is to say, seeing patients as individuals.

The distinction between an action ethics and a relational ethics perspective might seem forced. It is clear that in practical clinical work these two perspectives are intertwined because it is difficult to determine the right course of action and how to act in the best interests of the patient, unless a good relationship is established with the patient.

Virtues

Clinical ethics in our experience is theory-driven, but also sensitive to virtue considerations. As also pointed out by John-Stewart Gordon (in this volume), practical choice is not always the result of purely rational-theoretical deliberation (it may be so in some complex cases, in which I lack experience). More frequently, decision-making may involve sensitivity and experience. Human agents are susceptible to both cognitive errors and affective distortions because moral choices are affected intellectually and effectively by one's own personality (MacIntyre 1981). In that case no such decision-making procedure may be sufficient to preclude wrong actions in the practice of virtues. Moreover, according to the person-centred theory, simply following rules is an incomplete form of morality. A sort of legalism with too little attention to human inclinations is not enough to guarantee right choice and action.

Virtues in clinical ethics are therefore understood as a certain degree of perfection in intellectual dispositions and sensitivity, an essential personal component towards the realization of the patient's good. Virtues enable medical personnel to act with promptness and with facility in applying abstract rules and procedures to a particular patient in specific circumstances, and so to reach a prudent and compassionate choice (Pellegrino and Thomasma 1993).

Prudence is the most important action-guiding virtue; for its role in the decision-making process, it is also called 'practical wisdom'. However, some specific virtues are more strongly rooted in the professional tradition of medicine and nursing than in a simple general personalist ethics. In the clinical relationship there are especially rooted such relational virtues as compassion and caring, that is to say, a sympathetic attitude to the needs and concerns of the patient.

In our experience, mission is another important motivational resource for clinical ethical decision-making practice (Pijnenburg and Gordijn 2005). Mission is a personal identification with the social and moral meanings and values of clinical work as a 'helping profession', according to which doctors respond not in their own interests, but for the sake of the patient. According to our experience, the principle of mission has a role in preventing doctors' care from becoming merely routine and rationalized as a mechanistic application of techniques.

Conclusions

According to the methodology I have presented, decision-making in clinical ethics is based on circumstances and justified by an ethical theory. No adequate clinical ethics, in my view, can be based on unreflective foundations. Professional clinical ethics should always require an ethical methodology for the necessary moral discernment and judgement. Moreover, according to the person-centred ethical theory, there is no danger of infringing one moral rule in order to protect another one because the application of the moral rule always implies the application of a specified and ordered rule.

Clinical ethics applies general rules to particular cases with discernment, not immediately, which is why one needs a methodology. However, the knowledge of ethical theory and methodology does not exhaust the moral life and its decisions; one also needs appropriate attitudes and emotion through virtues to reach moral wisdom. A prerequisite for doing what is right for individual patients is establishing an ethically good relationship, which involves seeing and meeting the individual patient.

The relevant literature often reduces the subject of clinical ethics to a simple 'science of decisions', thus excluding the question of ethical judgement (Aulisio and Arnold 2003). I would assert, however, that the question of 'the right action' is fundamental, even in clinical ethics. The exclusion of ethical judgement would mean reducing ethical problems to a mere series of procedures to be followed, and clinical ethics to a question of techniques of communication or to one of overcoming the conflicts of interpersonal relations, thus betraying the very nature of clinical ethics, which is based on the question of 'the right action'. I would also suggest that rational discussion, which forms the basis of ethical rules, represents the only real and effective possibility of dialogue in a pluralist context. The two requirements – the decision to be made and the consent to reach – recognize a common root which consists of a rational decision that cannot be substituted by a mere collection of procedures.

Acknowledgements

I would like to thank the two reviewers for their helpful comments and suggestions.

References

Aulisio, M.P. and Arnold, R.M. 2003. Ethics consultation: In the service of practice. *Journal of Clinical Ethics*, 14(4), 276–81.
Breeur, R. 1999. Individualism and personalism. *Ethics Perspectives*, 6, 67–81.
Carrasco De Paula, I. 2004. Il concetto di persona e la sua rilevanza assiologia: I principi della bioetica personalista. *Medicina e Morale*, 2, 265–278.
Cataldo, P.J. 2001. The moral fonts of action and decision making, in *Catholic Health Care Ethics: A Manual for Ethics Committees*, edited by P.J. Cataldo and A.S. Moraczewski. Boston, MA: The National Catholic Bioethics Center, 2/1–2/5.
Childress, J.F. 2007. Methods in bioethics. Introduction: Questions about method, in *The Oxford Handbook of Bioethics*, edited by B. Steinbock. Oxford: Oxford University Press, 15–44.
Clouser, K.D. and Gert, B. 1990. A critique of principlism. *Journal of Medicine and Philosophy*, 15, 219–36.
Gert, B. 1990. Rationality, human nature, and lists. *Ethics*, 100(2), 279–300.
Gleeson, G. 2003. The withdrawal of life-sustaining treatment. Ethics and law: principles and practice. *Bioethics Outlook*, 14, 1–7.
Green, R.M. 1990. Method in bioethics: a troubled assessment. *Journal of Medicine and Philosophy*, 15, 179–97.
Jonsen, A.R. 1988. Of balloons and bicycles, or the relationship between ethical theory and practical judgment. *The Hastings Center Report*, 5, 14–16.
Jonsen, A.R. and Toulmin, S. 1991. *The Abuse of Casuistry*. Berkeley, CA: University of California Press.
Jonsen, A.R., Siegler, M. and Winslade, W.J. 2002. *Clinical Ethics*. New York: McGraw-Hill.
Kopelman, L.M. 1990. What is applied about 'applied' philosophy? *Journal of Medicine and Philosophy*, 15, 199–218.
MacIntyre, A. 1981. *After Virtue*. Notre Dame, IN: University of Notre Dame Press.

MacIntyre, A. 2006. *The Tasks of Philosophy. Selected Essays*. Cambridge: Cambridge University Press.

Moraczewski, A.S. 2001. The double effect, in *Catholic Health Care Ethics: A Manual for Ethics Committees*, edited by P.J. Cataldo and A.S. Moraczewski. Boston, MA: The National Catholic Bioethics Center, 2/1–2/5.

Pellegrino, E.D. and Thomasma, D.C. 1988. *For the Patient's Good: The Restoration of Beneficence in Health Care*. New York: Oxford University Press.

Pellegrino, E.D. and Thomasma, D.C. 1993. *The Virtues in Medical Practice*. New York: Oxford University Press.

Pijnenburg, M.A.M. and Gordijn, B. 2005. Identity and moral responsibility of healthcare organizations. *Theoretical Medicine and Bioethics*, 26, 141–60.

Chapter 11
Demands and Needs in Clinical Ethics Consultation in Georgia

Nino Chikhladze and Nato Pitskhelauri

Introduction

The health care system in Georgia as it operated from 1921 was characterized by a very bureaucratic and centralized form of governance, and non-effective economic mechanisms. Despite the declared preventive character of Soviet medicine, the emphasis was placed on treatment and hospital service. The sole indicator of the system's success was providing the population with hospital beds, which caused the development of an industrial character, discounting attributive indicators. Extensive development of the field created a negative circle: increasing the health care network required increasing investments, but the supply of money needed for intensification of medical processes was catastrophically declining. As a result, an imbalance was caused in the health care system. After this, it became quite problematic to fulfil the system's only main advantage – providing the population with access to medical treatment.

There were previously no ethical or judicial mechanisms of regulation. During the Soviet era in Georgia, legal activities meant only paraphrasing the Soviet government's given rules. In 1972, the government passed a law on health care, but the rights of patients were not protected and medical ethics principles were ignored. (An exception was the right of confidentiality of patients' personal data). In that model, the patient was not the subject but the object of the system, with no right to choose either the hospital or the doctor. The health care system soon became more and more corporate and ultimately it became uncontrollable by society.

Georgia in Transition

After the collapse of the Soviet Union, Georgia was restored to political independence. The change of political arrangements and the existing state governance, civil conflicts and the breakdown of traditional economic activity together caused an acute institutional vacuum with catastrophic consequences for the country. Georgia, like other post-Soviet countries, inherited a highly centralized and inefficient model of health care. While the expenditure on social needs sharply declined, a change from the Soviet model of health care, which had provided the population with free medical services for decades, took place (Jinjolava 1997: 96–100). The government of Georgia has carried out several reform initiatives for building a more effective health care system.

Reform in the Georgian Health Care System

A conception of population health protection in Georgia was developed, with the goal of creating an adequate health care model while entering into economic-market relations (Jorbenadze 1998:1–7). The model proposed to use the new economic relations and civilized democratic bases for the protection of citizens' rights. The reform's main goal was to provide the population with basic medical service.

In 1995 a new conception of health care reorganization was elaborated in Georgia, in which the political, economic and judicial components of state policy of health care were defined. The most important of them was to create a legal basis that would change the health care system from one oriented only on medical institutions to a system oriented on patients and with state financing for special medical programmes (Main Direction of Reorientation of Georgian Health Care System 1996). This was the beginning of regulation for a new health care system in Georgia.

Legislative Basis of the Health Care System

In the transitional period, the health care law did not work, so health care was in a legislative vacuum. The Soviet model left as its heritage a health care system with no experience of the legal system, having paternalistic relations with patients, and a tradition of isolating people from health care, leading to society in general being indifferent about it. One of the most important steps in the reforms was the creation of a legislative basis for the health care system. Since 1995, the Georgian parliament has passed many important laws, including 16 laws in the medical sphere, 12 laws to regulate social problems and one law about the protection of patients' rights.

In 1997 the law on health care was adopted. This is considered to be the framework law that determines the priorities and fundamental principles of the health care legislation of Georgia. During the preparation of these laws, documents of international organizations such as the UN, WHO, WMA, the European Community and European Council, together with appropriate laws of different countries, were used as models.

Nowadays Georgia belongs to the group of European countries with comprehensive legislation about the protection of patients' social and individual rights. Georgia is in the list of the top 10 countries which have enacted legislation about 'patients' rights'. From 1995 to 2007, the parliament of Georgia adopted the following laws, which have a bearing on this subject: the law on medical activity, the law on patients' rights, the law on human organ transplantation, the law on protection and promotion of infant natural feeding, the law on health care, the law on drug and pharmaceutical activity, the law on psychiatric care, the law on HIV/AIDS prevention, the law on abortion, the law on biomedical research involving human subjects, and the law on reproductive health and reproductive rights.

Top-down Approach for the Establishment of Ethical Committees

The basis for the creation of ethical committees in Georgia is determined by national legislation.

The first legislative act where we find the definition of a 'medical ethics committee' is the law on health care of 1997. The global goals of a medical ethics committee are defined as 'protection of patients' rights and the norms of medical ethics'. The law provides that: 'In order to ensure the patient's rights and the norms of medical ethics, medical institutions [shall] create committees for medical ethics' (The Law on Health Care, Chapter VI – Medical Institutions, Article 62).

The medical ethics committees' function is indicated in the law on patients' rights: 'Decisions about withholding or limiting the patient's information shall be authorized by the medical ethics committee or if such committee does not exist by another physician. Decisions about withholding or limiting the patient's information shall be entered in the medical record of the patient' (The Law on Patients' Rights, Chapter III – The Right of Information, Article 18).

In 1998, by the order of the President (Decree No. 15 of 12 January 1998), the Georgian Ministry of Labour, Health and Social Affairs was ordered to create a definition of medical ethics committees. At the first stage, due to the lack of appropriately trained professionals, it was considered wise to establish ethics committees which combined the functions of clinical ethics committees as well as research ethics committees. The first version of the draft regulation for the so-called medical ethics committee (required by Presidential Decree No. 15) was prepared. In 1999 two separate documents were drafted: the first one lays down principles for the establishment and operation of a clinical ethics committee and the second one regulates the activity of a research ethics committee. According to the latter document, a two-tiered network of committees on the regional level will be created in Georgia. (As of 2008, about 15 research committees had been established).

The National Council on Bioethics was established in Georgia in 2000 for the regulation of the ethical aspects of health care and biomedicine. The legal basis for establishment and functioning of the National Council on Bioethics was Order No. 157/0 enacted by the Minister of Labour, Health and Social Affairs (The Order of the Minister of Labour, Health and Social Affairs, No. 157/0 2000).

Aims of Medical Ethics Committees, Practical and Organizational Aspects

In the autumn of 2000, the Minister of Labour, Health and Social Affairs confirmed a charter for the regulation of medical ethics committees (The Order of the Minister of Labour, Health Care and Social Affairs No. 128/n 2000). The charter includes criteria for the creation of the medical ethics committees, their structure and composition, the functions of the medical ethics committee, etc. (Charter for Medical Ethics Committee 2000). According to this charter, 'For the humanization of medical practices in the country, to support patients' rights, dignity and personal autonomy', medical ethics committees should 'educate medical staff, show ethical aspects of problems arising in medical service, analyse and make corresponding recommendations'.

It is provided in the regulation that it is necessary to develop medical ethics committees in general hospitals, and in any kind of hospitals where there are intensive therapy and reanimation units, psychiatric hospitals, obstetrics/gynaecology hospitals, institutions for studying reproductive medicine, and centres of transplantation. Developing medical ethics committees is recommended in any kind of medical institution as well. However, in practice, medical ethics committees are not set up even in the types of medical institutions which are required by law to have them.

According to Chapter IV (Article 9) of the charter, the medical ethics committee must be multidisciplinary, and the medical ethics committee (Chapter IV, Article 10) must include at least one physician, nurse and a representative of the administration of each medical division of a general institution. Chapter IV (Article 11) provides that the medical ethics committee can include as members an ethics/bioethics professional, a priest, a lawyer and a representative of society.

The charter outlines the functions of the medical ethics committee, especially its educational activities in medicine. This can include the education of medical personnel, patients, patients' families and the community about the ethical dimensions of contemporary medical practice, the ethical aspects of making decisions concerning the relationship among doctors and patients and health protection. The committee should also: elaborate recommendations and main principles which will help medical staff to solve ethical problems arising in medical service, provide consultations for medical staff on clinical ethical aspects for patients and their relatives, and undertake retrospective study of ethical aspects of the decisions taken about past treatment of patients.

The organizational aspects of the medical ethics committee are also defined. It is provided that the medical ethics committee shall hold meetings as frequently as is necessary for its functioning, and meetings shall be held at least once a month.

Clinical Ethics Committees and Clinical Ethics Consultation

The National Council on Bioethics has prepared several recommendations since its inception in 2000. Although there have been considerable legal developments related to the establishment and development of clinical ethics committees in Georgia, very few clinical ethics committees have actually been established. In one of its recommendations concerning clinical ethics committees, the National Council on Bioethics explicitly recommended that the Minister of Labour, Health and Social Affairs should further support the establishment of clinical ethics committees.

Most of the committees were established in 2003, soon after the National Council on Bioethics issued its recommendation about the establishment and development of clinical ethics committees based on the charter.

The survey about activity of clinical ethics committees in Georgia was carried out by the National Council on Bioethics and Georgian Health, Law and Bioethics Society in 2003.[1] Results of the survey were published in the proceedings of the bilateral meeting organized by the Council of Europe within the framework of the cooperation programme to strengthen the rule of law in Georgia (Research and Medical Ethics Committees 2003).

Questionnaires were sent to health care institutions. According to the survey, just nine of them had a clinical ethics committee. Just three of these nine committees had their own regulations developed on the basis of the charter. The number of members of the clinical ethics committees ranged from five to 13.

Problems in the methodological foundation and implementation of clinical ethics committees in Georgian hospitals have been solved, but the question of their effectiveness remains.

Currently the attitudes and views of the health care professionals and administrators on the value of clinical ethics committees are not known and seem unclear. There is a need for further research in Georgia on topics such as: the experience in ethical decision-making of medical doctors and other health care professionals and their attitudes towards ethics consultation; the knowledge of medical doctors and other health care professionals, stakeholders, patients and their relatives about the ethical principles and legal requirements reflected in Georgian patients' rights legislation; the functioning of clinical ethics committees.

At present in Georgia, the demands for clinical ethics committees in society are weak, but the needs really exist in society. It is a situation where the demand and the actual level of need do not correspond with each other.

Conclusion

Clinical ethics committees have been designed to help in the implementation of ethical principles and the legal requirements reflected in the Georgian patients' rights legislation. But according to the results of survey and assessment by the National Council on Bioethics and the Georgian Health, Law and Bioethics Society, the members of clinical ethics committees do not have sufficient competencies and knowledge on ethical issues.

---

1 Since then, another such survey has not been undertaken in Georgia.

The main reasons are that the members of committees don't have formal education in bioethics and there's lack of training programmes in clinical ethics consultation in Georgia. And the result is a 'closed system' of a clinical ethics committee without the capability to make competent ethics consultations and hence to improve the existing situation.

The benefits of the existing top-down approach to clinical ethics committees in Georgia are:

- The creation of a legal basis for the establishment of clinical ethics committees.
- The elaboration of the concept and the regulation of ethics committees.
- The establishment of clinical ethics committees.

However, in the 10 years since 1998, the effectiveness of clinical ethics committees in Georgia has been very low. We suggest that the reason for this is not only a lack of trained professionals but also a lack of information about patients' rights, the principles of medical law, and the ways of making decisions about ethical dilemmas in Georgian society.

Analysis of the existing situation shows that the top-down model should be replaced by a bottom-up model. Patients, medical professionals and society must have more information about the mission of clinical ethics committees. It is necessary to increase not only bioethics education at all levels (undergraduate, postgraduate, continuing professional development), including special training for CEC members, but also public education and involvement.

Research and evaluation of the functioning and effectiveness of clinical ethics consultation is lacking in Georgia. Research in this area should be encouraged for the further development of clinical ethics committees based on appropriate evidence. The competence of ethics committee members is an issue deserving more attention. Clinical ethics committees must intensify their work towards achieving their main goals to protect the health, rights and dignity of patients and society.

References

Charter for Medical Ethics Committee. Tbilisi. 2000.
Jinjolava, T. 1997. *Social and economical aspects of reorientation of Georgian public health system: Strategy of social and economical reform in the transition.* Georgia: Diogene Publishers.
Jorbenadze, R. 1998. Some outcomes of the reorientation of the health care system of Georgia. Research papers, Volume I: 1–7. Tbilisi: Tbilisi State Medical University Press.
Main Direction of Reorientation of Georgian Health Care System. 1996. Tbilisi: Ministry of Health Care of Georgia.

Presidential Decree No. 15. 1998.
Research and Medical Ethics Committees. 2003. Proceedings of the bilateral meeting organized by the Council of Europe within the framework of the cooperation programme to strengthen the rule of law. Tbilisi: Ministry of Labour, Health and Social Affairs of Georgia.
The Law on Health Care. 1997. Tbilisi.
The Law on Patients' Rights. 2000. Tbilisi.
The Order of the Minister of Labour, Health Care and Social Affairs of Georgia No. 128/n 2000.
The Order of the Minister of Labour, Health and Social Affairs of Georgia No. 157/0 2000.

Chapter 12
Clinical Ethics Consultation in Croatia[1]

Ana Borovecki

Introduction

Almost 20 years have passed since fundamental political changes occurred in the European transitional societies. Many of those societies have become part of the European Union or are on the way to becoming members. However, the following quotation by the Russian philosopher L.S. Frank still resonates within the structures and corridors of power of those societies:

> Political revolution that is not grounded in social evolution at the basic level of satisfaction of 'simple' human economic, physical and psychological needs could only reproduce the same totalitarian pattern under a new ideological label. (Tichtchenko and Yudin 1997: 1)

When speaking of bioethics in the transitional society, the statement can be made that the general situation has improved for many countries, especially for those countries that are now members of the European Union. Nevertheless, after analysing the literature published over recent years on bioethical issues in European transitional societies, one still finds a certain pattern emerging. Examining publications on bioethics since the early 1990s, one can perceive a number of particular bioethical issues that are discussed. Certain issues have remained a constant and recurrent problem, others are more specific to certain countries, while other issues have changed over time. Significant issues of ethical debate are corruption and double standards in the health care system. These have remained significant problems for most European transitional societies (Miller et al. 2000, Pellegrino 1995). The issues of patients' rights, ethics committees, nursing ethics, and those connected with ethics of research, such as the use of placebos, conflict of interests, research integrity and academic misconduct are also widely discussed (Coker and McKee 2001, Vrhovac 2002). The abuse of psychiatry for political purposes and organ trafficking are in the focus of debate in some of the transitional societies (Polubinskaya and Bonnie 1996, Thau and Popescu-Prohovara 1992). It is also apparent from the literature that standards for

---

1 This research is part of the scientific project, 'The position of patients in the Health Services of the Republic of Croatia in terms of legislation and in reality', financed by the Ministry of Science, Education and Sport of the Republic of Croatia.

the institutionalization of bioethics in European countries in transition, including important legal frameworks such as the statutes of ethics committees and legislation on patients' rights, are only formally proclaimed within different legal provisions, while their actual implementation in everyday practice is deficient or non-existent (Glasa 2000).

At the same time, on the Western horizons of Europe a new practice is coming into full swing – clinical ethics consultation. This new practice is certainly no novelty for the rest of the world. Ethics consultation emerged with the development of the field of bioethics in the early 1980s in the USA (Spike and Greenlaw 2000). The idea behind this practice is to improve the quality of patient care by identifying, analysing and attempting to solve ethical problems (end-of-life issues, patient autonomy, genetics, abortion, religious and cultural issues, professional conduct, truth-telling and confidentiality, justice issues, beneficence) in the practice of clinical medicine (Yen and Schneiderman 1999). In clinical ethics, the focus is on the ethical aspects of the factual clinical situation with attention to all the relevant clinical factors involved (the situation of the patient with their expectations, pain, fears, and the professional and personal experience of care givers) (Gastmans 2002: 81). However, the bioethical issues in the European countries in transition, as previously stated, present a different spectrum of issues: better implementation of legal frameworks for patients' rights, corruption, establishment of ethics committees, and inequalities in health care provision (Borovecki et al. 2006). Is the issue of implementation of clinical ethics consultation services really important in the transitional societies? Apparently, yes. Even though the level of structural frameworks that supports health care systems in European transitional societies is experiencing many problems (Borovecki et al. 2005), ethical dilemmas are an inseparable part of everyday medical practice. Despite the fact that in all the transitional countries in Europe there are almost no trained ethical consultants, physicians have expressed positive attitudes towards ethics consultation (Aleksandrova 2008). This chapter aims to explore possible approaches to the implementation of clinical ethics consultation services in European countries in transition. Croatia has been taken as the model for this analysis.

The Croatian Situation and Clinical Ethics Consultation Services

The development of the field of ethics in Croatia came into full swing in the 1990s. At that time the focus was on two issues. The first was the development of the field and the implementation of ethics education in all medical schools. This has been gradually achieved and now ethics education is part of the undergraduate and postgraduate curricula at all four medical schools in Croatia (Borovecki et al. 2004). The second issue was development of legal frameworks. As a result of this process a number of legal requirements for ethics committees, patients' rights issues and biomedical research have been developed. However, the Croatian situation regarding the creation of legal norms can be characterized as a 'failure to thrive' situation, similar to many transitional societies.

Perhaps the best example of this is the situation regarding ethics committees and biomedical research. Although established in 1997 in the Law on Health Protection, ethics committees in Croatia are still struggling in their everyday work. The reason for this difficult situation can be found in the inadequate and often confusing legal provisions governing them. Croatia used to have only one type of ethics committee, the so-called 'mixed type', which functioned as both a health care ethics committee and a research ethics committee. It usually operated in different health care institutions. Research ethics committees as such could only be found in research institutes and medical schools. There were also ethics committees in professional organizations, but they only dealt with professional issues. Additional ethical standards were also created with the formation of the National Bioethics Committee for Medicine of the Government of the Republic of Croatia in 2001. In 2003 the new Law on Drugs and Medical Products was implemented. According to this law, the review of research protocols was now transferred to the independent central research ethics committee. This approach was in accordance with tendencies reported in the literature on the establishment of institutional review boards (IRBs) and territorial organization practices. According to the Law on Drugs and Medical Products and its newest version, the Law on Drugs 2007, research protocols should be reviewed by an independent central research ethics committee at the Ministry of Health. In 2007 new regulations on clinical research and good clinical practice were introduced. Here it is stated that a centralized review by an IRB is obligatory for all clinical and non-intervention drug research and clinical research of medical devices. However, other types of scientific academic research are not reviewed centrally, unless they deal with clinical research on drugs and medical devices. Such academic research is to be reviewed by the IRB at institutions of higher education (such as research institutes and universities) or by the IRB at the ministry in charge of approval of scientific academic research. At the same time, the articles in the newest version of the Law on Health Protection 2005, which provide the legal framework for the work of ethics committees in health care institutions, still state that the review of research protocols (it does not say which type of research) is one of the tasks done locally as part of the functions of an ethics committee. This creates confusion in regard to health care ethics committees since a research protocol can possibly be reviewed on a national and local level at the same time. Furthermore, the implementation of the legal standards concerning patients' rights is also experiencing the same fate – failure to thrive (Borovecki et al. 2006).

Nevertheless, improvement of the legal provisions is not the only remedy for the Croatian situation. The health care system in Croatia presents itself as a hierarchical and bureaucratic entity. The therapeutic aim of a medical institution is sometimes at risk of being subordinated to bureaucratic organizational aims (Borovecki et al. 2005). Moreover there is a risk of institutional violence. This risk is even greater in a transitional society such as Croatia. Power games, even political involvement in medical decision-making, are not uncommon in transitional settings. Furthermore, a legalistic and bureaucratic organization is the characteristic of the legal regulation of health care as a whole, and health care professions in transitional countries such as Croatia are no exception. Ethical regulations are taken lightly and their breach is not uncommon (Marusic 2005). Moreover, the Croatian health care institutions tend to be regarded as health factories. The number of beds, the number of patients processed, and the level of technical sophistication in these health factories are the most important factors in evaluation of their work. Little if any attention is paid to the age, personal characteristics, religious beliefs, and gender differences of patients or to ethical problems that arise in the process of providing health care.

Therefore it is no wonder that clinical ethics consultation services do not exist in Croatia nor are they mandatory. However, in everyday clinical practice, one is constantly confronted with a number of ethical problems that arise and which are not adequately treated, such as truth-telling, patient autonomy, Do Not Resuscitate orders, involvement of the patient and the patient's family in the medical decision-making process, and end-of-life decision-making. One can say that in this respect Croatia does not differ greatly from other transitional countries. Recently, a study was published about Bulgarian hospital physicians' attitudes towards ethics consultation. The majority of the respondents expressed a need for having ethical consultation in their hospitals (Aleksandrova 2008). One can reasonably assume that if one was to undertake such a survey in Croatia the same answers would emerge. However, the implementation of clinical ethics consultation services in Croatia, as in the majority of transitional societies in Europe, would have many obstacles in its way.

Can this situation be improved? What do we need for clinical ethics consultation to be implemented in Croatia? To what should we pay special attention while introducing such services in Croatia? What would be the best approach?

Implementing Clinical Ethics Consultation Services in Croatia

Pierre Boitte emphasizes that the reality that governs health care institutions whose prime example is the everyday life of a hospital, is primarily a clinical one. This means that clinical judgements and decisions are the focal point of everyday interaction within hospital walls. Clinical judgement enables health professionals to make decisions in given situations case by case. This judgement consists of a balance between theoretical knowledge and the unknown factors of the illness itself. The quality of this judgement is achieved by experience and practice. Sometimes, within this clinical reality, there are cases and situations that create areas of uncertainty, where clinical judgement needs to be complemented with certain additional qualities that can only be found in ethical reflection (Boitte 1998).

Ethical reflection is thus important for health care institutions and through this reflection the ethical function of a health care institution is observed. Health care institutions, at least in the best sense of their ethical practice, have ethical characteristics that are about relationships. They consist of intricate webs of relationships between people. They have attributes relevant to ethics; they promote values embodied in medical ethics, reinforcing certain kinds of behaviour and discouraging transgressions. They create and promote ethical cultures within their walls, with a purpose; they protect the well-being of patients, foster their healing process, and help patients and their families to cope with disease. Health care institutions embody particular organizational cultures that, good or bad, affect people and reflect certain values. Also, health care institutions have certain purposes, and they can be evaluated and held accountable as to whether or not they fulfil their purposes, particularly those affecting and effecting health care (Emanuel 2000). According to Boitte:

> To defend the role of an ethical function in hospitals means in this perspective to agree to take into account this critical reflection in the biomedical practices, considering at the same time the outside parts of the critical reflection, the proximity of actual caring and research practices and the institutionalization of those two activities. (Boitte 2005: 170)

For Boitte, critical reflection does not consist in formulating regulations in order to try to contain or bring limits to practice (which very often do not take care of those normative processes) but rather in promoting commitment in the persons who are fully engaged in biomedical innovations, especially those who practise medicine and care for people. This will enhance the ethical aspects of the decision-making process. In other words, we have to avoid only medical logic or managerial logic being taken into account when decisions concerning specific cases are made or when problems arise. In order to be relevant, ethics must consist of more than just intervention at the last moment. It must be present in every department with each patient to help other occupations – doctors or nurses and those cared for – to take responsibility (Boitte 2005). In an institutional setting such as a hospital, it is only through a gradual and long-term process of self-development of each participant in the caring process that we can avoid a bureaucratic mentality and 'window-dressing' tendencies in ethical decision-making, thus fostering the ethical function. This task is not easy and could take years. However, it is the only sound and permanent choice for Croatia or any other transitional country to avoid pitfalls of bureaucratic mentality within the health care system. Nevertheless, this creation of an ethical function in hospitals should only be regarded as a small part of the creation of the ethical function in the health care system itself. In order to initiate real change in an ethical climate in a transitional health care system, changes should be made on all levels.

Patient Education

Patient education should also be undertaken within this framework. Croatia has recently regulated patients' rights by law. In November 2004 the Law on the Protection of Patients' Rights was adopted. The key reasons for its adoption were the alignment of domestic health legislation with the Council of Europe Convention for the Protection of Human Rights and Dignity of the Human Being with regard to the Application of Biology and Medicine of 1997, which Croatia ratified in 2003, but also the more detailed application of the provisions of the World Health Organization's Declaration on the Promotion of Patients' Rights in Europe of 1994 (known as the Amsterdam Declaration). Pressure from NGOs, especially those directly related to health issues, accompanied by media emphasis on the frequent violations of patients' rights in the Croatian health care system and society, was also one of the reasons why the adoption of the Act was initiated. The legislation on patients' rights was a significant step in drawing closer to international standards of protection of patients' rights. However, legislation alone has not had a significant effect on the actual position of patients in the Croatian health care system, and currently many problems are being experienced in regard to its adequate implementation. This legislation is only one element in the process of protecting and improving patients' rights as human rights. It is indisputable that, with the legislation on patients' rights in Croatia, processes began which, by the logic of the development of democracy and civilization, will not be halted. However, legislation is only one, albeit an important, element in the process of protection and improvement of patients' rights as human rights. The second, no less important, element in that process is the development of a culture of respect and protection of human rights overall, and the human rights of sensitive categories of people. Citizens as patients, especially when needing medical treatment, certainly fall into such a category. In the opinion of the author of this chapter, with the political will shown through legislation and other strategic documents in the field of health and social politics, the keys to realizing this goal are information and education in human rights, that is, patients' rights, at all levels; in public and on the professional and scientific level (Babic-Bosanac et al. 2008).

Education of Health Care Providers

Educational efforts should be aimed also at health care providers, from the beginning of their university education to the level of permanent professional education. Through these educational efforts, professionalism should be regarded as a complex practice in which accountability is the most important core competence. Therefore, the place of medical ethics plays a central role in professional conduct. Professionalism has to be viewed in terms of accountability and normative and technical justification, not as a simple compliance with external standards. In that respect, a possible approach could be found in the concept of 'reflective professionalism' (Verkerk et al. 2007). A good professional in our times does not only exhibit technical proficiency that allows them to do things right, but they must also do the right thing. Morality is therefore an interpersonal endeavour (Verkerk et al. 2004).

The emphasis should be on the relationship between human beings on the one hand and the integration of human actions and being on the other hand (Gastmans 2002). The emphasis here should not be on methods and materials but on continuity. It is by a personal, all-encompassing approach that non-moral personal, societal and institutional factors influencing moral development can be better interwoven into the intricate web of ethical decision-making.

Changes in the Role of Ethics Committees in Hospitals

With the necessary changes in the Croatian health care system, hospital ethics committees could become the means for creating a new subtle study process within the hospital setting. Hospital ethics committees can indirectly improve the quality of care by providing support to clinicians and patients as they face difficult clinical decisions. They could help to create the desired kind of reflective and critical culture within the health care institutions, which would be essential for clinical governance to be a genuine rather than a cosmetic change (Boitte 1998). From the standpoint of quality control, ethics committees can also be good catalysts for the improvement of physician-patient communication. This will require transformation of the membership structure of committees, allowing representatives of patients' rights, NGOs and representatives of the local community to be members, which is not the case in Croatia at the moment. Not only could hospital ethics committees be instrumental in improving the quality of care in health care institutions, but they themselves should follow quality standards. Such an approach would also include the selection criteria for their members, putting emphasis on knowledge and expertise rather than on the social perception of the status of members in their professions or the preferences of the hospital administration.

Through this omnipresence of an ethical function within health care institutions, a process of gradual change could take place in the hospital climate. This process would paint a clear picture of a health care institution and provide us with data that would enable us to see how the ethical consultation process should take place and the structures through which it could be implemented. Unless we do this, we risk implementing ethical consultation services through a top-down approach, which is not the best approach for a transitional society. Such a society usually perceives top-down rules and regulations as foreign to its everyday life, something that should be bent and avoided where possible. In that case, the method of ethical consultation is less relevant, in terms of matters such as how it is done, who does it (ethics committee, consultant), and what is the best professional background of the consultant (physician, ethicist, psychologist, philosopher, theologian). The most important thing in implementing ethical consultation services in a transitional country such as Croatia is to give the process power and legitimacy within the institution. This can only be done by careful analysis and the creation of space for ethical reflection within health care institutions.

In conclusion, with the changes proposed here, the situation of clinical ethics consultation services in Croatia could be adequately improved. Since the Croatian case shows a number of similarities with other countries in transition, the proposed solution for the Croatian problems may possibly provide a paradigm for solving similar problems in other countries in transition in Europe and in other parts of the world as well. For more views on clinical ethics consultation services in transitional countries, see the contribution in this volume by Silviya Aleksandrova.

References

Aleksandrova, S. 2008. Survey on the experience in ethical decision-making and attitude of eleven University Hospital physicians towards ethics consultation. *Medicine, Health Care and Philosophy*, 11(1), 35–42.

Babic-Bosanac, S., Borovecki, A. and Fister, K. 2008. Patients' rights in the Republic of Croatia: Between the law and reality. *Medicinski Glasnik*, 5(1), 37–43.

Boitte, P. 1998. The role of the clinical ethicist in the hospital. *Medicine, Health Care and Philosophy*, 1(1), 65–70.

Boitte, P. 2005. For an ethical function in hospitals, in *Clinical Bioethics: A Search for the Foundations*, edited by C. Viafora. Dordrecht: Springer, 169–80.

Borovecki, A., ten Have, H. and Oreskovic, S. 2004. Developments regarding ethical issues in medicine in the Republic of Croatia. *Cambridge Quarterly of Healthcare Ethics*, 13(3), 263–6.

Borovecki, A., ten Have, H. and Oreskovic, S. 2005. Ethics and the structures of health care in the European countries in transition: Hospital ethics committees in Croatia. *British Medical Journal*, 331(7510), 227–9.

Borovecki, A., ten Have, H. and Oreskovic, S. 2006. A critical analysis of hospital ethics committees: Opportunity or bureaucratic cul-de-sac? *Drustvena istrazivanja*, 15(6), 1221–38.

Coker, R. and McKee, M. 2001. Ethical approval for health research in Central and Eastern Europe: An international survey. *Clinical Medicine*, 1(3), 197–9.

Emanuel, L.L. 2000. Ethics and the structures of healthcare. *HEC Forum*, 9(2), 151–68.

Gastmans, C. 2002. Towards integrated clinical ethics approach: Caring, clinical and organizational, in *Healthy Thoughts: European Perspectives on Health Care Ethics*, edited by R.K. Lie and P.T. Schotsmans. Louvain, Paris; Sterling, VA: Peeters, 81–102.

Glasa, J. (ed.) 2000. *Ethics committees in Central and Eastern Europe*. Bratislava: Charis IEMB.

Marusic, A. 2005. Ethics in health care and research in European transition countries: Reality and future prospects. *British Medical Journal*, 331(7510), 230.

Miller, W.L., Grodeland, A.B. and Koshechkina, T.Y. 2000. 'If you pay, we'll operate immediately'. *Journal of Medical Ethics*, 26(5), 305–11.

Pellegrino, E.D. 1995. Guarding the integrity of medical ethics: Some lessons from Soviet Russia. *JAMA*, 273(20), 1622–3.

Polubinskaya, S. and Bonnie, R. 1996. New code of ethics for Russian psychiatrists. *Bulletin of Medical Ethics*, 117(April), 13–19.

Spike, J. and Greenlaw, J. 2000. Ethics consultation: High ideals or unrealistic expectations? *Annals of Internal Medicine*, 133(1), 55–7.

Thau, C. and Popescu-Prahovara, A. 1992. Romanian psychiatry in turmoil. *Bulletin of Medical Ethics*, 78(May), 13–16.

Tichtchenko, P. and Yudin, B. 1997. The moral status of fetuses in Russia. *Cambridge Quarterly of Healthcare Ethics*, 6(1), 31–8.

Verkerk, M.A., Lindeman, H., Maeckelberghe, E., Feenstra, E., Hartoungh, R. and de Bree, M. 2004. Enhancing reflection: An interpersonal exercise in ethics education. *Hastings Centre Report*, 35(4), 31–8.

Verkerk, M.A., de Bree, M.J. and Mourits, M.J.E. 2007. Reflective professionalism: Interpreting CanMEDS' 'professionalism'. *Journal of Medical Ethics*, 33(11), 663–6.

Vrhovac, B. 2002. Conflict of interest in Croatia: Doctors with dual obligations. *Science and Engineering Ethics*, 8(3), 309–16.

Yen, B., and Schneiderman, L. 1999. Impact of pediatric ethics consultations on patients, families, social workers, and physicians. *Journal of Perinatology*, 19(5), 373–8.

Chapter 13
Clinical Ethics in the Netherlands: Moral Case Deliberation in Health Care Organizations

Margreet Stolper, Sandra van der Dam, Guy Widdershoven and Bert Molewijk

Introduction

The management of health care institutions should not only focus on ethical questions in the primary caring process. It should also pay attention to ethical questions regarding the organization of care and regarding the position the institutions want to take within societal developments in health care. Such instruments as health ethics committees and the formulation of codes of conduct and protocols which are now well known are important instruments, yet they are not sufficient. Therefore, in the near future, I will stimulate the management of health care institutions to take ethics into account within every quality management policy. A possible way to promote this role of ethics is the organization of a structural dialogue among patients, care givers and management in order to discuss ethical questions (translated: Letter of the Minister of the Department of Public Health, Welfare and Sports (VWS)[1] to the House of Representatives of the Netherlands, 2000).

In the Netherlands, interest in clinical ethics has increased considerably in the last few years. Health care institutions are increasingly forced to account for their activities. This has led to an adaptation of institutional policies towards a stronger focus on efficiency and transparency. The development of a national certification system for health care institutions (i.e., a benchmark) leads to more competition among the health care institutions. Next to this, there is also an increased attention to enhancing the (moral) competencies of health care professionals in order to deal better with moral dilemmas. As a consequence, there is an increased demand for training and educational programmes that promote professionals' moral competencies (Verkerk et al. 2007). In 2005, a national report by the Centre of Ethics in Health Care (CEG)[2] appeared, focusing on the quality and quantity

---

1 The Department of Public Health, Welfare and Sports in the Netherlands is commonly abbreviated as VWS (*Volksgezondheid, Welzijn en Sport*).

2 Centre of Ethics and Health (*Centrum voor Ethiek en Gezondheid*). CEG was instituted in 2001 by the Minister of VWS as a cooperative of the national Health Council

of clinical ethics in health care institutions. Based on a national survey (CEG 2005), the report describes a shift in focus from big moral issues towards small everyday ethics. The report concludes that many health care professionals lack basic ethical knowledge and skills that may help them to deal with moral issues. Moreover, the report observes a lack of awareness of the fact that ethics is linked to everyday forms of care. In line with the above citation, the CEG advised the Dutch government to pay more attention to structural moral deliberation among health care professionals. The CEG also recommended an ongoing connection between moral case deliberation and institutional policy (CEG 2005). Almost at the same time, the Dutch Minister of Health Care, Welfare and Sports (VWS) placed more attention on ethics in health care in general and asked for more structural attention to moral deliberation within health care institutions (Minutes, VWS 2005). This was the beginning of an ongoing process in which many clinical ethics committees (or health ethics committees) transformed their role from that of distant expert with a focus on policy and guidelines, into the so-called 'steering group'. In general, a steering group aims to develop the moral competencies of health care professionals and to guarantee an ethics climate throughout the whole institution.

The focus on the moral competency of health care professionals fits well within the theoretical frameworks of dialogical ethics and pragmatic hermeneutics. Both frameworks emphasize that the domain of ethics and ethics expertise should not be restricted to academic ethics and ethicists in health ethics committees. Health care professionals already frequently participate in ethical deliberations and discussions since they actually have to deal with moral questions. Moral case deliberation (MCD) gives health care professionals the possibility to exchange their views and the difficulties they encounter on moral questions in order to enhance their moral competencies. Based upon the theoretical assumption that every human being possesses moral experiences and the wisdom of expertise, health care professionals who participate in MCD are regarded as moral experts. The role of the facilitator of MCD is to help professionals to make their moral knowledge explicit and to further a dialogue. It is presupposed that the facilitator has practical moral expertise themselves. Yet it is not clear what knowledge and competencies the facilitator needs to support the group process. What kind of attitude and ethics knowledge is needed? And finally, what is the role of ethics theory in MCD?

This chapter focuses on these questions by describing the practice and theory of moral case deliberation. First we give an outline of the meaning of the concept of MCD and several reasons why organizations introduce MCD. Next we give a description of the theoretical background of MCD and the way we monitor and facilitate MCD projects through research. By describing a pilot training programme in which health care professionals are trained as facilitators of MCDs,

---

and the Council of Public Health. The function of CEG is to involve society by finding and formulating answers in order to construct an effective policy in the field of medicine and biology. The aim of this task is to satisfy the statutory duty of care.

we will highlight the specific approach of the Moral Deliberation Group at Free University Medical Centre. Finally, the evaluation of this pilot will serve as a basis for discussing some main characteristics of our approach and for drawing some conclusions.

Moral Case Deliberation

What is a Moral Case Deliberation?

A moral case deliberation is an interactive session in which health care professionals systematically reflect on one of the moral question(s) that has emerged in concrete personal experience (i.e., a case). Usually it involves a heterogeneous group, such as a multidisciplinary team or a group of health care professionals from different settings with different professional backgrounds. In general, there are three levels of distinctive goals of MCDs: (1) the case level: to reflect on the case and improve the quality of care within the case, (2) the professional level: to reflect on what it means to be a good professional and to enhance the professional's moral competencies, and (3) the institutional or organizational level: reflection on policy issues and on prerequisites for improvement of the quality of care at that level.

An MCD session takes in general 60–90 minutes and is structured and facilitated by a facilitator. The facilitator structures the meeting by means of a conversation method (depending on the specific goal of the MCD). Some methods focus on the moral case itself and aim towards a well-considered decision, while other methods use the moral case to focus on the attitude of a professional in order to enhance moral competencies (Steinkamp and Gordijn 2003, 2004). The conversation methods aim to foster an open and ongoing dialogue. This implies a respectful and critical attitude of the participants in which they question each other in order to understand each others' perspectives; an attitude that is focused on an inquiry of each others' judgements and presuppositions, not on debate and rhetoric.

The expertise of the facilitator of an MCD consists of fostering an open and safe atmosphere to promote a sincere and constructive dialogue (Abma et al. 2009). The aim of the dialogue is to reflect on the professional quality of the work of the participants, the ideas behind their professional behaviour and their presuppositions about good care. The facilitator does not give advice, nor does he or she morally justify a specific decision. The facilitator acts as a Socratic guide by supporting a critical inquiry of moral convictions and moral questions. Besides using general conversation skills, the facilitator of an MCD keeps an eye on the moral dimension of the case, applies one or more conversation methods, supports the joint reasoning process, and helps the group in planning concrete actions in order to improve the quality of care.

Why Moral Case Deliberation?

Moral case deliberation can be performed on an ad hoc basis. It can also be implemented in a more structural way. In order to reach the latter goal, long-term projects between the university and the health care organizations are being set up with a duration of two to six years. These projects consist of several implementation phases in which various ethics activities (such as MCDs) are planned (see section 2, 'Facilitating Moral Case Deliberation'). The overall aim of the moral deliberation projects is to use the structural embedding of MCD as a means for other goals, such as enhancing professional quality and fostering quality of care. There are various reasons why Dutch health care organizations might embrace an MCD project. Reasons often mentioned include: to enhance professional quality (i.e., increasing the acting repertoire of the health care givers) or to improve cooperation and mutual understanding after a recent merger or reorganization. MCD can also be regarded as a structural part of an institutional educational policy with the aim of an ongoing reflection on the justification and improvement of the quality of care. Another possibility is to use MCD as part of a quality assurance policy.

Moral case deliberation differs from clinical ethics consultation (Molewijk et al. 2008b, 2008c, Ranson et al. 2006).[3] Clinical ethics consultation (CEC) is the support of a decision-making process by an ethical expert. The report of the ASBH Taskforce on the Core Competencies for Health Care Ethics Consultation stresses the procedural and expert approach of the ethics consultant in discussing 'the ethics facilitation approach'. A central goal of the ethics consultant is to answer the question, 'Who is the appropriate decision-maker?' in a morally and legally appropriate way (ASBH Task Force 1998, Aulisio et al. 2003). The ethics consultant focuses more on the answer to the question, 'What is morally right?', whereas the facilitator within the moral deliberation focuses more on the process by which the group members reach this answer on their own (Molewijk et al. 2008b).

The differences between clinical ethics consultation and moral case deliberation are not only practical, they also have a theoretical background. Whereas CEC is based upon a view of ethics as individual problem-solving, MCD focuses on moral learning through dialogue. In the next paragraph we will clarify the underlying theoretical background of MCD.

Theoretical Background of Moral Case Deliberation

The design of the MCD projects at Free University Medical Centre and the methods of MCD are inspired by a combination of pragmatic hermeneutics and dialogical ethics (Gadamer 1960, Molewijk et al. 2008a, Rudnick 2007). A fundamental

---

3   Ranson, S., Molewijk, B. and Widdershoven, G.A.M. 2006. *Deliberating on Deliberation: An Evaluation on Empirical Evaluation Studies on Ethics Consultation and Moral Deliberation.* Unpublished paper presented at the EACME conference 28–30 September 2006 in Louvain, Belgium.

claim of pragmatic hermeneutics is that ethics and morality starts with actual experience. This means that theories and concepts are subordinate: they may be useful, but ultimately they should be based upon and made applicable to concrete practices. This approach to ethics goes back to Aristotle, who claimed that moral wisdom and moral knowledge originate from reflections on and within concrete situations. Moral knowledge is dependent on experience (Widdershoven 2005, Widdershoven and Abma 2007). This means that the construction and meaning of morality is inherently contextual and temporal. The meaning of good care, for example, is not given beforehand, but arises out of a dialogue among open-minded people in practice. Knowledge from ethical theories may play a role in a dialogue but it cannot claim epistemological authority. Following this, moral case deliberation always starts with concrete personal experiences; hypothetical thought experiments or definitions of ethical concepts are not the starting point of MCD.

Monitoring and Facilitating MCD Projects through Research

All MCD projects are monitored and facilitated by means of quantitative and qualitative research methods within the framework of a responsive evaluation research design. This is an interactive process-oriented methodology, based on the same theoretical inspirations as MCD (Abma et al. 2009). This approach reframes the traditional way of evaluation (i.e., determining the effectiveness of programmes on the basis of given policy goals) into a process of interpreting the results of a programme by engaging stakeholders and their issues of concern (Abma et al. 2001, Abma 2006, Abma and Widdershoven 2006). This approach aims to enhance the mutual understanding of a situation by fostering ongoing dialogues about relevant issues among various stakeholders. The stakeholders, groups of people whose interests are at stake, participate actively in the evaluation process and they are involved in monitoring the project. They become equal partners in the evaluation process by being involved in the formulation of research questions, the selection of participants and the interpretation of findings. Through dialogue the participants share their issues and concerns, but also respond to those of others, to reach an understanding of important issues of other stakeholders (Abma et al. 2009). The underlying notion is to acknowledge the plurality of the interests, values and perspectives of all the stakeholder groups. This research design includes collecting data by both qualitative and quantitative research methods (such as semi-structured interviews, focus groups, participative observation, questionnaires).

Facilitating Moral Case Deliberation: Training for Health Care Professionals

Now that we have presented the practical and theoretical features of moral case deliberation (including the role of responsive evaluation), we will focus on the training of health care professionals as MCD facilitators, which is a part of the final implementation phase. By elaborating on the training and its evaluation, we will demonstrate the actual meaning and consequences of our approach.

Following the idea that MCD should support the existing moral expertise of practitioners, our claim is that the facilitation of MCD can and in the end should also be performed by practitioners. This, however, requires a specific training programme. How should one train health care professionals to become facilitators of MCDs? What kind of skills and ethics knowledge do they need? How should we train these skills? In order to answer these questions we will share our experiences concerning a pilot training programme for health care professionals in two psychiatric hospitals in the south of the Netherlands (Molewijk et al. 2008a).

Pilot Training Facilitating Moral Case Deliberation

A pilot training programme facilitating MCD was offered to employees in two different psychiatric hospitals (an intramural health care institution and an extramural one) in the south of the Netherlands. The training was part of a long-term project in which MCD was implemented in several phases:

1. Moral sensitization by means of various pilot activities.
2. Transmission of moral expertise and competencies to health care professionals.
3. Training health care professionals to become facilitators of MCD; and
4. Forming an organizational structure and institutional policy to embed the moral deliberation activities (Molewijk et al. 2008a).

These phases overlap with each other.

Both institutions participated in a joint training programme in which health care professionals were trained to become facilitators of MCD. This was special because normally these institutions do not often cooperate (among other things, due to competitive market mechanisms). The training was facilitated by the Moral Deliberation Group and offered three times for groups of 10 participants from various professions (nurses, psychologists, managers, etc.). In the first training programme, members of the board of directors also participated.

Organization

The training programme consisted of six meetings of four hours spread over half a year. The participants were trained in three different conversation methods. The participants prepared for every meeting by studying some basic literature about ethics or a specific topic, for example, a conversation method. Usually this consisted of one or two articles or a chapter of a book. During the meetings the participants were expected to practise their role as a facilitator of MCD. Between the meetings, participants were expected to practise these methods. The exercises were arranged by themselves in their own multidisciplinary team or in other teams. The participants were encouraged to practise in pairs. Experiences of these exercises were extensively discussed during the following meeting.

The purpose of the training was to teach the participants to act as facilitators in MCD. This means generally that the facilitators should be able to foster a sincere and constructive dialogue on a moral question. The meetings were organized around the following general aims: to learn to coach a group, to feel familiar with the conversation methods in order to foster a dialogue, to learn to distinguish moral issues from other issues (such as psychological or technical problems) by themselves and with the participants, to learn to moderate a collaborative endeavour, and finally, to learn some basic knowledge about ethical theories, concepts, arguments and reasoning. Every meeting started with an opening and some announcements followed by a collective reflection on the experiences with practising MCD. Next, the homework including the literature was discussed. Then the participants exercised with one of the conversation methods. In total, three different methods were used. One participant would act as a facilitator during 20 minutes. The other participants would act as members of the MCD. Each exercise was jointly evaluated by discussing the experiences of the facilitator trainee, the other participants, and the trainer. During the exercises every participant could ask for help or advice from the trainer; the trainer intervened when necessary by asking the facilitator for clarity or by asking the facilitator and the group, 'What are you doing and why are you doing that? What are the alternatives?'

Method of Evaluation

The training was evaluated by using the methodology of responsive evaluation. A PhD student conducted participatory observations, analysed the written meeting reports, the notes of the oral evaluation after each meeting, and the notes of the semi-structured interviews. The data were analysed by the PhD student; interpretations and conclusions were shared and checked by a senior ethicist (who also acted as the trainer in the training programme) and a senior academic in health care ethics.

Furthermore, in-depth interviews were held with each participant two months after the end of the training programme. The participants were asked about their experiences with the training programme, their opinion about the content and organization, and their expectations and experiences regarding the practical application of the training. Two years later some participants were approached again with a questionnaire containing questions about their experiences as facilitator of MCDs (success factors and failures) and the frequency of facilitating the MCD in a timeframe of a year.

Results

In general the participants were satisfied with the training. The analysis of the interviews shows that they became more sensitive to moral issues in daily practice and had an increased awareness of the variety of perspectives. At the same time the training contributed to a less ad hoc behaviour. The content of the meetings were evaluated as highly satisfactory and the practical exercises as a useful way to become more familiar with the conversation methods. However, some of the participants criticized the number of conversation methods (three) related to the number of meetings (six). Some participants also criticized the preparatory literature on the grounds that it was too academic and lacked feasibility.

The interviews clarified the reasons why some participants were not very active during and after the training. Lack of motivation was the main reason. They had not participated voluntarily, but were sent by their boss. Finally, the interviews revealed criticism regarding the composition of the group. The mix of different professionals from various levels in the organization resulted in an unequal balance of power, with the effect that some participants were afraid of negative consequences. As a result they experienced less openness and transparency, which is alarming because both are core features of MCD.

The participatory observations showed among other things that those who had little previous experience with MCD needed more time and attention to become acquainted with the conversation methods, the recognition of moral issues in general, and gaining a clear picture of MCD, and therefore were less able to focus on developing the specific role of facilitator of MCD.

One of the main results from the written questionnaire after two years was the lack of clarity among the trained facilitators about how many hours and in which team/department they were allowed to facilitate MCD. It remains necessary to practise as a facilitator of MCD, both during and after the training.

Discussion

In general, projects of clinical ethics following the approach of the Moral Deliberation Group of Free University Medical Centre are well received and successful (Molewijk et al. 2008a, 2008b, 2008c). However, with respect to the experiences of the pilot training programme, there were some critical notes concerning two main topics: (1) the attitude of a facilitator of MCD and the way knowledge and skills are trained, and (2) the pitfalls in the organization of an MCD.

The evaluation of the training showed that participants with little experience with MCD needed relatively more time and attention to have an idea of MCD, to feel familiar with the conversation methods and to learn to identify the moral issues. This comes at the expense of learning to develop their role as facilitator of MCD. In response to this criticism, we decided to formulate a pre-condition for participation in training, that every participant should have experienced an MCD at least six times. By setting this pre-condition, we can be sure that the facilitator trainee already knows what it means to participate in an MCD, and therefore can more easily focus on the specific requirements of becoming a facilitator of MCD in the training. With experience and knowledge about

MCD, participants will be able to pay more attention to the specific role of the facilitator of MCD.

Furthermore, the evaluation shows lack of motivation of some participants as a hindering factor for active participation in the training. Therefore we decided to develop a recruitment policy. This recruitment and selection procedure can also support the implementation and embedding of the training. We concluded that it should be the concern of the health care organization to develop an implementation policy, and, for instance, to create opportunities for the participants to practise their MCD facilitator's role during and after the training.

Both in interviews and in the written evaluation, some organizational elements of training were criticized, like the number of conversation methods and the preparatory literature. This shows the need for a balance between theory and practice. In response to these criticisms we adapted the training by reducing the number of conversation methods (two instead of three conversation methods) and lengthening the training with one extra meeting. Furthermore, we diminished the literature and emphasized the practical exercises in and between the meetings by using reflection reports written by the participants. This point is connected with the view on the role, knowledge and skills of the facilitator of MCD. As we mentioned earlier the main goal of MCD is to foster an open and sincere dialogue with the aim of promoting the moral competencies of health care professionals. A supporting Socratic attitude of the facilitator is more important than theoretical ethical knowledge. This does not mean that theory has no role to play. One might consider using theoretical elements in a follow-up of an MCD session or in the training programme. In line with our hermeneutic philosophy, however, theory should always be closely related to practice, and applied to practice. The appropriate place of theory (and the sort of theory) is a further question to be addressed in our MCD projects. Such questions can, we think, only be answered by doing experiments in practice.

An issue for discussion in our MCD sessions and projects is the absence of the patient. Although the patient perspective is always brought in, the patient is usually not physically present.[4] This is questionable since MCD assumes that all participants are morally equal. Some implicit and explicit considerations may justify the absence of the patient. For example, a main pillar and also a significant condition of MCD is an open atmosphere to promote a sincere and constructive dialogue. This could be compromised if the patient were present. For example, when a nurse has problems with the behaviour of a patient, they might feel barriers to speaking openly and freely about their ideas and feelings when the patient is physically part of the conversation. Furthermore, there are certain preconditions for the patient to participate in the conversation. The patient should be capable of understanding the conversation before they can

---

4   In rare MCD cases, it happens that the health care professionals only become aware of the perspective of the patient because it is an explicit step within the conversation method of an MCD.

take part in it. Especially with psychiatric patients this is not always the case. Recently several health care organizations have experimented with different forms of MCD (or clinical ethics consultation) in which the patient or a patient representative is involved (Fournier 2005, Richter 2007). At GGNet, a large institution for mental health care in the east of the Netherlands, both patients and patient representatives are currently participating in MCD sessions together with health care professionals and family representatives. Pitfalls and successes of these developments should and will be made public in order to learn from these initiatives, since a true dialogue on good care also implies a dialogue *with* patients (and not only about patients).

Conclusion

According to the approach of the Moral Deliberation Group, the main goal of moral case deliberation (MCD) is to educate health care professionals and to improve their moral competence. The focus of this approach is a joint inquiry about what is good within the context of a concrete case. This chapter has described the theoretical and practical implications of an MCD project focusing on a pilot training programme for facilitators of MCD. The findings show that the organization and embedding of an MCD project are easily underestimated. Implementing MCD is not only a matter of planning an MCD project and training health care professionals to become MCD facilitators. It is a complex and difficult process with several dimensions. To ensure the quality of the expertise of the facilitators and the MCD sessions, one needs the assistance of external experts in ethics and implementation strategies. This means a permanent supply of (extra) training and supervision for the trained facilitators of MCD, especially after the training. This is also needed in order to keep an eye on the quality of MCD. Moral case deliberation can only support and develop the moral expertise of health care professionals if it is structured by experienced facilitators, who themselves need to be properly trained.

References

Abma, T.A. 2006. The practices and politics of responsive evaluation. *American Journal of Evaluation*, 27(1), 31–43.
Abma, T.A., Greene, J., Karlsson, O., Ryan, K., Schwandt, T.S. and Widdershoven, G.A.M. 2001. Dialogue on dialogue. *Evaluation*, 7(2), 164–80.
Abma, T.A., Molewijk, B. and Widdershoven, G.A.M. 2009. Good care in ongoing dialogue: Improving the quality of care through moral deliberation and responsive evaluation. *Health Care Analysis*, 17(3), 217–35 (published online: 13 January 2009).

Abma, T.A. and Widdershoven, G.A.M. 2006. Moral deliberation in clinical psychiatric nursing practice. *Nursing Ethics*, 13(5), 1–12.

ASBH Task Force on Standards for Bioethics Consultation. 1998. *Core Competencies for Health Care Ethics Consultation: The Report of the American Society for Bioethics and Humanities*. Glenview, IL.

Aulisio, M.P., Arnold, R.M. and Youngner, S.J. (eds) 2003. *Ethics Consultation: From Theory to Practice*. Baltimore and London: The John Hopkins University Press.

CEG. 2005. Centre of Ethics and Health (*Centrum voor Ethiek en Gezondheid*). *Rapport Signalering Ethiek en Gezondheid* [*Annual Report on Ethics and Health*] *2005*. The Hague: Centre of Ethics and Health.

Gadamer, H.G. 1960. *Wahrheit und Methode* [*Truth and Method*]. Tübingen: J.C.B. Mohr.

Fournier, V. 2005. The balance between beneficence and respect for patient autonomy in clinical medical ethics in France. *Cambridge Quarterly of Health Ethics*, 14(3), 281–286.

Minutes, VWS. 2005. *Volksgezondheid, Welzijn en Sport, Agenda ethiek en gezondheid 2006* [*Department of Public Health, Welfare and Sports, Agenda on Ethics and Health*] *2006*. The Hague: Department of Health Care, Welfare and Sport of the Netherlands.

Molewijk, B., Abma, T., Stolper, M. and Widdershoven, G.A.M. 2008a. Teaching ethics in the clinic: The theory and practice of moral case deliberation. *Journal of Medical Ethics*, 34, 120–24.

Molewijk, B., Verkerk, M., Milius, H. and Widdershoven, G.A.M. 2008b. Implementing moral case deliberation in a psychiatric hospital: Process and outcome. *Medicine, Health Care and Philosophy*, 11, 43–56.

Molewijk, B., van Zadelhoff, E., Lendemeijer, B. and Widdershoven, G.A.M. 2008c. Implementing moral case deliberation in Dutch health care: Improving moral competency of professionals and the quality of care. *Bioethica Forum*, 1(1), 57–64.

Ranson, S., Molewijk, B. and Widdershoven, G.A.M. 2006. *Deliberating on Deliberation: An Evaluation on Empirical Evaluation Studies on Ethics Consultation and Moral Deliberation*. Unpublished paper presented at the EACME conference 28–30 September 2006 in Louvain, Belgium.

Richter, G. 2007. Greater patient, family and surrogate involvement in clinical ethics consultation: The model of clinical ethics liaison service as a measure for preventive ethics. *HEC Forum*, 19(4), 327–40.

Rudnick, A. 2007. Processes and pitfalls of dialogical bioethics. *Health Care Analysis*, 15, 123–35.

Steinkamp, N. and Gordijn, B. 2003. Ethical case deliberation on the ward: A comparison of four methods. *Medicine, Health Care and Philosophy*, 6(3), 235–46.

Steinkamp, N. and Gordijn, B. 2004. *Ethik in der Klinik: Ein Arbeitsbuch* [*Ethics in the Clinic: A Workbook*]. Cologne and Munich: Springer-Verlag.

Verkerk, M.A., de Bree, M.J. and Mourits, M.J.E. 2007. Reflective professionalism: Interpreting CanMEDS' 'professionalism'. *Journal of Medical Ethics*, 33, 663–6.

Walker, M.U. 1998. *Moral Understandings: A Feminist Study in Ethics*. New York and London: Routledge.

Widdershoven, G.A.M. 2005. Interpretation and dialogue in hermeneutic ethics, in *Case Analysis in Clinical Ethics*, edited by R. Ashcroft, A. Lucassen, M. Parker, M. Verkerk and G.A.M. Widdershoven. Cambridge: Cambridge University Press, 57–76.

Widdershoven, G.A.M. and Abma, T.A. 2007. Hermeneutic ethics between practice and theory, in *Principles of Health Care Ethics*, edited by R.E. Ashcroft, A. Dawson, H. Draper, and J.R. McMillan. Chichester: Wiley, 215–22.

Chapter 14
Clinical Ethics Consultation and Bedside Rationing

Daniel Strech

Introduction

Priority-setting and rationing occur at all levels in almost all health care systems around the world. Countries with very different health care systems and levels of health care spending all contend with the same problem of how to reconcile a steadily increasing demand for health care services with limited or even declining financial resources. If health care rationing is inevitable, it should be done in a fair and efficient way. Several ethical concepts have been developed which are especially demanding of transparency, explicitness and consistency of allocation decisions on the macro- and meso-level (Daniels and Sabin 2002, Emanuel 2000). While these normative requirements are largely undisputed in academic discourse, they have not yet been widely implemented in everyday health care practice. Especially at the micro-level of the health care system, that is, the clinical practice and the patient-physician relationship, little research has focused on how to manage decisions on bedside rationing (BSR) (Pearson 2000) and what role clinical ethics consultation could play during the decision-making process (Hurst et al. 2008).

To overcome this situation, first of all we need empirical information about how physicians currently deal with resource constraints at the bedside and about the practical challenges and opportunities in optimizing just processes of allocation of scarce health care resources at the hospital level. Next to empirical data about practice settings, justified conceptual frameworks are needed to provide sound guidance for the implementation of consistent and fair decision-making when it comes to BSR.

This chapter first discusses the need for transparent and ethically acceptable criteria for BSR based on the findings of a systematic review of qualitative research with physicians. The practical relevance of support in BSR through clinical ethics consultation (CEC) is then demonstrated. After referring briefly to existing ethical approaches to health care rationing, a framework, 'clinical ethics consultation and bedside rationing', which consists of five major steps, will be presented and critically discussed.

The Status Quo of Bedside Rationing

With respect to the need for empirical data, we can draw on quantitative surveys and qualitative research with physicians on health care rationing that provide important information about how financial constraints influence clinical decision-making and the doctor-patient relationship, and about the criteria that physicians use to allocate scarce resources across individual patients. Along with the complexity and variety of ethical approaches to BSR, the results of empirical interview studies on BSR are also complex and manifold. BSR can be the consequence of shortage of different kinds of resources, including diagnostic and therapeutic interventions, physician time or intensive-care beds. A variety of different study methodologies, with different cultural backgrounds and different researchers' perspectives focusing on the same ethical dilemmas, further increases the complexity. In addition, we face contradictory evidence within and between different studies.

To reduce the probability of a one-sided and potentially biased presentation of the results of qualitative and quantitative research on BSR, systematic reviews of these studies were performed (Strech et al. 2008b, Strech et al. 2009). Some results from the review of qualitative research that are relevant for the following argumentation will be presented below. References were identified by systematically screening major electronic databases, e.g., MEDLINE and EMBASE, as well as manuscript references. To be included in the final analysis, studies had to meet the following criteria:

1. Provide qualitative data through in-depth interviews, focus groups or surveys with open-ended questions.
2. Be conducted in a developed or high-income country.
3. Include practising physicians (GPs and specialists) as participants; and
4. Focus on questions of rationing or resource allocation in health care.

Ten out of 554 references (Jecker and Berg 1992, Ayres 1996, Stronks et al. 1997, Jones et al. 2004, Schultheiss 2004, Berney et al. 2005, Carlsen and Norheim 2005, Hurst et al. 2005, Prosser and Walley 2005, Reeleder et al. 2005) were finally included in the systematic review after assessment of relevance and synthesized by thematic analysis. For a more detailed description of the methodology of systematic reviews of empirical bioethics, see Strech et al. (2008c).

How Physicians Allocate Scarce Resources at the Bedside

Several social and psychological factors were identified to heavily influence BSR. In particular, they can be divided into: 1) context-related, 2) doctor-related, and 3) patient-related factors. Context-related factors include the situatedness of the doctor-patient encounter, e.g., whether it is at the 'end of the day' or 'on a Friday night'. Other context-related factors are the availability of resources, the hospital's operating budget, the influence of the pharmaceutical industry or the access to relevant information. Doctor-related factors that influence BSR contain the lack of economic competence and the implicit categorization of the patient, e.g., whether they are 'performers' or 'good' or 'bad' patients. Doctors also report that they are influenced by their personal involvement with the patient. These factors contribute to another, more general finding. Doctors perceive themselves of being incapable to maintain consistent standards of care and BSR decisions: 'I am absolutely inconsistent' is a typical statement. Moreover, the patient's individual characteristics and capabilities can strongly influence BSR. For example, a patient's ability to express his or her wishes or to exhibit a demanding behaviour might be a decisive factor in whether he or she is allocated a certain resource or not: 'Those that shout the loudest get the most'. Other influencing factors are the patient's preferences, socioeconomic status, and ability to exercise pressure.

The highly subjective nature and variability of these determinants underline the need for more explicit and consistent approaches to BSR. Such an approach, e.g., cost-conscious guidelines (Eccles and Mason 2001), should clearly define which patients should get which services under which medical conditions. Only by this means can arbitrariness, and thus harm to the patient and unjust distribution of health care resources, be avoided on the one hand and trust in the health care professionals (HCPs) and their institutions be maintained on the other (Goold 2001). Our review shows that sometimes factors such as the patient's individual ability to exercise pressure or the physician's implicit categorization of a patient currently might determine whether a patient receives an intervention or not. Although BSR will always be influenced by case-specific factors inherent in daily medical practice, which certainly constrains the application of ethical principles and rationing standards (Berney et al. 2005), this fact does not per se eliminate the need to develop explicit and consistent rationing standards or to involve ethics consultants in the decision-making process. However, our review reveals a remarkable ambivalence in physicians' attitudes towards explicit standards of care. On the one hand, several describe a need for relieving the burden of implicit BSR from physicians and consecutively call for more explicit, standardized measures of BSR. On the other hand, another set of quotations suggests physicians' inability to maintain or adapt consistent standards of care. This inability, however, apparently does not result from an inherent feature of medical practice or from irrevocable structures of our health care systems, but rather from a personal psychological motive, the desire to satisfy the patient's preferences.

How Should We Ration?

International surveys of physicians confirmed that physicians see rationing as a matter of fact that is widely prevalent in everyday medical practice (Allan and Innes 2004, Bovier et al. 2005, Hurst et al. 2006). This supports the point of view that the crucial question in the current debate is not *whether* or not physicians should ration, but *how* they can ration in a fair and efficient manner, that is, which thresholds and which processes are acceptable (Ubel 2000, Daniels and

Sabin 2002). According to the findings of the systematic review, physicians apply different *implicit* rationing strategies, such as deferral and deflection of patients, remaining silent, early discharge or delay of interventions. The fact that these measures are less transparent and not readily controllable underlines the need for the implementation of some sort of CEC that might increase transparent and consistent and thus *explicit* rationing mechanisms. Only if rationing is performed according to explicit, transparent, and general standards can it be performed in a 1) consistent, 2) medically rational and 3) ethically fair way (since it allows an equal treatment). In fact, the review reveals a further argument: 4) CEC as well as standardized measures for explicit rationing can relieve physicians from the emotional distress resulting from implicit rationing and, moreover, might put less pressure on the patient-physician relationship.

Role Conflicts and Controversial Prioritization Criteria

Our results demonstrate that BSR might lead to various role conflicts for physicians. It is by now widely acknowledged that the traditional picture of a physician as acting in an encapsulated physician-patient dyad is no longer adequate, since the physician in fact maintains multiple accountabilities (Shortell et al. 1998). There is further empirical evidence for this observation in the studies of the systematic review. BSR leads to several role conflicts and ethical tensions, e.g., the tension between professional autonomy and health authority guidelines or the tension between physicians' private (financial) interests and the patients' health interests. CEC might help to disentangle these tensions somewhat and develop strategies to disburden physicians from the emotional stress and frustration which accompanies them.

Moreover, the high variability of allocation criteria presented in this review calls into question the consistency of physicians' rationing decisions at the bedside. In contrast to the aforementioned psychological and social factors of influence, ethical criteria were rarely mentioned and their exact meaning remained unclear. In other words, BSR seems to be only poorly influenced by explicit and transparent ethical criteria (see also Hurst et al. 2005). One major approach to overcome this shortcoming could be that CEC has to break down abstract and theoretical ethical criteria and translate them into physicians' daily practice of BSR.

The following conceptual framework has to be interpreted considering these preliminary remarks. The framework describes the different aspects that CEC can add to the current situation of BSR. Nevertheless, bringing forward these requirements for a just process of BSR might be limited due to characteristics in the local practice setting and in national law. Finally, we have to acknowledge that BSR as an issue for CEC challenges the point of view that CEC should stick to conflicts which only affect a single patient and analyse conflicting values only against the background of this patient's situation. Reasons for opening up CEC to issues of BSR have been demonstrated in the previous paragraphs:

1. Improvement of transparency and consistency in rationing mechanisms.
2. Reduction of emotional distress and role conflicts of physicians.
3. Lowering pressure on the patient-physician relationship.
4. Translation of abstract ethical criteria such as justice into physicians' daily practice.

Framework

The presented findings clarify the range of problems CEC faces when it comes to counselling on BSR. The following framework attempts to refine the requirements for helpful and effective CEC on issues such as BSR. With regard to the status quo of BSR mentioned above, the framework's aims are twofold. First, the framework aims at making BSR more just and improving the quality of patient-centred care. Second, it aims to relieve the burdens of BSR on physicians.

This framework consists of five elements:

1. Awareness: improve awareness and train general concerns of justice and cost-effectiveness measures in decision-making by HCPs.
2. Clarification of success requirements: clarify the success requirements and applicability for a consistent, efficient, and fair process of BSR in the specific institutional context.
3. Critical appraisal: improve the skills of HCPs in critical appraisal and assessment of the relevance of internal and external evidence for cost-effectiveness and economic analysis.
4. Decision-making under ethical constraints: improve consistent application of external and internal CE-evidence in BSR while respecting individual variations and further ethical constraints (e.g., severity of disease, end-of-life decisions).
5. Evaluation of process: evaluate the institution-specific process of resource allocation for its applicability and appropriateness.

As Samia Hurst and Marion Danis point out, the ethical-procedural framework 'accountability for reasonableness' from Norman Daniels and James Sabin is not straightforward when applied to issues of BSR in an isolated way (Daniels and Sabin 2002, Hurst and Danis 2007). The framework from Daniels and Sabin consists of four conditions that should be fulfilled to guarantee fair processes and a reasonable rationale in rationing decisions. Those conditions are: transparency about the grounds for decisions (publicity), appeals to rationales that all can accept as relevant to meeting health needs, fairness, and procedures (such as appeals and enforcement) for revising decisions in the light of challenges to them. Together these elements assure 'accountability for reasonableness'. Hurst and Danis point out that the substantial content of a reasonable rationale is too vague for use in clinical practice. Additionally, the reasoning strategy that could be applied in this setting has not yet been specified. Criteria such as publicity might be difficult to apply when those decisions are not clearly legitimated by national law. Based on Daniels and Sabin's four conditions, Hurst and Danis argue for a model called 'rationing by clinical judgment' that requires six further specified elements:

1. Physician's reasoning based on general considerations of justice.
2. Respect for individual variations.
3. Decisions based on reciprocity.
4. Consistent application of the same process.
5. Explicit process; and
6. Iterative re-examination of the process and its application (Hurst and Danis 2007).

In contrast, the framework 'clinical ethics consultation on bedside rationing', presented here, does not focus on the perspective of the physician but on the tasks for CEC that arise in the context of dealing with scarce financial resources at the hospital level. This specific framework does explicitly reconsider elements from the two frameworks of Daniels and Sabin and Hurst and Danis but specifies them for the demand of CEC and further complements these elements by additional tasks relevant for CEC on BSR.

Awareness

One general task for CEC is to improve awareness and train general concerns of justice in decision-making by HCPs (physicians, nurses, health care management). While HCPs have become more familiar with the principle of respect for patient autonomy (informed consent) over the last two decades and also learned much about professionalism in the current era of evidence-based medicine, most of them are not aware of the various traditional theories of justice. First, in-house training organized by CEC or ethics committees could provide basic knowledge about different theories of justice (utilitarian, egalitarian, and prioritarian), about the difference between procedural and substantial criteria for justice and about more specific substantial criteria relevant for BSR, such as severity of disease and life-rescue decisions. Moreover, HCPs also have to be trained at least in basic knowledge about different approaches in economic analysis, such as cost-benefit or cost-utility analysis. As an overall aim, HCPs should understand that different theories of justice, different procedural and substantive criteria, and different approaches in economic analysis imply different normative assumptions and therefore will lead to different outcomes. Ethics consultants can communicate these issues in real cases when different and conflicting approaches for just decision-making are at stake. Furthermore, it might be up to hospitals ethics committees to organize continuing and practice-orientated training in this field. Next to this rather theoretical knowledge on moral deliberation and ethical decision-making, other elements of training in the context of BSR should improve skills in the communication of competing duties and rationing decisions to patients (Pearson 2000).

Clarification of Success Requirements

One further issue for CEC is to clarify the requirements for successful implementation of explicit measures of BSR in the specific institutional context. Here, the following questions are at stake: 'What is the institutional status quo of financial scarcity?', 'What is current practice (of implicit rationing) in the specific institutional context?', 'What are the specific clinical, judicial, economical, and ethical circumstances that need to be considered with respect to the specific institutional context?' and 'What are the attitudes and expectations of the HCPs in the specific institution?'. In order to make BSR more transparent and consistent, one important role of CEC is to assess the institutional-specific status quo related to this set of questions. Based on this specific knowledge, requirements for successful implementation of explicit BSR can be clarified.[1] As shown in the systematic review mentioned above, answers to these questions might vary considerably between different national and international hospitals and their specific practice settings. In-depth interviews with German chief and senior clinicians at primary care hospitals, secondary care hospitals (community hospitals), and tertiary care hospitals (university hospitals) revealed that different hospital-specific strategies and structures exist to contend with the demands of rationing decisions (Strech et al. 2008a). Some of these strategies result in informal arrangements, and advantages or disadvantages for certain groups of HCP. It can be important to be aware of these specific situations and to know more about the experiences, attitudes, and expectations of BSR among HCPs for the prior detection of possible barriers to just and consistent procedures of BSR.

Finally, from the judicial perspective, BSR can be illegal and HCPs might face litigation if they are motivated to be more explicit and transparent about their rationing decisions. This, for example, is what German physicians fear while being caught in the double-bind paradox of the German law wanting unlimited health care yet without unlimited spending.

Critical Appraisal of Economic Analysis

If not all medical services with net benefits can be given to every patient, from a utilitarian as well as from a prioritarian perspective, allocation decisions are better informed by referring to CE data and have to be complemented by further procedural and material ethical criteria (see the section on 'training'). Judgements about the relevance and context-specific applicability of CE data have to be made by physicians as well as by hospital managers. However, these judgements can be

---

[1] See also the chapter by László Kóvács in this volume, which argues for the consideration of the professional conditions of a hospital before implementing new elements of CEC.

supported by CEC through process skills such as facilitation, the input of ethical theories such as justice and equity, as well as ethics consultants' knowledge about the beliefs and perspectives of patients.

In the following, some major issues in the critical appraisal of economic analysis that are relevant for HCPs at the hospital level are summarized. A critical appraisal of CE data generally addresses the following key questions that build the common framework of evidence-based decision-making: 'Are the results valid?', 'What were the results?', and 'Will the results help in caring for my patients?' In the following, some issues from economic analysis relevant for HCPs will be illustrated. For a more detailed presentation of the critical appraisal of economic analysis with relevance for HCP at the hospital level, see, for instance, Drummond et al. (1997) and O'Brien et al. (1997).

When assessing data validity, one has to pose a question such as the following: 'Does the study protocol adequately reflect the clinical practice patterns and prices of health care services of my daily practice? In other terms, HCPs have to consider to what extent the observed cost data are transferable to their specific practice settings. If the study protocol does not reflect routine clinical practice or current prices of health care services, some form of adjustment might be necessary. Adjustment is achieved by various economic approaches which are used to model the primary dataset. However, whether the adjustment of CE data on the hospital level is valid and legitimate from an economical and judicial point of view has to be answered in the specific national or at least in the specific institutional context.

Another important question, for instance, is: 'What are the local opportunity costs?' By diverting resources from one intervention, what health benefits will be forgone from other interventions no longer being applied? A variety of further relevant questions and issues in the context of appraising economic analysis exists. However, as was stated above in this chapter, CE data can inform the decision but cannot make a choice.

Decision-making and Ethical Constraints

With regard to medical decision-making under conditions of scarce resources, the principal aim of CEC should be to improve consistent and fair consideration of CE data while respecting individual variations by acknowledging further ethical constraints (e.g., the severity of disease, end-of-life decisions). In doing so, other ethical aspects of BSR, such as role conflicts and moral conflicts of HCPs, are expected to decrease because the decision-making process is determined by prior attention of justice and because relevant reasons (such as ethical constraints) are considered systematically. However, even with adequate and reasonable ethical consultation, BSR performed by HCPs will never be a pleasurable task. The principal dilemma of BSR is that, on the one hand, there may be tension between respect for individual variation and general considerations of justice and the demand for consistency in medical decision-making. On the other hand, the underdetermination of CE evidence for specific cases and the further ethical constraints involved in BSR require flexibility in rationing decisions.

According to the framework 'accountability for reasonableness' from Daniels and Sabin, the necessity of flexibility and thus the fact of variations in prioritization and rationing decisions call for criteria that lead to a fair process of decision-making. The four conditions of fair process have been accepted as necessary for rationing decisions at the macro- and meso-level of health care from various scholars in the field of health care ethics. However, while seen as necessary, these four conditions have at the same time often been judged as insufficient because they lack more substantial criteria that specify the relevance condition. The international debate on just rationing decisions has highlighted the following substantial criteria that might serve as ethical constraints when interpreting and balancing CE evidence in specific cases: end-of-life decisions, severity of disease, medical need, lack of alternative treatment options, degree of evidence, and normal opportunity range. CEC should improve the attention of HCPs to these criteria rather than criteria such as age, compliance or role in society, which have been criticized from an ethical point of view (Hurst et al. 2005).

In another scenario, cost-conscious guidelines might be helpful to support decision-making such as BSR. Cost-conscious guidelines are based on the best available CE evidence (Eccles and Mason 2001) and would allow an explicit and more systematic balancing of different allocation criteria. Instead of referring to external and internal CE evidence and their intuitive clinical judgement, physicians can draw on evidence-based guidance to make allocation decisions at the bedside. In this case, CEC becomes important if the specific situation of the patient requires deviation from the recommended course of action. By referring to the substantive criteria mentioned above, CEC can enhance the ability of HCPs to elaborate clearly the underlying reasons for deviating from cost-conscious guidelines.

Evaluation of Process

Even if necessary and helpful, the involvement of CEC in BSR remains a major challenge. In the international sphere of CEC there are only minor experiences with this kind of consultation. No reports on experiences with the recommendations given in this chapter exist. Therefore, to monitor the institution-specific processes of BSR for its applicability and appropriateness is an essential requirement of CEC. Providers of CEC should document the process and underlying reasons for decision-making in specific situations of BSR. This can serve as a basis for review and critique later on. In accordance with the publicity condition of a fair process of rationing, the decisions and underlying reasons should also be publicly available in some form and thus accessible to critique by those affected. In reality, however, institutional transparency about rationing decisions strongly depends on the judicial context. As mentioned above, in some countries, HCPs find themselves confronted with a legal paradox that does not legitimate rationing decisions made by HCPs at the micro-level but at the same time does not explicitly ration health care by any other means.

Conclusion

HCPs increasingly contend with the necessity of cost-containment that sometimes also results in health care rationing. This chapter has presented various reasons for opening up CEC to those rationing issues, namely: improvement of transparency and consistency in rationing mechanisms, reduction of emotional distress and role conflicts for HCPs, decrease of conflicts that might occur in the patient-physician relationship, and translation of abstract ethical criteria such as justice into the daily practice of HCPs. However, opening up the practice field of CEC to counselling in rationing decisions also indicates that ethics consultants need to expand their knowledge of economics. Furthermore, the involvement of clinical ethics consultants in rationing decisions at the hospital level can conflict with national law. It is up to politics and law to solve these kinds of paradox in the first instance. This framework provides guidance for CEC in situations of BSR. Whether CEC can apply certain elements of this framework to guide decision-making even in situations where national law contradicts this kind of decision is a matter for discussion.

References

Allan, G.M. and Innes, G.D. 2004. Do family physicians know the costs of medical care? Survey in British Columbia. *Canadian Family Physician*, 50, 263–70.

Ayres, P.J. 1996. Rationing health care: Views from general practice. *Social Science & Medicine*, 42(7), 1021–5.

Berney, L., Kelly, M., Doyal, L., Feder, G., Griffiths, C. and Jones, I.R. 2005. Ethical principles and the rationing of health care: A qualitative study in general practice. *British Journal of General Practice*, 55(517), 620–25.

Bovier, P.A., Martin, D.P. and Perneger, T.V. 2005. Cost-consciousness among Swiss doctors: A cross-sectional survey. *BMC Health Services Research*, 5, 72.

Carlsen, B. and Norheim, O.F. 2005. Saying no is no easy matter: A qualitative study of competing concerns in rationing decisions in general practice. *BMC Health Services Research*, 5, 70.

Daniels, N. and Sabin, J.E. 2002. *Setting Limits Fairly*. Oxford: Oxford University Press.

Drummond, M.F., Richardson, W.S., O'Brien, B.J., Levine, M. and Heyland, D. 1997. Users' guides to the medical literature. XIII. How to use an article on economic analysis of clinical practice. A. Are the results of the study valid? Evidence-Based Medicine Working Group. *Journal of the American Medical Association*, 277(19), 1552–7.

Eccles, M. and Mason, J. 2001. How to develop cost-conscious guidelines. *Health Technology Assessment*, 5(16), 1–69.

Emanuel, E.J. 2000. Justice and managed care: Four principles for the just allocation of health care resources. *Hastings Center Report*, 30(3), 8–16.
Goold, S. 2001. Trust and the ethics of health care institutions. *Hastings Center Report*, 31(6), 26–33.
Hurst, S.A. and Danis, M. 2007. A framework for rationing by clinical judgment. *Kennedy Institute of Ethics Journal*, 17(3), 247–66.
Hurst, S.A., Hull, S.C., DuVal, G. and Danis, M. 2005. Physicians' responses to resource constraints. *Archives of Internal Medicine*, 165(6), 639–44.
Hurst, S.A., Reiter-Theil, S., Slowther, A.M., Pegoraro, R., Forde, R. and Danis, M. 2008. Should ethics consultants help clinicians face scarcity in their practice? *Journal of Medical Ethics*, 34(4), 241–6.
Hurst, S.A., Slowther, A.M., Forde, R., Pegoraro, R., Reiter-Theil, S., Perrier, A., Garrett-Mayer, E. and Danis, M. 2006. Prevalence and determinants of physician bedside rationing: Data from Europe. *Journal of General Internal Medicine*, 21(11), 1138–43.
Jecker, N.S. and Berg, A.O. 1992. Allocating medical resources in rural America: Alternative perceptions of justice. *Social Science & Medicine*, 34(5), 467–74.
Jones, I.R., Berney, L., Kelly, M., Doyal, L., Griffiths, C., Feder, G., Hillier, S., Rowlands, G. and Curtis, S. 2004. Is patient involvement possible when decisions involve scarce resources? A qualitative study of decision-making in primary care. *Social Science & Medicine*, 59(1), 93–102.
O'Brien, B.J., Heyland, D., Richardson, W.S., Levine, M. and Drummond, M.F. 1997. Users' guides to the medical literature. XIII. How to use an article on economic analysis of clinical practice. B. What are the results and will they help me in caring for my patients? *Journal of the American Medical Association*, 277(22), 1802–6.
Pearson, S.D. 2000. Caring and cost: The challenge for physician advocacy. *Annals of Internal Medicine*, 133(2), 148–53.
Prosser, H. and Walley, T. 2005. A qualitative study of GPs' and PCO stakeholders' views on the importance and influence of cost on prescribing. *Social Science & Medicine*, 60(6), 1335–46.
Reeleder, D., Martin, D.K., Keresztes, C. and Singer, P.A. 2005. What do hospital decision-makers in Ontario, Canada, have to say about the fairness of priority setting in their institutions? *BMC Health Services Research*, 5(1), 8.
Schultheiss, C. 2004. Im Räderwerk impliziter Rationierung: Auswirkungen der Kostendämpfung im deutschen Gesundheitswesen. Teil II: Methoden der Rationierung [Caught in implicit rationing: Consequences of cost-containment in the German healthcare system, original in German]. *Psychoneuro*, 30, 568–74.
Shortell, S.M., Waters, T.M., Clarke, K.W. and Budetti, P.P. 1998. Physicians as double agents: Maintaining trust in an era of multiple accountabilities. *Journal of the American Medical Association*, 280(12), 1102–8.
Strech, D., Börchers, K., Freyer, F., Neumann, A., Wasem, J. and Marckmann, G. 2008a. Ärztliches Handeln bei Mittelknappheit: Ergebnisse einer qualitativen

Interviewstudie [Clinical decision-making in the face of financial scarcity: Findings of in-depth interviews, original in German]. *Ethik in der Medizin*, 20(2), 94–109.

Strech, D., Synofzik, M. and Marckmann, G. 2008b. How physicians allocate scarce resources at the bedside: A systematic review of qualitative studies. *Journal of Medicine and Philosophy*, 33, 80–99.

Strech, D., Synofzik, M. and Marckmann, G. 2008c. Systematic reviews of empirical bioethics: Conceptual challenges and practical recommendations. *Journal of Medical Ethics*, 34, 472–7.

Strech, D., Persad, G., Marckmann, G. and Danis, M. 2009. Are physicians willing to ration health care? Conflicting findings in a systematic review of survey research. *Health Policy*, 90, 113–24.

Stronks, K., Strijbis, A.M., Wendte, J.F. and Gunning-Schepers, L.J. 1997. Who should decide? Qualitative analysis of panel data from public, patients, healthcare professionals, and insurers on priorities in health care. *British Medical Journal*, 315(7100), 92–6.

Ubel, P.A. 2000. *Pricing Life: Why it's Time for Health Care Rationing*. Cambridge, MA: The MIT Press.

PART III
Evaluation of Clinical Ethics Consultation

There is an increasing call for evaluation of CEC services. Evaluation not only provides an opportunity to demonstrate responsible use of the resources which currently are invested into CEC structures in many countries but also to critically reflect structure, aims and the methods used for CEC. In comparison with other aspects of the field there is little conceptual and empirical work on CEC. At the same time the existing body of literature indicated not only that there are many but also quite heterogeneous methods and criteria which may be used to evaluate CEC services. By means of case studies as well as systematic literature review the following three chapters shall provide an overview about current approaches to evaluation of CEC and the conceptual as well as methodological challenges associated with this enterprise.

Chapter 15

Experience in Ethical Decision-making and Attitudes Towards Ethics Consultation of Regional Hospital Physicians in Bulgaria

Silviya Aleksandrova

Background

Bulgaria, as a country in transition and already a member of the European Union, is currently subject to profound political and social reforms. Meeting new standards of care as well as addressing new problems posed by developments in medicine presents a serious challenge to health professionals. More and more ethical decisions are required in everyday clinical practice.

The goal of ethics consultation is to improve the quality of patient care by identifying, analysing, and attempting to resolve the ethical problems that arise in the practice of clinical medicine (Yen and Schneiderman 1999). Ethics consultation emerged in North America in the 1970s but more formal consultative services were introduced in the early 1980s (Spike and Greenlaw 2000, Yen and Schneiderman 1999). The modern role of the ethics consultant varies; they are either the primary decision-maker, or they facilitate the interaction between parties (Aulisio et al. 2000, Hoffman et al. 2000, Reiter-Theil 2000, 2003, Steinkamp and Gordijn 2001). Some authors believe that physicians in general should not offer ethics consultations, and others believe that only philosophers should. However, Bernstein and Bowman (2003) argue that a physician who is a specialist in the problem of the patient and who is additionally trained in ethics may be well positioned to help the patient and the health care team. He or she would have intimate knowledge of the risks and benefits of treatment and the relative value added of specific treatment alternatives. From the family's perspective, a specialist could add a level of credibility and authoritativeness of information in a bioethics consultation. Formal training in ethics, on the other hand, would enhance a physician's ability to explore many of the more nuanced ethical questions. Ethics consultation can also be provided by an ethics committee (Forde et al. 2008, Hurst et al. 2007) as an expert model, representative model or process model.

Ethics consultation does not exist in Bulgaria and neither is there a long tradition of ethics education. Until 1991, there was not a separate ethics course in the medical curriculum. In comparison, Hurst et al. (2007) conducted a survey in four European countries in which half of the respondents reported some form of training in ethics. Moreover, physicians with greater confidence in their knowledge of ethics were more likely to have used such services when available. Considering the experience of other countries in ethics consultation, we were interested in studying ethical decision-making in everyday practice in Bulgaria. To this end, in 2004 we conducted a cross-sectional survey among 126 physicians working in Pleven University hospital. The issues under study were: occurrence, nature of and strategies used to address ethical dilemmas in clinical practice; physicians' attitudes towards ethics consultation; and physicians' opinions on the personal characteristics and skills of an ethics consultant. The study revealed that almost all of the responding physicians encountered ethical dilemmas and their main source of advice was a colleague involved in the case and the head of the department. The most common ethical problems were relationships with patients and relatives and teamwork. About 90 per cent of the physicians expressed a positive attitude to ethics consultation although they had no experience with it. They would request ethics consultation mainly for help in resolving conflicts and out of concern for the rightness of a decision or practice. The most important quality of the ethics consultant, according to the respondents, was clinical competence. A special qualification in ethics was put in just fifth place (Aleksandrova 2008).

Objective

The aims of this study were to investigate regional hospital physicians' experience in ethical decision-making and their attitudes towards ethics consultation. It is one step towards fulfilling the need for further research and development of ethics consultation services, as identified in the 2004 survey.

Methods

The cross-sectional study included four regional general hospitals for acute illnesses situated in the central northern part of Bulgaria: Gabrovo, Lovech, Ruse and Veliko Tarnovo. Each hospital served on average a population of about 250,000 and had approximately 100–150 physicians. Physicians working in diagnostic and laboratory facilities with limited personal contact with patients were excluded from the study.

Data collection was performed using the method of self-administered questionnaire. The survey instrument was drafted based on a review of the ethics consultation literature and developed to be relevant to the context of the medical practice situation in Bulgaria. The questionnaires were distributed and collected by the head nurses of the clinical departments. Each questionnaire was supplied with a special envelope to be sealed after completion to ensure confidentiality.

As there was no direct contact with the principal investigator, the questionnaire contained a detailed introductory section explaining the concept of ethics consultation to the respondents, the aim of the survey, and instructions on how to fill in the questionnaire.

The questionnaire consisted of 14 multiple-choice questions including also a category 'other' for expressing a different opinion. Eleven of the questions were essential and three considered identification variables. All of the variables except 'Years of professional experience' were qualitative: six of them were of binominal type and seven were nominal variables with the possibility of more than one preferred answer. The essential questions were designed to provide information about: (1) the occurrence and nature of ethical dilemmas and strategies to address them in clinical practice; (2) physicians' attitudes towards ethics consultation; and (3) physicians' opinions on the personal characteristics and skills of an ethics consultant. The identification variables included gender, years of professional experience and the clinical specialty of physicians participating in the survey.

Statistical analysis was performed using Microsoft Office Excel software using descriptive statistics to summarize response frequencies. To compare differences between groups, Chi-square (χ^2) test and Student's unpaired t-test were used. The differences were significant at the level $P < 0.05$.

Results

Respondent Characteristics

In total 420 questionnaires were distributed, of which 293 were returned, giving a response rate of 69.8 per cent. It is worth mentioning that for some identification variables there was less compliance. For example, three persons did not mark their gender; nine persons did not record their years of professional experience and 33 subjects did not mention their clinical specialty. These participants may not have felt confident about the anonymity of the study.

General and socio-demographic data are presented in Table 15.1. Gender distribution favoured females slightly at 56.5 per cent (a result in accordance with the feminization of the profession). There was no significant difference between the four hospitals ($\chi^2 = 4.05$, df = 3, P > 0.1) so data on gender has been considered collectively in the below discussion. Considering length of service, respondents with 21–30 years of experience represented 44 per cent, followed by those with 11–20 years (34.2 per cent). Physicians with fewer than 10 years and more than 30 years of service were equally represented (10.9 per cent). There was no significant difference in the length of service for the separate hospitals ($\chi^2 = 10.54$, df = 9, P > 0.1). As for the specialty of the respondents, 33 physicians did not identify their specialty and 11 others did not have a specific specialty. The rest (249 physicians) were allocated into four groups for the purpose of further analysis:

Table 15.1 General and Socio-demographic Data of the Responding Physicians

Gender	Gabrovo n	Gabrovo %	Lovech n	Lovech %	Ruse n	Ruse %	Veliko Tarnovo n	Veliko Tarnovo %	Total n	Total %
Males	23	34.8	30	48.4	36	49.3	37	41.6	126	43.5
Females	43	61.2	32	51.6	37	50.7	52	58.4	164	56.5
Total	66	100	62	100	73	100	89	100	290	100
Not specified	1	-	-	-	2	-	-	-	3	
Length of service										
Fewer than 10 years	10		6		9		6		31	10.9
11–20 years	24		20		30		23		97	34.2
21–30 years	22		32		27		44		125	44.0
More than 30 years	8		4		4		15		31	10.9
Total	64		62		70		88		284	100
Not specified	3		-		5		1		9	
Specialty										
Obstetrics, gynaecology and paediatrics	9		16		8		15		48	19.3
Internal medicine, neurology and general medicine	36		13		25		32		106	42.6
Surgical specialties	10		15		20		27		72	28.9
Others	5		10		5		3		23	9.2
Total	60		54		58		77		249	100

- internal medicine, neurology and general medicine (106 physicians, 42.6 per cent)
- surgical specialties: surgery, orthopedics, urology, anaesthesiology, ophthalmology, otorhinolaryngology (72 physicians, 28.9 per cent)
- obstetrics, gynaecology and paediatrics (48 physicians, 19.3 per cent)
- others (23 physicians, 9.2 per cent).

Physicians' Views on the Occurrence and Nature of Ethical Problems Encountered

A high percentage (86.3 per cent) of respondents indicated that ethical problems have been discussed in their specialty. Only 40 physicians (13.7 per cent) answered 'no' to this question. There was no significant difference between gender or between physicians with fewer than 20 years and more than 20 years of service (P > 0.1). As for discussion of ethical problems by specialty, positive responses were slightly higher in paediatricians and gynaecologists (91.7 per cent) as compared with internal medicine specialists (86.8 per cent) and surgeons (86.1 per cent). However, the difference was statistically insignificant (P > 0.05).

Table 15.2 Discussion of Ethical Problems in Physicians' Practice

Responses	n	%
No	40	13.7
Yes	253	86.3
If yes, on what occasion?		
In scientific publications	20	7.9
At scientific conferences and other forums	81	32.0
In personal communication with colleagues	240	94.9
Other occasions	14	5.5
Total	253	*

Note: Results add up to more than 100 per cent because multiple responses were possible.

Furthermore, the participants were asked on what occasions they had discussed ethical problems. As is shown in Table 15.2, almost all respondents indicated that they had discussed ethical problems in personal communication with their colleagues (94.9 per cent). About one-third (32.0 per cent) indicated that such issues had been considered at conferences and other scientific forums, and only 7.9 per cent of participants responded they had done so in scientific publications.

Personal experience with ethical dilemmas was studied next. Table 15.3 shows that an impressive proportion of the responding physicians (94.5 per cent) have encountered ethical problems in their practice. Only 16 physicians gave negative responses. The most frequent ethical dilemmas were 'relationships with patients and relatives' (76.2 per cent) and 'teamwork' (64.3 per cent).

Table 15.3 Occurrence and Types of Ethical Dilemmas Encountered in Physicians' Practice

Responses	n	%
No	16	5.5
Yes	277	94.5
If yes, what type of dilemmas?		
Relationships with patients and relatives	211	76.2
Teamwork	178	64.3
End-of-life issues	99	35.7
Informed consent	76	27.4
Resource allocation	73	26.4
Confidentiality	51	18.4
Organ donation and transplantation	22	7.9
Violation/protection of patients' rights	19	6.9
Biomedical research	17	6.1
Problems of reproduction	9	2.5
Total	277	*

Note: Results add up to more than 100 per cent because multiple responses were possible.

Table 15.4 Occurrence and Types of Ethical Dilemmas Encountered in Physicians' Practice by Specialty

Ethical dilemmas	Obstetrics, gynaecology and paediatrics n	%	Internal medicine n	%	Surgical specialties n	%
Relationship with patients and relatives	38	80.8	80	80.0	50	72.5
Teamwork	37	78.7	69	69.0	42	60.9
End-of-life issues	17	36.2	37	37.0	28	40.6
Informed consent	14	29.8	19	19.0	27	39.1
Resource allocation	13	13.6	32	32.0	16	23.2
Confidentiality	12	25.5	17	17.0	13	18.8
Violation/protection of patients' rights	4	8.5	9	9.0	3	4.3
Problems of reproduction	6	12.8	1	1.0	1	1.4
Biomedical research	1	2.1	10	10.0	3	4.3
Organ donation and transplantation	3	6.4	3	3.0	14	20.3
Total	47	*	100	*	69	*

Note: Results add up to more than 100 per cent because multiple responses were possible.

The first was more frequent among women than among men (80.5 per cent to 71.7 per cent, t = 1.46, df = ∞, P > 0.1). The other types of ethical dilemmas were ranked as follows: 'problems at the end-of-life' (35.7 per cent), 'obtaining informed consent' (27.4 per cent), 'rationing of scarce resources' (26.4 per cent), 'confidentiality' (18.4 per cent), 'organ donation and transplantation' (7.9 per cent), 'violation/protection of patient rights' (6.9 per cent), 'experiments on human beings' (6.1 per cent), and 'problems related to reproduction' (2.5 per cent).

Interesting differences in the types of ethical dilemmas encountered emerged between specialties (Table 15.4). The first five groups of ethical problems were ranged similarly in the specialties. Rationing of scarce resources was mentioned more often as a problem in internal medicine (32.0 per cent to 13.6 per cent and 23.2 per cent respectively for gynaecology and surgery). Conduct of experiments with human beings was also a problem encountered more frequently in internal medicine (10.0 per cent to 2.1 per cent and 4.3 per cent respectively for gynaecology and surgery). Keeping confidentiality, on the other hand, was more problematic in gynaecology and paediatrics (25.5 per cent to 17.0 per cent and 18.8 per cent respectively for internal medicine and surgery). Problems with obtaining informed consent and organ donation and transplantation were more frequent in surgical specialties due to the nature of those specialties.

Table 15.5 Perceived Need and Main Sources of Advice/Help in Solving Ethical Problems

Responses	n	%
No	64	21.8
Yes	229	78.2
If yes, what are the main sources of advice/help?		
Colleague involved in the case	140	60.9
Head of the department	139	60.4
Colleague not involved in the case	29	12.6
Third party (friend, relative)	29	12.6
Others	11	4.8
Total answers 'Yes'	230	*

Note: Results add up to more than 100 per cent because multiple responses were possible.

Physicians' Perceptions about the Need for and Sources of Advice in Resolving Ethical Problems

Table 15.5 reflects the answers to the fundamental question: Have you needed advice/help in solving ethical dilemmas? And, if yes, what was the main source of advice? The majority (78.2 per cent) of the respondents pointed out that they needed some advice or help in solving ethical problems; for women this proportion was 81.7 per cent, higher than for men (73.8 per cent) ($\chi^2 = 2.87$, df = 1, P > 0.05). Gynaecologists and paediatricians needed advice/help more often than internal medicine specialists and surgeons (91.7 per cent to 76.4 per cent and 77.8 per cent respectively). However, the difference was insignificant ($\chi^2 = 5.07$, df = 2, P > 0.05). Physicians with fewer than 20 years of service reported greater need for advice/help than their more experienced colleagues (75.0 per cent, $\chi^2 = 2.54$, df = 1, P > 0.05).

As far as the main source of advice is concerned, almost equally trusted were the 'colleague involved in the case' (60.9 per cent) and the 'head of the department' (60.4 per cent). The other categories (colleague not involved in the case, third party, others) were less relevant.

Physicians' Attitudes towards Ethics Consultation

In accordance with the recognized need for advice/help in ethical decision-making, 88.2 per cent of respondents considered ethics consultation to be beneficial. Women were more convinced of the benefits of the ethics consultation than men (92.1 per cent for women and 86.5 per cent for men). The difference was statistically insignificant ($\chi^2 = 2.38$, k = 1, P < 0.1). As for opinions within different specialties, 95.8 per cent of gynaecologists regarded ethics consultation as potentially beneficial compared with 87.7 per cent of internal medicine specialists and 90.3 per cent surgeons (P > 0.05). Similarly, 93.8 per cent of gynaecologists and paediatricians would seek an ethics consultation compared with 79.2 per cent of internal medicine specialists and 86.1 per cent of surgeons. No relation with the years of service was found. Female physicians would choose to seek an ethics consultation more often than their male counterparts (87.8 per cent to 76.2 per cent respectively) and this difference is statistically significant ($\chi^2 = 6.74$, k = 1, P < 0.01).

The predominant dilemmas that might lead to requests for ethics consultation were ranked as follows (see Table 15.6): 'looking for help in resolving conflicts' (72.3 per cent), 'concern for the rightness of a decision or practice' (70.2 per cent), 'looking for help in interacting with patients and relatives' (39.3 per cent), 'anticipation of a bad situation' (34.7 per cent), 'uncertainty in a particular situation' (26.7 per cent), and 'desire to consider ethical aspects of a situation' (21.1 per cent). Triggers of requests for ethics consultation were similar in men and women. The only reason more common for women was 'looking for help in resolving conflicts' (78.1 per cent to 69.9 per cent) but the difference was insignificant (t = 1.44, df = ∞, P > 0.1). Physicians with more than 20 years of service chose 'looking for help in interacting with patients and relatives' more often than their colleagues with fewer than 20 years of experience (56.2 per cent to 43.1 per cent, t = 1.28, df = 92, P > 0.1).

Fifty-one physicians indicated that they would not request an ethics consultation. Of this group, 55 per cent responded that they mainly preferred to rely on their own

Table 15.6   Attitudes of Responding Physicians Towards Ethics Consultation

Questions and responses	n	%
Would ethics consultation be beneficial?		
No	31	11.8
Yes	262	88.2
Would you personally request ethics consultation?		
No	51	17.4
Yes	242	82.6
If yes, on what occasion?		
1. Looking for help in resolving conflicts	175	72.3
2. Concern for the rightness of a decision or practice	107	70.2
3. Looking for help in interacting with patients and relatives	95	39.3
4. Anticipation of a bad situation	84	34.7
5. Uncertainty in a particular situation	65	26.7
6. Desire to consider ethical aspects of a particular situation	51	21.1
Total answered 'yes'	242	*
If no, for what reasons?		
1. Preference to rely on own decision	43	55.1
2. Lack of conviction in the worth of ethics consultation	24	30.8
3. Therapeutic process would be delayed	23	29.5
4. Lack of trust in the qualification of the ethics consultant	13	16.7
5. I don't know to whom to refer	9	11.5
6. My clinical autonomy would be restricted	6	7.7
Total answered 'no'	78	*

Note: Results add up to more than 100 per cent because multiple responses were possible.

decision, 30.8 per cent did not believe in the usefulness of ethics consultation, 29.5 per cent thought that ethics consultation would just take time and would delay the therapeutic process, and 16.7 per cent didn't trust the qualifications of the ethics consultant. The percentages add up to more than 100 per cent as the respondents could choose more than one option.

Physicians' Views about the Personal Characteristics of an Ethics Consultant

Physicians' perceptions about the personal and professional characteristics of an ethics consultant are presented in Table 15.7. Only nine out of 293 physicians did not express their opinion on this question. The majority of the answers included more than three qualities of the consultant. The most valued were 'clinical competence' (60.9 per cent), 'ability to deal with conflicts' (60.2 per cent), 'communication skills' (55.3 per cent), 'tolerance of different views' (49.3 per cent), 'special qualification in ethics' (45.1 per cent) and 'competence in psychology' (38.4 per cent). Ranking of the qualities was the same for men and women, but women placed more weight on the first three qualities. The difference is insignificant ($P > 0.05$).

Clinical competence was ranked first by physicians from all specialties. Internal medicine specialists ranked communication skills second and special qualifications in ethics third. Gynaecologists and paediatricians gave equal weight to the ability to deal with conflicts and communication skills. Surgeons placed the status of a trusted senior colleague (termed 'professorship' for short in our study) immediately after communication skills and even higher than tolerance of different views. As for the influence of the length of service on physicians' opinions, those with fewer than 20 years of experience gave priority to communication skills (62.1 per cent), followed by ability to deal with conflicts (59.7 per cent) and clinical competence (56.5 per cent). Physicians with more than 20 years of service valued clinical competence most (66.7 per cent), followed by the ability to deal with conflicts (56.9 per cent) and special qualification in ethics (50.3 per cent).

Table 15.7 **What Qualities and Skills Should an Ethics Consultant Possess?**

Responses	**n**	**%**
Clinical competence	173	60.9
Ability to deal with conflicts	171	60.2
Communication skills	157	55.3
Tolerance of different views	140	49.3
Special qualification in ethics	128	45.1
Competence in psychology	109	38.4
Respected colleague (professorship)	108	38.0
Empathy	47	16.5
Total number of responders	284	*

Note: Results add up to more than 100 per cent because multiple responses were possible.

Discussion

This study is a continuation of the study conducted in 2004 of physicians practising at Pleven University hospital (Aleksandrova 2008). The first survey had a response rate of 88.9 per cent, which was attributed to the personal contact between the investigator and each of the participants. This time personal contact was not possible due to the inclusion of four regional hospitals located at some distance from one another. The achieved response rate of 69.8 per cent is still high compared with similar surveys (DuVal et al. 2001, 2004, Yen and Schneiderman 1999).

The coverage of more physicians than in the first survey allowed exploration of associations between identification variables and the issues under study. Most of the associations were not statistically significant, but the consistency of the results indicates the validity of the received information. Women, for example, reported a higher need for help in solving ethical dilemmas. They were also more convinced of the benefits of the ethics consultation and consequently they would personally look for such support more often. Gynaecologists and paediatricians reported discussion of ethical problems in their specialty at a higher percentage than the other specialties. They also reported a greater need for advice in solving ethical dilemmas and a higher appreciation of the potential benefits of ethics consultation. Physicians with more than 20 years of service were more conservative, suggesting they still follow a more traditional understanding of ethics as dealing with norms and rules of behaviour. They would request ethics consultation mainly for help in interacting with patients and relatives, and the clinical competence of the ethics consultant is of the utmost importance for them.

Considering the situations in which ethical problems are discussed, the low percentage of respondents seeking access to ethics publications deserves attention. Partially this can be explained by a lack of publications on ethical problems as a whole in the national medical literature. However, another explanation could be the lack of access to such literature in regional hospitals as well as lower interest in scientific work in non-university hospitals.

At the same time, regional physicians recognized encounters with ethical problems in a higher percentage than the university hospital physicians from the 2004 study (94.5 per cent to 84.8 per cent). The main ethical problems were distributed similarly in both studies. In the regional hospitals, we found a big difference between the first two dilemmas (relationship with patients and relatives, at 76.2 per cent, and teamwork, at 64.3 per cent) and the other options in the questionnaire (biomedical research, reproductive problems, transplantation issues). This result can be explained by the fact that biomedical research is usually undertaken in university hospitals. As for the patients in need of transplantation, they are referred to larger hospitals. The lower percentage of reported problems in reproductive medicine could be attributed to the fact that patients with severe reproductive problems are treated in larger hospitals so that in regional hospitals the main reproductive issue is that of abortion. According to the liberal abortion law adopted in Bulgaria in 1990, every pregnant woman can request an abortion until the twelfth week of gestation regardless of the reason for this request. Therefore Bulgarian physicians, who potentially lack the relevant philosophical background and who are used to a secular way of thinking, simply do not perceive abortion as a problem posing ethical dilemmas.

The higher percentage of problems related to confidentiality in gynaecology and paediatrics was an expected result. In obstetrics and gynaecology, the character of the work itself is delicate, related to intimate parts of human life and such issues, if they become known to third parties, can bring harm to the patients and their families. In paediatrics the work with infant patients can challenge the obligation to maintain confidentiality, given the necessity to seek proxy decision-making from parents or guardians. As for the higher percentage of problems related to reproduction in gynaecology, problems of biomedical research in internal medicine, and transplantation problems in surgery, they are typical for these specialties.

We also observed that regional physicians needed help in solving ethical dilemmas as much as university hospital physicians but that they relied more on their own resources (colleague involved in the case and the head of the department) for ethical decision-making. This is due to the autonomy of the work of regional hospitals and difficulties in consulting with other institutions. The greater need for advice reported by younger colleagues is another expected result insofar as they are still not confident in their practice.

Considering the reasons for not requesting an ethics consultation, the most common reason was the preference to rely on one's own decision. Similar findings have been reported by other authors, who attributed this to the medical culture of conflict aversion and anxiety of being judged by outsiders (Forde et al. 2008). Although not in the leading position among reasons, the answer 'I don't know whom to refer to' should be thoroughly considered. In the case of provision of ethics consultation by ethics committees, referral procedures should be familiar to clinicians in advance to ensure that they know what to expect and how to seek help (Forde et al. 2008). An interesting result was the perceived need for help when analysed by specialty. Gynaecologists and paediatricians appear to need more help than surgical specialties. There was no significant difference by specialty in the reasons to not seek ethics consultation. Some authors have found that surgeons in particular perceive that ethics consultation is unable to grasp the full picture from an external position (Orlowski et al. 2006).

Last but not least, according to the respondents the ethics consultant should be clinically competent, able to deal with conflicts and have good communication skills. The stress on clinical competence, however, was not as high as that observed in the 2004 survey of the university hospital. On the other hand, 'professorship' was more valued in comparison with the first survey (38.0 per cent to 19.1 per cent). A special qualification in ethics was not regarded of the highest importance in either of the surveys. In that respect, some authors support the view that, in connection with moral questions, no formal training can confer the expertise needed (Varelius 2008). This might have been the understanding of the respondents in this survey as well.

Conclusion

Ethical dilemmas are inseparable from everyday medical practice. There are some differences between the university hospital and regional hospitals with regard to different ethical problems, ways of solving them and opinions on the qualities of the ethics consultant, but as a whole the results of this study confirm the results from the study conducted in 2004.

Considering the expressed need for advice on the one hand and the regional hospitals' autonomy and reliance on one's own resources in solving dilemmas on the other hand, additional ethics training could be offered to clinicians. Moreover, those with more than 10 years of service did not have an ethics course in their medical studies. Better ethics education will increase sensitivity to ethical issues in practice and could serve as a basis for the bottom-up development of ethics consultation services.

The survey confirmed the positive attitude to ethics consultation previously noted, which strengthens the basis for development of ethics consultation.

References

Aleksandrova, S. 2008. Survey on the experience in ethical decision-making and attitude of Pleven University Hospital physicians towards ethics consultation. *Medicine, Health Care and Philosophy*, 11(1), 35–42.

Aulisio, M.P., Arnold, R.M. and Youngner, S.J. 2000. Health care ethics consultation: Nature, goals, and competencies. A position paper from the Society for Health and Human Values – Society for Bioethics consultation task force on standards for bioethics consultation. *Annals of Internal Medicine*, 133, 59–69.

Bernstein, M. and Bowman, K. 2003. Should a medical/surgical specialist with formal training in bioethics provide health care ethics consultation in his/her own area of specialty? *HEC Forum*, 15(3), 274–86.

DuVal, G., Clarridge, B., Gensler, G. and Danis, M. 2004. A national survey of US internists' experiences with ethical dilemmas and ethics consultation. *Journal of General Internal Medicine*, 19, 251–8.

DuVal, G., Sartorius, L., Clarridge, B., Gensler, G. and Danis, M. 2001. What triggers requests for ethics consultations? *Journal of Medical Ethics*, 27 (supplement I), 124–9.

Forde, R., Pedersen, R. and Akre, V. 2008. Clinicians' evaluation of clinical ethics consultation in Norway: A qualitative study. *Medicine, Health Care and Philosophy*, 11(1), 17–25.

Hoffman, D., Tarzian, A. and O'Neil, J.A. 2000. Are ethics committee members competent to consult? *Journal of the American Society of Law, Medicine & Ethics*, 28(1), 1073–105.

Hurst, S., Reiter-Theil, S., Parries, A., Forde, R., Slowther, A., Pegoraro, R. and Danis, M. 2007. Physicians' access to ethics support services in four European countries. *Health Care Analysis*, 15(4), 321–35.

Orlowski, J., Hein, S., Christensen, J.A., Meinke, R. and Sincich, T. 2006. Why doctors use or do not use ethics consultation. *Journal of Medical Ethics*, 32(9), 499–502.

Reiter-Theil, S. 2000. Ethics consultation on demand: Concepts, practical experiences and case studies. *Journal of Medical Ethics*, 26(3), 198–203.

Reiter-Theil, S. 2003. Balancing the perspectives: The patient's role in clinical ethics consultation. *Medicine, Health Care and Philosophy*, 6, 247–254.

Spike, J. and Greenlaw, J. 2000. Ethics consultation: High ideals or unrealistic expectations? Editorial. *Annals of Internal Medicine*, 133, 55–7.

Steinkamp, N. and Gordijn, B. 2001. The two-layer model of clinical ethics and a training program for the Malteser Hospital Association. *HEC Forum*, 13(3), 242–54.

Varelius, J. 2008. Is ethical expertise possible? *Medicine, Health Care and Philosophy*, 11(2), 127–32.

Yen, B. and Schneiderman, L. 1999. Impact of pediatric ethics consultations on patients, families, social workers, and physicians. *Journal of Perinatology*, 19(5), 373–8.

Chapter 16
Ethical Decision-making in Nursing Homes: A Literature Study

Georg Bollig

Introduction

A qualitative study using interviews with elderly people, their relatives and health care professionals from Norway showed that all participant groups experience ethical problems involving the adequacy of health care for elderly people in Norway. These included ethical problems concerning communication and conflicts between patients, relatives and health care professionals (Schaffer 2007). Worldwide, the population of elderly people and those suffering from dementia is increasing (Ferri et al. 2005). Of people living in nursing homes, 70–80 per cent suffer from dementia (Sandgathe Husebø and Husebø 2004). In advanced dementia, patients cannot decide on their own anymore and physicians, nurses and relatives have to make difficult decisions for them, often without knowing the patient's wishes.

Ethics consultation or ethics committees can be useful tools for decision-making in cases of people with advanced dementia (Gerhard and Bollig 2007). According to Chichin and Olson (1995), the frequency of ethical dilemmas in long-term care settings is likely to increase. Ethical problems that occur frequently in nursing homes are, for example, insecurity about the patient's wishes, questions about hospitalization versus treatment in the nursing home, type of treatment options to offer, or the use of restraints. In Germany and Austria there is now some discussion about the need for ethics committees in nursing homes and pilot projects involving moral deliberation and ethics consultation in nursing homes are proceeding (Bockenheimer-Lucius 2007, Bockenheimer-Lucius and May 2007, Reitinger et al. 2007a).

The background for this study was that in Norway both clinicians and politicians want to improve systematic work with ethics in the primary health care service and especially in elderly care and nursing homes. At present systematic ethics work and ethics committees are only located in hospitals and this work is coordinated by the Section of Medical Ethics at the University of Oslo. This study was undertaken to investigate what ethical problems occur in nursing homes and what strategies the staff use to solve or cope with ethical problems and dilemmas. The aim of this study was to investigate the following scientific questions:

1. What are the ethical challenges in nursing homes?
2. What kinds of strategies are used to handle these challenges?

Methods and Materials

A literature search was conducted using the databases MEDLINE, EMBASE, Pub Med, CINAHL, PsycINFO and Norart. Articles from Norway and other countries, published in English, German, Danish, Swedish and Norwegian, were included. Search keywords used were 'ethics', 'primary health care', 'nursing home' and 'long-term care'. For the Norwegian database, Norart, the search keywords were 'etikk', 'kommunehelsetjeneste' and 'sykehjem'. Other relevant articles were found on the Internet, in the reference lists of articles and books, and other sources. To illustrate the problems of practitioners in the field, both empirical research and descriptive work including personal experiences or letters to the editor, etc., are included in the section on results. Some of the methods found in the literature, such as, for example, the ethics café, have not yet been investigated scientifically.

Results

There are many ethical issues involved in primary health care, care for the elderly and especially in nursing homes. Few relevant empirical studies were identified. According to Peile, the first step to deal with ethical problems or dilemmas is to become aware of the ethical aspects of a given situation and to recognize a problem as an ethical one. Ethics education should aim at helping people to think by themselves instead of presenting them with solutions (Peile 2001). A qualitative study with semi-structured interviews of 14 nurses in nursing homes concluded that most nurses reported a situation as an ethical dilemma when it was associated with a feeling of 'discomfort' (Slettebo and Bunch 2004a). A simple definition of what an ethical dilemma is has been given by Pedersen: 'An ethical dilemma is present, if there is doubt or insecurity about what is right or wrong, good or bad' (personal communication with R. Pedersen, 20 September 2007).

Ethical Challenges in Nursing Homes

Despite the high frequency of ethical problems or dilemmas occurring in nursing homes all around the world every single day, they are often overlooked or neglected. This is probably due to their ordinariness and presence in everyday life situations (like bathing, feeding, etc.). Powers (2001) used qualitative methods with in-depth interviewing of residents, their families and nursing home staff in a nursing home. As a result of her study, she suggested a taxonomy of everyday ethical issues with four domains: learning the limits of intervention, tempering the culture of surveillance and restraint, preserving the integrity of the individual, and defining community norms and values. Everyday ethical issues can be divided into 'behaviour issues', 'treatment issues' or 'resource issues' (Powers 2001). Everyday ethical issues are, among others, refusal to bathe, offensive behaviour, expectoration in the dining room and overt sexuality in public places (Sansone 1996). According to Reitinger et al. (2007a), everyday ethics are about recognizing the basic needs of elderly people, the amount of time used to care, discussing dilemmas with colleagues and including others (physician, nurse assistant, volunteers, kitchen personal, etc.) in decision-making. Ethical issues can arise from situations such as admission to the nursing home, running away, bathing, conflicts with relatives, admission to hospital, treatment with nutrition and fluid, dying with dementia, or bereavement of the staff (Reitinger et al. 2007b). To have time and space to reflect on ethical issues would enable nursing home staff to make 'good decisions' in their care for nursing home residents (Reitinger et al. 2007a). Freedom to choose, personal safety and the right to have privacy are important everyday ethical issues in nursing homes (Rapelje 1992). One of the most frequent ethical dilemmas is conflict or dissension between staff, patient and relatives (Elander et al. 1993). Although these situations represent frequent ethical issues, they do not receive as much public attention as life-and-death issues.

Ethical problems in nursing homes are often more complex than those in hospitals (Glasser et al. 1988, Libow et al. 1992, Sansone 1996). Some of the significant differences between hospitals and nursing homes are that nursing home patients are more vulnerable, physicians play a limited role in the nursing home, and fewer nursing homes have established ethics committees (Hirsh 1987). Ethical dilemmas that occur frequently in nursing homes are mostly linked to dementia and the need for surrogate decision-making (Olson 1993). From Olson's experience as a gerontologist at Mount Sinai Medical Center in New York, serving approximately 3,000 elderly people, there are many ethical issues in long-term care (Olson et al. 1993):

- Placement of people
- Allocation of scarce resources
- How to maintain autonomy
- Informed consent
- Privacy
- Dilemmas around end-of-life treatment

Ethical dilemmas faced by the directors of 50 nursing homes included resource allocation issues, policy issues, management of care issues, client autonomy/competence issues and interpersonal issues (Harrison and Roth 1992). A survey of 59 long-term care facilities in the USA showed that the four major ethical issues occurring in 88 per cent of the facilities were: withholding or withdrawing artificial nutrition and hydration, treatment and care of patients with cognitive impairment, family conflicts and the use of restraints (Hogstel et al. 2004).

A survey of ethical problems in 225 American nursing homes showed the following ethical dilemmas (Weston et al. 2005):

- Assessing the resident's decision-making capacity (79 per cent)
- Decisions not to resuscitate (78 per cent)

- Decisions not to hospitalize (77 per cent)
- Tube-feeding issues (74 per cent)
- Implementing advance directives (70 per cent)
- Ascertaining resident's health care preferences (68 per cent)
- Identifying surrogate decision-makers (59 per cent)
- Withholding/withdrawing life-sustaining treatments (48 per cent)

The Elderly Person's Perspective

Relatively little is known of the perspective of the elderly residents and their relatives about ethical problems in nursing homes. The elderly in general are not a group accorded priority in the health care system and this has become even more of a problem since the introduction of diagnosis-related groups (DRG). This problem was addressed by Knight as long ago as 1994:

> Unfortunately, the DRG system often works against the elderly by excluding them from certain hospitals or forcing them out of hospitals before they are ready for discharge, even though support services at home are limited. (Knight 1994: 915)

Scarce resources in the care for the elderly are not only a problem of poor countries. Norwegian doctors and nurses are of the opinion that basic medical care for the elderly is not sufficient and that more personnel are needed in the care of the elderly (Forde et al. 2006). The increase of ethical problems in nursing homes is connected to both a shortage of resources and a lack of competence in this field of health care. In 2006 the Norwegian parliament promised to improve support for the care for the elderly and for nursing homes in Norway, including systematic work with ethics (Det Kongelige Helse- og Omsorgsdepartementet 2006).

Disagreement about medical treatment for life-threatening disease between relatives of incompetent patients and staff members in nursing homes is frequent. This has been shown in an epidemiological, descriptive cross-sectional study with interviews of nursing home residents (101 competent and 106 incompetent), 142 relatives and 207 staff members (Moe and Schroll 1997). The conclusion was that treatment preferences should be discussed before an acute situation occurs, especially in incompetent patients. To ascertain the patient's wishes, advance directives, living wills and proxy appointment can be used (Olson 1993). One major problem is the lack of communication between the patient, the relatives and the physician about advance directives and the end of life. Very few elderly people have expressed their wishes for end-of-life care and many people seem to be unable to talk openly about death (Lloyd-Williams et al. 2007). In a qualitative study by Schaffer (2007), 25 health professionals, six elderly people and five family members took part in semi-structured interviews. Elderly Norwegians were concerned about care or treatment given at the end of life, decision-making for themselves and others, discussion with family members and quality of health care services for the elderly in Norway. None of them had expressed their wishes for end-of-life care to their physicians. The relatives interviewed in the same study mentioned dissatisfaction with health care services, discussion of or involvement in end-of-life care and concerns about other family members as ethical problems (Schaffer 2007). The patient's perspective on end-of-life care has been studied by Singer et al., who used in-depth, open-ended, face-to-face interviews and content analysis with 38 long-term care patients. They identified five domains of quality in end-of-life care: receiving adequate pain and symptom management, avoiding inappropriate prolongation of dying, achieving a sense of control, relieving burden, and strengthening relationships with loved ones (Singer et al. 1999). Existing nursing home ethics committees rarely involve patients or their relatives directly as participants. In a study in the US, patients were included in 8 per cent and family members in 15 per cent of nursing home ethics committees, whereas administrators were included in 93 per cent and medical directors in 82 per cent of such committees (Glasser et al. 1988).

Strategies Used to Handle the Ethical Challenges

According to Hogstel et al., health care professionals should remember that: 'The choice of treatment or no treatment should not be what the physician, staff, spouse, adult child, or friend would want, but what the resident would want' (2004: 368). In a survey by Racine and Hayes (2006), 95 per cent of health care providers in the community in Quebec, Canada, think that a clinical ethics service is needed in a community health care service.

Several methods and approaches for discussion of ethical issues in nursing homes are described in the literature. Methods used, or proposed, to handle ethical problems in nursing homes are:

- (In)formal discussions
- Reflection groups (ethics peer groups)
- Ethics consultant/ethics team
- Ethics committee
- Ethics café
- Ethics rounds
- Gaming/role-play

(In)formal Discussions

The usual method is an informal or formal discussion between health care professionals (nurses and physicians) alone or with the patient and/or his or relatives. Hayley et al. (1996) suggested that most ethical issues in the nursing home can be resolved in an open discussion between the resident (when possible), relevant family members, the physician and nursing home staff members. Preparatory conversations between patient, relatives, physician and nursing home staff about advance directives and the patient's wishes and views about different treatment options can be useful to avoid unnecessary life-prolonging treatments and hospital admissions (Husebø and Husebø 2005). As mentioned above, Slettebo and Bunch (2004a) have shown that nurses mainly use negotiation, explanation and restraint to solve ethically difficult care situations in nursing homes.

Reflection Groups (Ethics Peer Groups)

Reflection groups with colleagues or a multidisciplinary team are used in some nursing homes in Norway, most of them without a systematic approach to reflection of ethical questions or guidance of an ethics expert. A combination of using the nurses' own experience and a theory of ethics called casuistry could lead to a more systematic way to find acceptable solutions for ethically difficult situations in nursing homes (Slettebo and Bunch 2004b).

Ethics Consultant/Ethics Team

An approach that is not often used in nursing homes is to appoint an ethics consultant or ethics team, who gives advice or helps with immediate consultations on a ward. In Chichin and Olson (1995), the team is described as consisting of members from the disciplines of social work, nursing, medicine and administration. After implementation, the particular team was called in on 12 cases within the first six months. All cases were related to issues of withholding or withdrawing treatment at the end-of-life.

Ethics Committee

Weston et al. (2005) stated that the need for ethics committees in long-term care is evident. A survey of nursing home committees in the USA, using questionnaires which were posted to administrators of 4,504 long-term care facilities, revealed that of the 29 per cent which responded, few (8 per cent) had established ethics committees. Their tasks were: policy review (in 81 per cent), advisory case review (in 67 per cent) and education (in 45 per cent) (Glasser et al. 1988). In other studies, ethics committees existed in 10 per cent and 34 per cent of nursing homes (Brown et al. 1987, Osborne et al. 2000). Nursing home ethics committees fulfil the same tasks as hospital ethics committees. These can be: education, case review and analysis, and policy development (Bockenheimer-Lucius and May 2007, Brown et al. 1987, Osborne et al. 2000, Sansone 1996). The usual tasks of ethics committees in the USA are: discussing cases, education and forming policies (Glasser et al. 1988, Hogstel et al. 2004, Weston et al. 2005). Ethics committees in nursing homes rarely exist in European countries such as Germany and Austria (Bockenheimer-Lucius 2007, Bockenheimer-Lucius and May 2007, Reitinger et al. 2007). Ethical guidelines and an ethics committee have already been established in the Bergen Red Cross nursing home (Husebø 2006), however, while other pilot projects with ethics committees in nursing homes are in the starting phase in Norway.

The composition of nursing home ethics committees in the USA showed that the most frequent members were administrators (93 per cent), nursing directors (89 per cent), medical directors (82 per cent), whereas patients (8 per cent) and family members (15 per cent) are seldom involved in decision-making in an ethics committee (Glasser et al. 1988). The conclusion of the same study was that a broader inclusion of patient perspectives is necessary for nursing home ethics committees.

One option to improve ethical deliberation and decision-making is education. According to Hogstel et al. (2004), nursing home staff should be educated in advance directives, the legal hierarchy of medical decision-makers, the benefits and burdens of specific treatments and medical futility.

That it is possible to implement ethics committees on a state-wide basis in the USA has been shown in New Jersey by the 'NJ SEED' programme. Between 1998 and 2001, a five-module curriculum was provided to 700 professional staff and state-wide a network of 15 long-term care regional ethics committees was introduced. The ethics committees consisted of multidisciplinary members such as administrators, activity therapists, consumers, doctors, nurses, social workers, chaplains, nutritionists, nurse aides, and others. Case consultations of the regional ethics committees dealt with initiation and/or withdrawal (or withholding) of tube feeding (nine out of 12 cases), withholding of other treatments (e.g., pacemakers, dialysis, and hospitalization), patients' rights, decision-making capacity, conflicts between patients, family/provider preferences and advance directives. As a result of this project, all nursing homes in New Jersey now have access to an ethics committee (Weston et al. 2005).

Ethics Café and Ethics Rounds

Ethics cafés (Bachmann and Rippe 2004) have been started in Zürich in Switzerland. The aim is to discuss ethical issues with different groups (physicians, nurses, patients and relatives). Discussions are held in plenary sessions and/or small groups. The discussion is led by a moderator with profound ethics knowledge who works as a sort of 'midwife' in order to encourage the discussion; this approach is called *Mäeutik* (Bachmann and Rippe 2004). Ethics rounds (Olson et al. 1993) have been established at the Jewish Home and Hospital for the Aged in New York City, USA, since 1985. Ethics rounds are meetings for health care professionals, patients and relatives, and aim at encouraging a dialogue across disciplines, education and discussion of ethical issues for a broad range of people. The meetings include a case presentation and a formal presentation by a guest speaker and are not aimed at making decisions. This approach has been complemented with an ethics education programme.

Gaming/Role-play

Gaming and role-play have been used as educational tools for health care professionals and other nursing home staff. Through acting in different roles one can enhance the understanding of others' values and positions (Wilson et al. 1988). Wilson et al. developed a role-play simulation game called 'Resolving Ethical Dilemmas', which has three objectives: to encourage understanding of the roles and responsibilities of all team members, to promote understanding of personal versus professional values, and to promote understanding of the difficulties and dilemmas involved in decision-making related to long-term care and the elderly.

Discussion

Findings from the literature revealed that there are two major groups of ethical issues in nursing homes. The first group can be described as 'everyday ethical issues' such as autonomy, informed consent, use of restraints, offensive behaviour, refusing medication, food and/or bathing, and others. The second group consists of 'big ethical issues', mostly dealing with life-or-death matters including decisions to withhold or withdraw life-sustaining treatment (including artificial nutrition and hydration), to hospitalize a patient or not, to treat or not (e.g., antibiotics, etc.), to give curative or palliative care, etc. One can agree with Olson (1993) that dementia and the need for surrogate decision-making is one major cause for ethical dilemmas in nursing homes. In the literature, as well as in the public debate, more attention is paid to the 'big ethical issues', especially those around end-of-life treatment and decision-making. Maybe many of the everyday ethical issues are often overlooked in nursing homes because of their ordinariness. One has to try to become aware of these everyday ethical issues (Peile 2001, Powers 2001). Whereas 'everyday ethical issues' are important and need attention, ethics committees and consultant teams' case discussions mostly deal with withdrawal of life-sustaining treatment (Chichin and Olson 1995, Weston et al. 2005). Good care for the elderly is connected to end-of-life care and the possibility to die with dignity in the nursing home. According to Gjerberg and Bjorndal (2007), there are four factors which can help to enable a 'good death'. These are good pain and symptom management, safety, no futile life-prolonging treatment, and taking care of the relatives. These findings are similar to the suggestions of Singer (1999). One important factor is to recognize and to consider the wishes of patients and their relatives. Peile suggested that forums for ethical discussion should be established throughout primary care sites and include staff and patients. More timely and effective discussions about and planning for the end-of-life should be a routine measure. Advanced care planning should be the result of a series of such discussions (Larson and Tobin 2000). This underlines that advance directives have a role in enabling end-of-life discussions between the patient, his or her relatives and the physician and staff. Planning for the end-of-life has to be a process including repeated discussions rather than a meeting where all future decisions can be made at once. Strategies for enhancing end-of-life discussions are most productively linked to the physicians' interpersonal communication skills, a patient-centred model of care, a focus on quality of remaining life and innovative clinical models for implementing these discussions earlier in the care process (Larson and Tobin 2000). Some authors suggest that bringing palliative care into nursing homes can be helpful to take patients' and relatives' wishes into account. Schaffer stated that:

> Health care services for the growing frail older population need to be reframed to integrate a palliative care philosophy that supports patient and family goals for cure or prolongation of life, while promoting peace and dignity during illness and the dying process. (2007: 255)

To implement systematic work with ethics in nursing homes it is paramount to sensitize and educate nursing home staff, but probably also patients, relatives and the public about the importance of ethical issues in care of the elderly. A combination of education and case discussions seems reasonable in the starting phase. Many methods to handle ethical problems in nursing homes are described in the literature. These are (in)formal discussions, reflection groups (ethics peer groups), ethics consultant/ethics team, ethics committee, ethics café, ethics rounds and gaming/role-play. Therefore a variety of different approaches to enhance awareness about ethical problems and to deliberate on them seems possible. Various methods of ethical case deliberation (clinical pragmatism, the Nijmegen method of ethical case deliberation, Hermeneutic dialogue and Socratic dialogue) can be used and the method may even be chosen depending on the type of moral problem (Steinkamp and Gordijn 2003). Probably one has to combine different approaches, for example, discussion groups on the wards and ethics committees where people are able to transfer certain problems to a higher level of ethics competence or to deliberate with a broader perspective. My suggestion is a three-step approach to ethical decision-making in nursing homes (Figure 16.1). The different steps can be individualized to meet different needs as well as geographical conditions. For a small rural nursing home education and open discussions might be a good start, whereas large institutions, like the Bergen Red Cross nursing home with 174 patients, need their own ethics committee or ethics consultation team. It is also possible to use all three steps in one nursing home side by side. As we do not know yet which option is the best, research must be an essential part of the implementation process and it would be wise to study different approaches in different regions in order to learn more about the topic. Surveys from nursing homes should be combined with qualitative in-depth interviews in order to evaluate the different approaches such as ethics peer groups/reflection groups, ethics consultation services and ethics committees. Interviews with nursing home patients and relatives could help us to learn more about their views and wishes on ethical challenges and decision-making in nursing homes.

Figure 16.1 A Three-step Approach to Ethical Deliberation and Decision-making in Nursing Homes

Implementation of ethics in nursing homes is both needed and possible, as Weston et al. (2005) have already shown. The implementation of systematic ethics work can help to ascertain the patient's wishes and enable the physician, staff and others to deliberate about ethical problems in the course of decision-making. Hopefully this could lead to a reduction of conflicts between the patient, the relatives, the staff and the physician, and higher levels of consent about treatment and care. Possible outcome measures could be the number of cases with consent after ethical deliberation, or if people perceive that they have reached a 'good decision'. Good decisions could be reached more often if options and ethical issues were discussed openly before making a decision. To implement ethics education and ethical deliberation in nursing homes, time and financial support is needed. In times of cost-effectiveness and economical restraints, one should remember the following when seeking to finance such efforts: 'Ethics cost, whether you have them or not' (Harvey 2001: 936).

Conclusion

Many ethical problems in nursing homes are linked to dementia and uncertainty about the patient's actual wishes. Although many ethical decisions have to be made in nursing homes on a daily basis, and many ethical dilemmas occur, there is a lack of systematic work in the field of ethics in nursing homes. The need for ethics committees in nursing homes has been advocated by many authors. The implementation of ethics peer groups, ethics consultation or ethics committees could probably help to solve many ethical dilemmas in nursing homes. This could lead to a broader inclusion of the patients' and relatives' perspectives and open discussions about the ethical aspects of 'everyday ethical issues' (e.g., the use of restraints) as well as 'big ethical issues' (e.g., decision-making in end-of-life care). The implementation should be individualized to meet different needs as well as geographical and cultural conditions. A three-step approach to ethical decision-making in nursing homes is proposed. Research should be an integral part of the implementation of ethics services in nursing homes.

References

Bachmann, A. and Rippe, K.P. 2004. [Ethics cafés-idea, concept and general practice: Invitation for reflection]. *Pflegezeitschrift*, 57(12), 868–9.
Bockenheimer-Lucius, G. 2007. [Ethics committee in a long-term care facility: challenge and a chance for an ethical decision-making culture]. *Ethik in der Medizin*, 19, 320–30.
Bockenheimer-Lucius, G. and May, A.T. 2007. [Ethics committees in long-term care facilities: A curriculum]. *Ethik in der Medizin*, 19, 331–9.
Brown, B.A., Miles, S.H. and Aroskar, M.A. 1987. The prevalence and design of ethics committees in nursing homes. *Journal of the American Geriatric Society*, 35(11), 1028–33.
Chichin, E.R. and Olson, E. 1995. An ethics consult team in geriatric long-term care. *Cambridge Quarterly of Healthcare Ethics*, 4, 178–84.
Det Kongelige Helse- og Omsorgsdepartementet. 2006. Stortingsmelding nr. 25 (2005–2006). Mestring, muligheter og mening. Framtidas omsorgsutfordringer. [Ministry of Health and Care Sciences. Future care challenges]. Oslo: Akademika AS.
Elander, G., Drechsler, K. and Persson, K.W. 1993. Ethical dilemmas in long-term care settings: Interviews with nurses in Sweden and England. *International Journal of Nursing Studies*, 30, 91–7.
Ferri, C.P., Prince, M., Brayne, C., Brodaty, H., Fratiglioni, L., Ganguli, M., Hall, K., Hasegawa, K., Hendrie, H., Huang, Y., Jorm, A., Mathers, C., Menezes, P.R., Rimmer, E. and Scazufca, M. 2005. Global prevalence of dementia: A Delphi consensus study. *Lancet*, 366(9503), 2112–7.
Forde, R., Pedersen, R., Nortvedt, P. and Aasland, O.G. 2006. [Enough resources to the care of the elderly?]. *Tidsskrift for den Norske Lægeforening*, 126, 1913–16.
Gerhard, C. and Bollig, G. 2007. [Palliative care for patients with advanced dementia]. *Palliativmedizin*, 8, 69–72.
Gjerberg, E. and Bjorndal, A. 2007. [What is a good death in a nursing home?] *Sykepleien Forskning*, 3, 174–80.

Glasser, G., Zweibel, N.R. and Cassel, C.K. 1988. The ethics committee in the nursing home: Results of a national survey. *Journal of the American Geriatric Society*, 36, 150–56.

Harrison, J.K. and Roth, P.A. 1992. Ethical dilemmas faced by directors of nursing. *Journal of Long Term Care Administration*, 20(2), 13–16.

Harvey, J. 2001. Ethics cost, whether you have them or not. *British Medical Journal*, 232, 936.

Hayley, D.C., Cassel, C.K., Snyder, L. and Rudberg, M.A. 1996. Ethical and legal issues in nursing home care. *Archives of Internal Medicine*, 156, 249–56.

Hirsh, H.L. 1987. Nursing home ethics committees: To be or not to be. *Nursing Homes and Senior Citizen Care*, 36(3), 12–15.

Hogstel, M.O., Curry, L.C. and Burns, P.G. 2004. Ethics committees in long-term care facilities. *Geriatric Nursing*, 25, 364–9.

Husebø, S. and Husebø, B.S. 2005. [Care at the end of life or active euthanasia?]. *Tidsskrift for den Norske Lægeforening*, 125, 1848–9.

Husebø, S. 2006. [The dying old: Guidelines for ethical decisions about withdrawal of life-sustaining treatments]. *Omsorg*, 4, 43–5.

Knight, J.A. 1994. Ethics of care in caring for the elderly. *Southern Medical Journal*, 87, 909–17.

Larson, D.G. and Tobin, D.R. 2000. End-of-life conversations: Evolving practice and theory. *Journal of the American Medical Association*, 284, 1573–8.

Libow, L.S., Olson, E., Neufeld, R.R., Martico-Greenfield, T., Meyers, H., Gordon, N. and Barnett, P. 1992. Ethics rounds at the nursing home: An alternative to an ethics committee. *Journal of the American Geriatrics Society*, 40(1), 95–7.

Lloyd-Williams, M., Kennedy, V., Sixsmith, A. and Sixsmith, J. 2007. The end of life: A qualitative study of the perceptions of people over the age of 80 on issues surrounding death and dying. *Journal of Pain and Symptom Management*, 34, 60–66.

Moe, C. and Schroll, M. 1997. What degree of medical treatment do nursing home residents want in case of life-threatening disease? *Age and Ageing*, 27(2), 133–7.

Olson, E. 1993. Ethical issues in the nursing home. *Mount Sinai Journal of Medicine*, 60, 555–9.

Olson, E., Chichin, E.R., Libow, L.S., Martico-Greenfield, T., Neufeld, R.R. and Mulvihill, M. 1993. A center on ethics in long-term care. *The Gerontologist*, 33(2), 269–74.

Osborne, T., Lacy, N.L., Potter, J.F., Crabtree, B.F. and American Health Care Association. 2000. The prevalence, composition, and function of ethics committees in nursing facilities: Results of a random, national survey of American Health Care Association members. *Journal of the American Medical Directors Association*, 1(2), 51–7.

Peile, E. 2001. Supporting primary care with ethics advice and education. *British Medical Journal*, 323, 3–4.

Powers, B.A. 2001. Ethnographic analysis of everyday ethics in the care of nursing home residents with dementia. *Nursing Research*, 50(6), 332–9.

Racine, E. and Hayes, K. 2006. The need for a clinical ethics service and its goals in a community healthcare service centre: A survey. *Journal of Medical Ethics*, 32, 564–6.

Rapelje, D.H. 1992. Ethical issues in long-term care. *Leadership in Health Services*, 1, 10–11.

Reitinger, E., Heller, A. and Heimerl, K. 2007a. [Ethical decisions in care of the elderly]. *Betreuungsrechtliche Praxis*, 2, 58–62.

Reitinger, E., Wegleitner, K. and Heimerl, K. (eds). 2007b. *Stories that concern us: Learning from ethical challenges in the care of the elderly*. Vienna: IFF-Palliative Care und OrganisationsEthik Eigenverlag.

Sandgathe Husebø, S. and Husebø, S. 2004. [Ethical end-of-life decision-making in nursing homes]. *Tidsskrift for Den norske lægeforening*, 124, 2926–7.

Sansone, P. 1996. The evolution of a long-term care ethics committee. *HEC Forum*, 8, 44–51.

Schaffer, M.A. 2007. Ethical problems in end-of-life decisions for elderly Norwegians. *Nursing Ethics*, 14(2), 242–57.

Singer, P.A., Martin, D.K. and Kelner, M. 1999. Quality end-of-life care: Patients' perspectives. *Journal of the American Medical Association*, 281, 163–8.

Slettebo, A. and Bunch, E.H. 2004a. Solving ethically difficult care situations in nursing homes. *Nursing Ethics*, 11(6), 543–552.

Slettebo, A. and Bunch, E.H. 2004b. Ethics in nursing homes: Experience and casuistry. *International Journal of Nursing Practice*, 10, 159–65.

Steinkamp, N. and Gordijn, B. 2003. Ethical case deliberation on the ward: A comparison of four methods. *Medicine, Health Care and Philosophy*, 6, 235–46.

Weston, C.M., O'Brien, L.A., Goldfarb, N.I., Roumm, A.R., Isele, W.P. and Hirschfeld, K. 2005. The NJ SEED Project: Evaluation of an innovative initiative for ethics training in nursing homes. *Journal of the American Medical Directors Association*, 6, 68–75.

Wilson, C.C., Netting, F.E. and Henderson, S.K. 1988. Gaming as a method for learning to resolve ethical dilemmas in long-term care. *Health Education*, 19(1), 42–4.

Chapter 17

Evaluation of Clinical Ethics Consultation: A Systematic Review and Critical Appraisal of Research Methods and Outcome Criteria

Jan Schildmann and Jochen Vollmann

Background

Clinical ethics consultation (CEC) has been advocated as an instrument to facilitate decision-making in situations in which patients, families or members of the health care team perceive ethical challenges regarding the care of an individual patient. The implementation of the first CEC services in health care institutions can be dated back to the USA at the beginning of the 1970s (Fletcher and Brody 1995, Kosnik 1974, Vollmann 2006). Ethics committees, as one form of ethics consultation service, have been supported in US case law (e.g., in the case of Karen Ann Quinlan) and by the US President's Commission for the Study of Ethical Problems in Medicine and Biomedical and Behavorial Research (US President's Commission 1983). In its accreditation guidelines, the Joint Commission on Accreditation of Health Care Organizations (JCAHO) recommends the provision of mechanisms to resolve ethical dilemmas for US health care institutions (JCAHO 1995). Repeatedly, the results of surveys conducted indicate that the number of US hospitals offering ethics consultation services has increased during the last few decades (Youngner et al. 1983, Fox et al. 2007).

In Europe the implementation of CEC services was delayed by about 20 years compared with the development in the USA (Hope and Slowther 2000). In 1997 the German organizations of Roman Catholic and Protestant hospitals – which form about one-third of all hospitals in the country – issued a joint statement in which they recommended the implementation of clinical ethics committees (Deutscher Evangelischer Krankenhausverband und Katholischer Krankenhausverband Deutschlands 1997). In 2006 the Central Ethics Commission of the German Medical Association (ZEKO) recommended the implementation of CEC services for health care institutions (Bundesärztekammer 2006). On the European level, the European Clinical Ethics Network (ECEN) was founded in 2005 in order to explore conceptual, methodological and practical aspects of CEC. The network currently comprises members of about a dozen countries (Molewijk and Widdershoven 2007).

Multiple goals of CEC have been defined in the literature. These goals refer to the quality of the structure and process of clinical ethics consultation as well as to possible outcomes and the impact of these services. The provision of CEC services by knowledgeable and competent ethics consultants and the improvement of patient care are examples for different types of evaluation criteria. In 1995 a conceptual framework for evaluation research of CEC was developed as part of a conference on 'Evaluation of Care Consultation in Clinical Ethics' conducted by US specialists for clinical ethics consultation (Tulsky and Fox 1996). In this context, four domains of possible outcomes of CEC were suggested, which may serve as a basis for evaluation studies in this field:

1. 'Ethicality' defined as the promotion of 'practices consistent with ethical norms and standards'.
2. 'Satisfaction' of the participants of CEC.
3. 'Resolution of conflict' by CEC; and
4. 'Education' of those participating in CEC (Fox and Arnold 1996).

In the following, empirical studies to evaluate the outcome of clinical ethics consultation have been advocated in the literature on the basis of mainly three reasons. The first reason is that evaluation furthers transparency and accountability of CEC and those offering this service. This is not only important in the light of limited financial and personal resources which are allocated to clinical ethics consultation services but also to foster trust and confidence between patients, families and members of the health care team as a necessary prerequisite for the successful and sustained implementation of clinical ethics consultation. A second reason which has been cited in favour of evaluation is the potential impact of the results of such studies on the quality of the service. If, for example, service users are dissatisfied with the time that elapses from request to the actual provision of clinical ethics consultation, this aspect may be reconsidered by ethics consultation providers. A third reason which can be put forward for evaluation of outcomes of ethics consultation is that such research may stimulate reflection about the provision of consistent CEC services regarding the underlying conceptual assumptions, the method used to perform CEC, and the goals defined for this service (Aulisio et al. 2000, Hope and Slowther 2000, Lo 2003).

There has been a paucity of empirical work with respect to the evaluation of outcomes of CEC up to the mid-1990s. A review by Tulsky and Fox published in 1996 generated 42 pieces of empirical research on the work of CEC services (Tulsky and Fox 1996). Whereas most studies provide information about the number of ethics consultations provided in a certain time span and characteristics of the cases for which CEC had been requested, the authors identified one single pre/post study comparing the characteristics of subjects before and after the introduction of a clinical ethics programme. During the last decade, several evaluation studies on the outcomes of clinical ethics consultation have been published, including one prospective, multicentre, randomized controlled trial (Schneiderman et al. 2003). In addition, there have been several reviews which reflect and comment critically on the methods and outcomes used in evaluation studies of CEC (Craig and May 2006, Williamson 2007). However, there is no systematic review of evaluation studies on the effects of clinical ethics consultation of which the authors are aware. The potential benefits of such a review are, first of all, the systematic and transparent gathering of data for the purpose of a descriptive analysis of similarities and differences between the various evaluation studies conducted so far. Secondly, the results of such a review can serve as a basis for a critical appraisal of descriptive as well as normative aspects of evaluation studies on clinical ethics consultation. Third, the summary of available data facilitates the identification of research questions and by this promotes further development of CEC.

In this chapter the results of a systematic review on studies evaluating the outcomes of CEC are presented. For the purpose of this chapter there is a detailed presentation of the methods used in the evaluation studies identified as part of the review and a description of the outcome criteria which have been defined in the respective research projects. The discussion will focus on selected aspects of the methodological quality of the studies as well as the normative relevance of the outcome criteria which have been used by the researcher to demonstrate the effects of CEC.

Methods

The literature search was performed in a four-step approach based on recommendations for systematic reviews of bioethical literature by Strech et al. (2008). The performed steps were:

1. Formulation of the review question and definition of key terms.
2. Definition of relevance criteria for the literature review.
3. Definition of a search algorithm and performance of literature review by using an electronic database; and
4. Definition and use of ancillary search strategies.

As a first step the review question was formulated. For the purpose of this study the review question was formulated as follows: *Which outcomes of evaluation studies on clinical ethics consultation have been published in the literature?* The terms *outcomes*, *clinical ethics consultation* and *evaluation studies* were identified as 'key terms' of the review question which needed further definition. For the purpose of the review, the term *clinical ethics consultation* has been defined as prospective case consultation of patients, relatives and members of the health care team in the case of ethical conflicts which are related to the care of a patient. *Outcomes* have been defined as effectiveness of ethics consultation as measured

Table 17.1 Relevance Criteria and Respective Exclusion Criteria

Relevance criteria	Topics excluded
Clinical ethics consultation	Research ethics consultation
Prospective case consultation	Retrospective case consultation
Case consultation	Policy development, educational or other activities performed by ethics consultant(s)/committee(s)
Ethics consultations	Ethical case discussions without ethics consultant/consultation team
Evaluation studies	Case reports, conceptual studies
Evaluation of outcomes	Evaluation studies on epidemiology, structure or process of CEC only
Respondents of evaluation study (*participants of ethics consultation*)	Surveys of patients, family members or health care professionals who did not participate in ethics consultation

by the attainment of a specified end result. *Evaluation studies* as the third 'key term' have been defined as the systematic application of a described social research procedure to collect empirical data.

As the second step, criteria to determine the relevance of retrieved articles were defined. A first list of relevance criteria was developed on the basis of the review question prior to the literature search. The final list of relevance criteria outlined in Table 17.1 is the result of an iterative process of the application of the predefined relevance criteria and modifications which have been developed during the process of the literature review. Table 17.1 summarizes the relevance criteria and respective topics which do not fall under these criteria.

As part of the third step, a database was selected and a search algorithm developed. PubMed, which has been selected as the database for this review, is a service of the US National Library of Medicine, which includes over 17 million citations from MEDLINE (including BIOETHICSLINE) and other life science journals for biomedical articles back to the 1950s. Search terms used for the database search included medical subject headings [MeSH] – the controlled vocabluary of PubMed – as well as relevant textwords [TW] used in the abstracts or (in the case of a lack of abstract) in the introduction of a convenience sample of four articles on evaluation of ethics consultation (Forde et al. 2008, Fox 1996, Schneiderman et al. 2003, Tulsky and Fox 1996). All identified search terms were gathered in three groups depending on whether they related to the *method* of a study (e.g., 'empirical study' [MeSH]), the *intervention* (e.g., 'ethics consultation' [MeSH]) or to *outcome* (e.g.. 'mortality' [MeSH]). All terms within one of the three groups were connected with the Boolean operator OR, the three groups were connected with the operation AND. The PubMed literature search was limited to articles in English and German language and covered articles which had been added to the database between 1 January 1970 and 31 December 2007. Table 17.2 summarizes MeSH terms and textwords which form part of the search algorithm.

Table 17.2   MeSH and Textwords Used for the Search Algorithm

Method	Intervention	Outcome
Medical Subject Headings [MeSH]		
Data collection	Ethics consultation	Outcome assessment (health care)
Health care surveys	Ethicists	Length of stay
Evaluation studies as topic	Ethical review	Medical futility
Empirical research	Ethics committees, clinical referral and consultation/ethics	Patient care planning
Textwords [TW]		
Evaluation	Ethics consultation	Effect
Trial	Ethics consultations	Effectiveness
		Evaluate
		Useful
		View

As the final step of the systematic literature review, two ancillary literature search strategies were used for the purpose of gathering articles on the evaluation of outcomes of CEC: 1) the bibliographies of those articles retrieved by the PubMed research which were identified as relevant were reviewed for further publications which might fulfil the defined relevance criteria; and 2) all first-named authors of relevant articles identified up to this point were entered in PubMed together with the term 'ethics consultation' and any articles generated were checked for relevance.

For the literature search using the PubMed database, all abstracts were read and a decision regarding the inclusion or exclusion of the article based on the predefined relevance criteria was made. Where no abstract was available, articles with a potentially relevant content (as indicated by title) were ordered and the decision was made after reading the full text version. Decisions about the relevance of articles identified as part of the review of the bibliographies were made on the basis of the title and the text which refers to the reference. All articles identified as fulfilling the relevance criteria were read in full text and a final decision with respect to the relevance of the paper for this review was made. The content of the publication was analysed with respect to relevant information on the evaluation methods used in the studies and the outcome criteria defined to determine the effect of CEC.

Results

The PubMed review using the above mentioned search algorithm generated 159 hits and 10 articles that fulfilled the relevance criteria (Dowdy et al. 1998, Forde et al. 2008, La Puma et al. 1988, La Puma et al. 1992, McClung et al. 1996, Orr and Moon 1993, Schneiderman et al. 2000, Schneiderman et al. 2003, White et al. 1997, Yen and Schneiderman 1999). By means of reviewing the bibliographies of these 10 publications, another two relevant articles could be identified (Orr et al. 1996, Perkins et al. 1988). Two additional publications were gained by using PubMed to search for articles published by the first-named authors of the 12 relevant publications identified up to this point (Cohn et al. 2007, Schneiderman et al. 2006). The 14 papers that could be identified as a result of the systematic literature review report results of 12 different evaluation studies, of which three papers report different results from one trial (Cohn et al. 2007, Schneiderman et al. 2003, Schneiderman et al. 2006).

Research Methods

Twelve of the 14 articles identified as relevant for the review question report the results of studies which used predominantly quantitative research methods, whereas two papers present the results of research projects in which semi-structured interviews and qualitative data analysis were used (Forde et al. 2008, Perkins et al. 1988). In both of the qualitative studies, the participants were exclusively physicians. In five quantitative studies, patients and health care professionals participated as evaluators of CEC (Cohn et al. 2007, McClung et al. 1996, Schneiderman et al. 2000, Schneiderman et al. 2003, Schneiderman et al. 2006, Yen and Schneiderman 1999, White et al. 1997). In three other studies interviewees were health care professionals only (La Puma et al. 1988, La Puma et al. 1992, Orr and Moon 1993, White et al. 1997). In one study only patients and relatives were asked about their perspective (Orr et al. 1996). Two studies are randomized controlled trials (Cohn et al. 2007, Schneiderman et al. 2000, 2003, 2006), one study is a prospective controlled trial (Dowdy et al. 1998), whereas one study uses data from an earlier trial as a control group (La Puma et al. 1992).

Chart review (Cohn et al. 2007, Dowdy et al. 1998, La Puma et al. 1988, La Puma et al. 1992, Orr and Moon 1993, Schneiderman et al. 2000, Schneiderman et al. 2003, Schneiderman et al. 2006, Yen and Schneidermann 1999) was used most frequently to elicit data for evaluation of the outcomes of CEC. The majority of structured interviews or questionnaires contained questions with a Likert-scale answer format. In addition, open-ended questions that allowed for narrative comments by respondents had been used as part of the instruments in some studies.

Table 17.3   Methods of Data Collection in Quantitative Studies

Method of data collection	Number of studies
Chart review	7
Structured interviews	4
Structured questionnaires	4
Hospital bill	1

Table 17.3 summarizes the different methods of data collection used in studies with a predominantly quantitative design.

Three papers provide information about the development of the quantitative measurement instruments used to elicit the perceptions and views of respondents. White et al. (1997) report that their instrument was based on elements of quality of CEC as outlined in the literature. Orr et al. (1996) based the content of their structured questionnaire on an analysis of an exploratory study in which patients and family members were asked about their assessment of CEC. La Puma et al. (1992) refer to their instrument as 'pretested' without giving further information. The publications identified in this review neither provide information on the process of operationalizing the criteria to evaluate CEC nor do they indicate values regarding content validity or reliability of the instruments used in the studies. With respect to the two qualitative studies included in this review, Forde et al. (2008) provide an account about their method of data gathering using a three-step approach of 'structuring', 'categorizing' and 'interpreting' of data. In contrast, the authors of the second qualitative study (Perkins et al. 1988) only mention the source of data (physicians requesting clinical ethics consultation and chart review) without providing information about the process of data analysis and interpretation.

Outcome Criteria

The majority of studies investigated participants' overall assessment of the CEC services (see Table 17.4). Five studies assessed the views of patients as well as health care professionals on CEC (Cohn et al. 2007, McClung et al. 1996, Schneiderman et al. 2000, Schneiderman et al. 2003, Schneiderman et al.

Table 17.4 Outcomes of CEC as Investigated in Quantitative Studies

Participants' views on clinical ethics consultation with respect to:	Number of studies
Overall assessment of CEC	9
Analysis/clarification of ethical issues in CEC	7
Impact of CEC on medical treatment	7
Information/educational benefit of CEC	6
Provision of (emotional) support as part of CEC	4
Resolving of ethical conflict by CEC	3
Stressfulness of CEC	3
Respect for participants' values in CEC	2
Fairness of CEC	1
Helpfulness of opinion rendered by CEC	1
Improvement of communication between different parties by CEC	1
Participants' agreement with decision of CEC	1
Possibility to present own views in CEC	1

2006, Yen and Schneiderman 1999, White et al. 1997), whereas in three other quantitative studies (La Puma et al. 1988, La Puma et al. 1992, Orr and Moon 1993, White et al. 1997) and in the two qualitative studies (Forde et al. 2008, Perkins et al. 1988) only physicians' perceptions and views were explored. In one study the assessment of perceptions and views was restricted to patients or surrogates only (Orr et al. 1996). Table 17.4 summarizes criteria used to evaluate CEC in structured questionnaires or interviews. The function of CEC with respect to the clarification of ethical issues, the perceived impact of CEC on medical treatment, and information and education for members of the health care team as well as other participants are identified as the variables most frequently used to evaluate CEC.

In addition to eliciting participants' perception and views, three studies applying predominantly quantitative methods used objective outcome measures to determine the impact of CEC (Cohn et al. 2007, Dowdy et al. 1998, Schneiderman et al. 2000, 2003, 2006). Mortality of patients and so-called 'nonbeneficial life-sustaining treatments' of patients who eventually died in hospital were investigated as outcome criteria in these studies. One of these studies investigated the effect of CEC on financial resources spent for health care treatment (Dowdy et al. 1998). In this study, the researchers also investigated the communication process about treatment decisions as documented in the chart as an objective outcome criterion of CEC.

The two studies which used a qualitative design both explored physicians' experiences and satisfaction with CEC. Perceptions with respect to the identification and analysis of ethical issues as part of CEC have been evaluated in both studies. With respect to possible outcomes of CEC, the study by Perkins et al. (1988) also explored self-perceived changes in confidence regarding ethical decision-making and perceived impact on patient care. In addition to face-to-face interviews, chart review was used in this study as an additional source of data collection to substantiate the findings from the interviews.

Discussion

This chapter provides information about methods of data collection and the outcome criteria of evaluation studies on the effects of CEC. In recent years there have been several comments on the methods used to evaluate CEC (Craig and May 2006, Lo 2003, Williamson 2007). However, up to this point no systematic review on this issue has been published of which the authors are aware. A transparent, systematic review of empirical data is a prerequisite for a sound analysis and critical appraisal of the empirical studies which have been conducted to determine the impact of CEC.

Search strategies applied in this review included the use of the PubMed database and the reference list of relevant articles gained by using the search algorithm described in the method section. The presentation and discussion of the results at a joint session of the participants of the international conference of CEC, held on 11–16 February 2008 at the Institute for Medical Ethics and History of Medicine, Ruhr-University Bochum, and the members of the European Clinical Ethics Network (ECEN) did not generate any new studies which had been missed as part of this review. However, it is likely that there are more evaluation studies published than are summarized in this review. Examples are written reports on the quality of health care and outcomes, which are frequently issued by health care institutions, or papers published in journals which do not appear in the PubMed database. In addition relevant papers may have been missed when using the PubMed database because the keywords used in these publications do not match MeSH terms or the textwords which form part of the search algorithm used in this study.

The focus of this systematic review has been limited to studies which investigate the outcomes of CEC. Studies on structural and procedural aspects are not included in this analysis. An earlier review conducted by Tulsky and Fox (1996) indicates that such studies form a relevant amount of the empirical work done in this field so far. In the light of the mainly process-orientated focus of ethical deliberation, studies evaluating procedural aspects provide information on the quality of an important feature of ethics consultation. The focus of this study on outcomes reflects the current awareness and interest in clinical medicine to judge the value of interventions on the basis of their impact on clinical practice. Moreover, outcomes are frequently used to justify the resources allocated to health care services. In this respect providers of CEC frequently are already, and probably increasingly will be, asked to present the practical impact of their work. In addition to the fact that evaluation studies on the impact of CEC fit well with the current mainstream thinking of the 'medical outcome movement' (Fox 1996), one may argue that the design of such studies can stimulate our thinking about the provision of a consistent approach of CEC with respect to its aims, structure, procedure and methods.

The systematic review generated only two studies which used a qualitative method of data gathering (Forde et al. 2008, Perkins et al. 1988). These studies explored the perception of physicians with respect to the potential value of CEC. The exploratory character of qualitative studies has the advantage that topics deemed relevant for participants of CEC can be elicited and further analysed (see also the chapter in this volume by Georg Bollig). One example in this respect may be the exploration of factors which contribute to a positive (or negative) perception of CEC. Further analysis on topics elicited by means of semi-structured interviews can be done either by conducting further qualitative interviews which are adapted to the issues brought up in past interviews or in the form of empirical quantitative studies in which hypotheses triggered as a result of qualitative studies may be tested. In addition to its explorative character, the results gained by qualitative studies may have an explanatory function. One example for the potential use of qualitative studies in this respect are the repeated findings of quantitative studies with respect to a discrepancy between the perceived benefit of CEC on the side of health care professionals (high) versus patients and surrogates (significantly lower) (Cohn et al. 2007, McClung et al. 1996, Yen and Schneiderman 1999).

The majority of identified evaluation studies use a predominantly quantitative approach. With the exception of three studies (La Puma et al. 1992, Orr et al. 1996, White et al. 1997), the respective papers provide no information on important aspects of the methodological quality of the study. Information on the development of the instruments, including pre-tests and procedures to ensure content validity, as well as data on performance criteria such as reliability scores are missing in the papers analysed in this review. On this background the validity of the data gained by these studies is difficult to judge. This is moreover valid since it has been reported that participants of these studies may not have understood adequately some of the questions framed in the research instrument (Orr et al. 1996).

The outcome criteria used in the presented evaluation studies can be divided into *subjective criteria*, by which CEC participants evaluate the intervention and *objective criteria*, by which the effect or impact of CEC is described on the basis of parameters such as mortality or treatment measures. With respect to the subjective outcome criteria, participants' global judgement on CEC, the perceived impact on medical treatment and educational benefits are used frequently. In addition, participants' satisfaction regarding emotional support and a fair procedure as part of the CEC has been measured. The use of such criteria begs questions with respect to the relevant stakeholder of whom information should be elicited. While the earliest studies identified in this review focus on the perspective of physicians (Perkins et al. 1988, LaPuma et al. 1988, 1992, Orr and Moon 1993), there has been a trend towards eliciting data also from other groups involved with or affected by CEC, such as patients, surrogates and health care professionals other than physicians. This latter approach can be supported as a move away from an exclusively medical perspective. The differing judgements about CEC from the various groups participating in CEC (e.g., the mentioned discrepancy in satisfaction between health care professionals and surrogates) lead to the issue of the normative relevance of participants' satisfaction with CEC (Williamson 2007). It seems possible that a skilfully conducted CEC may still leave behind dissatisfied participants, given that this CEC made it very clear to all participants that dealing with the ethical dilemma in question will inevitably have negative consequences regardless of the option which will be chosen. Another possible cause for dissatisfaction may be the experience that the aim for a consensus between the different parties generates a decision which seems to be unethical to one or several participants of CEC. Questions regarding the normative relevance or more specifically the ethical acceptability of outcome criteria seem even more difficult to answer with respect to the objective outcome criteria. As has been pointed out in earlier analyses, the reduction of intensive treatment, days in hospital or costs are contingent criteria and do not themselves function as parameters for good or bad CEC (Craig and May 2006, Lo 2003). The task of balancing burdens and benefits has to be made in every single case and in the light of present or former preferences of the affected patient. For this reason normative criteria such as 'nonbeneficial treatment' cannot be based on descriptive facts such as days spent in an intensive care unit prior to death.

In summary, the findings in this review indicate that there is a scarcity of transparent information on the methodological quality of empirical studies on the evaluation of CEC. This is valid for adequate descriptions of the development of the research instruments used, pre-tests and information on scores of performance criteria such as content validity or reliability. With respect to empirically and ethically sound evaluation studies of CEC, a close interdisciplinary collaboration between researchers with a disciplinary background of empirical as well as normative sciences seems necessary to ensure the development of adequate instruments, a sound research design as well as a reflective interpretation of findings. Finally the use of a mixed method approach, integrating qualitative as well as quantitative methods in one research project, would be valuable regarding a more complete way to gather information and for an increase of the explanatory function of empirical research on CEC.

References

Aulisio, M., Arnold, R.M. and Youngner, S.J. 2000. Health care ethics consultation: Nature, goals and competencies. *Annals of Internal Medicine*, 133, 59–69.

Bundesärztekammer. 2006. Stellungnahme der Zentralen Kommission zur Wahrung ethischer Grundsätze in der Medizin und ihren Grenzgebieten: Zentrale Ethikkommission bei der Bundesärztekammer zur Ethikberatung in der klinischen Medizin. *Deutsches Ärzteblatt*, 103(A), 1703–5.

Craig, J.M. and May, T. 2006. Evaluation of the outcomes of ethics consultation. *Journal of Clinical Ethics*, 17, 168–80.

Cohn, F., Goodman-Crews, P., Rudman, W., Schneiderman, L.J. and Waldman, E. 2007. Proactive ethics consultation in the ICU: A comparison of value perceived by healthcare professionals and recipients. *Journal of Clinical Ethics*, 18, 140–7.

Deutscher Evangelischer Krankenhausverband und Katholischer Krankenhausverband Deutschlands e.V. (ed.) 1997. *Ethik-Komitee im Krankenhaus*. Stuttgart: Selbstverlag.

Dowdy, M.D., Robertson, C. and Bander, J.A. 1998. A study of proactive ethics consultation for critically and terminally ill patients with extended lengths of stay. *Critical Care Medicine*, 26, 252–9.

Fletcher, J. and Brody, H. 1995. Clinical ethics, in *Encyclopedia of Bioethics*, edited by W. Reich. New York: Macmillan, 399–412.

Forde, R., Pedersen, R. and Akre, V. 2008. Clinicians' evaluation of clinical ethics consultations in Norway: A qualitative study. *Medicine, Health Care and Philosophy*, 11, 17–25.

Fox, E. 1996. Concepts in evaluation applied to ethics consultation research. *Journal of Clinical Ethics*, 7, 116–21.

Fox, E. and Arnold, R.A. 1996. Evaluating outcomes in ethics consultation research. *Journal of Clinical Ethics*, 7, 127–38.

Fox, E., Myers, S. and Pearlman, R.A. 2007. Ethics consultation in United States: A national survey. *American Journal of Bioethics*, 7, 13–25.

Hope, T. and Slowther, A. 2000. Clinical ethics committees: They can change clinical practice but need evaluation. *British Medical Journal*, 321, 649–50.

JCAHO. 1995. *Comprehensive Accreditation Manual for Hospitals*, 66. Chicago: Joint Commission on Accreditation of Health Care Organizations.

Kosnik, A.R. 1974. Developing a health facility medical moral committee. *Hospital Progress*, 55, 40–44.

La Puma, J., Stocking, C.B., Darling, C.M. and Siegler, M. 1992. Community hospital ethics consultation: Evaluation and comparison with a university hospital service. *American Journal of Medicine*, 92, 46–51.

La Puma, J., Stocking, C.B., DiMartini, A. and Siegler, M. 1988. An ethics consultation service in a teaching hospital: Utilization and evaluation. *Journal of the American Medical Association*, 260, 808–11.

Lo, B. 2003. Answers and questions about ethics consultation. *Journal of the American Medical Association*, 290, 1208–9.

McClung, J.A., Kamer, R.S., DeLuca, M. and Barber, H.J. 1996. Evaluation of a medical ethics consultation service: Opinions of patients and health care providers. *American Journal of Medicine*, 100, 456–60.

Molewijk, B. and Widdershoven, G.A.M. 2007. Report of the Maastricht meeting of the European Clinical Ethics Network. *Clinical Ethics*, 2, 45.

Orr, R.D. and Moon, E. 1993. Effectiveness of an ethics consultation service. *Journal of Family Practice*, 36, 49–53.

Orr, R.D., Morton, K.R., deLeon, D.M. and Fals, J.C. 1996. Evaluation of an ethics consultation service: Patient and family perspective. *American Journal of Medicine*, 101, 135–41.

Perkins, H.S., Bunnie, S. and Saathoff, B.A. 1988. Impact of medical ethics consultations on physicians: An exploratory study. *American Journal of Medicine*, 85, 761–5.

Schildmann, J. and Widdershoven, G.A.M. 2009. Reflexiv-kritische Konzeptionalisierung von Ethik-Gremien, in *Handbuch für Ethik im Gesundheitswesen: Ethikdialog in der Wissenschaft (Bd.5)*, edited by T. Weidmann-Hügle and M. Christen. Basel/Bern: Schwabe & EMH Schweizerischer Ärzteverlag, 195–204.

Schneiderman, L.J., Gilmer, T. and Teetzel, H.D. 2000. Impact of ethics consultations in the intensive care setting: A randomized, controlled trial. *Critical Care Medicine*, 28, 3920–4.

Schneiderman, L.J., Gilmer, T., Teetzel, H.D., Dugan, D.O., Blustein, J., Cranford, R., Briggs, K.B., Komatsu, G.I., Goodman-Crews, P., Cohn, F., Young, E.W. 2003. Effect of ethics consultations on nonbeneficial life-sustaining treatments in the intensive care setting: A randomized controlled trial. *Journal of the American Medical Association*, 290, 1166–72.

Schneiderman, L.J., Gilmer, T., Teetzel, H.D., Dugan, D.O., Goodman-Crews, P. and Cohn, F. 2006. Dissatisfaction with ethics consultations: The Anna Karenina principle. *Cambridge Quarterly Healthcare Ethics*, 15, 101–6.

Strech, D., Synofzik, M. and Marckmann, G. 2008. Systematic reviews of empirical bioethics: Conceptual challenges and practical recommendations. *Journal of Medical Ethics*, 34, 472–7.

Tulsky, J.A. and Fox, E. 1996. Evaluating ethics consultation: Framing the questions. *Journal of Clinical Ethics*, 7, 109–15.

US President's Commission. 1983. US President's Commission for the study of ethical problems in medicine and biomedical and behavorial research: Decisions to forego life-sustaining treatment. A report on the ethical, medical and legal issues. Washington, DC.

Vollmann, J. 2006. Ethik in der klinischen Medizin: Bestandsaufnahme und Ausblick. *Ethik in der Medizin*, 18, 348–52.

White, J.C., Dunn, P.M. and Homer, L. 1997. A practical instrument to evaluate ethics consultations. *HealthCare Ethics Committee Forum*, 9, 228–46.

Williamson, L. 2007. Empirical assessments of clinical ethics services: Implications for clinical ethics committees. *Clinical Ethics*, 2, 187–92.

Yen, B.M. and Schneiderman, L.J. 1999. Impact of pediatric ethics consultations on patients, families, social workers, and physicians. *Journal of Perinatology*, 19, 373–8.

Youngner, S.J., Jackson, D.L., Coulton, C., Juknialis, B.W., Smith, E.M. 1983. A national survey of hospital ethics committees. *Critical Care Medicine*, 11, 902–5.

Index

Note: References to figures and tables are given in italics; references to footnotes are indicated by the letter 'n', e.g., 109n2 is note 2 on page 109

abortion 65n, 68–9, 68n–69n, 184–5
'accountability for reasonableness' framework 165–6, 169
agent values 80–2, 83–4, 115
American Society for Bioethics and Humanities (ASBH) 58–9
applied ethics 125–6
Aristotle 16, 39, 46–7, 153
artificial nutrition case narrative 54
Auer, Alfons 67
Aulisio, Mark P. 107n, 109n2
authoritarian approach 58–9

balancing method 14–15, 14n4
Beauchamp, Tom L. 14–15, 14n3, 14n4, 58
bedside rationing (BSR)
    allocation of resources 162–3
    framework for 165–9
    rationing strategies 163–4
    role conflicts 164–5
    systematic review 162
Birnbacher, Dieter 26–7, 108–10, 114, 116
Boitte, Pierre 142–3
bottom-up approach 13, 74–5, 92–4, 136
BSR *see* bedside rationing
Bulgarian ethics consultation study
    background 175–6
    health care providers' attitudes and experience 178–83, *179*, *180*, *182*
    methodology 176–7
    respondent characteristics 177–8
    study discussion 184–6

Caplan, Arthur 109, 110n
case-specific ethics consultation 92–3
casuistry 13–14, 120
CEC *see* clinical ethics consultation (CEC)

Centre of Ethics in Health Care (CEG) (Netherlands) 149–50, 149n2–150n
Chambliss, Daniel F. 79n2
Charter for Medical Ethics Committee (Georgia) 133–5
Childress, James F 14–15, 14n3, 14n4, 58
clinical ethicists 57–9
    competencies 109–13, 109n2, 110n, *183*
    expertise and moral judgement 114–16
    as facilitators 48–9
    role of 17, 18–19, 19n, 86–7, 108–9
    within moral deliberation project 40–2
clinical ethics
    as applied ethics 125–6
    development of 37–8
    hermeneutic aspects 40–48
clinical ethics committees
    changing role in Croatian hospitals 145–6
    in Georgia 133–6
    role in implementation of CEC *98*, 101–4
clinical ethics consultation (CEC) 1–2, 1n1, 203–5
    benefits for medical staff 86–8
    and conscience 65–70, 75–6
    and empirical research 31–3
    evaluation study 205–13
    as external moral authority 70–71
    implementation of 92–104
    in Croatia 142–6
    with regard to conscience 71–5
    outcomes of quantitative studies *209*
    physicians' attitudes towards (Bulgaria) 181–3

competencies
  discipline-specific 109n2
    analytical and reconstructive 110
    in consultancy practice 111–13
    expert knowledge 109–10, 109n2, 110n
    powers of judgement 110–11
  key 113, *183*
conscience
  as concept 66
  dynamics of 66–7
  and implementation of CEC 71–5
  professional 65–6, 65n, 67–70, 68n–69n, 70n
  reconciliation with CEC 75–6
conscientious objection 68–9, 68n
consequentialist ethics models 26–7
consultation theory 31–3
coordinator, role in implementation of CEC *98*, 99–100
Croatia
  current situation 139n, 140–2
  implementation of CEC 142–3
    health care providers' education 144–5
    patient education 144
    role of ethics committees 145–6
  legislation 144

Daniels, Norman 165–6, 169
Danis, Marion 165–6
data collection 24, 176–7, *208*
'decent agent' 83–4, 83n
decision-making
  in bedside rationing 168–9
  Bulgarian study 175–86
  and CEC 13–15, 16–18
  influence of conscience 67
  in nursing homes study 189–99, *198*
  prudence and mission 127
deliberation process 57–9
  see also moral case deliberation (MCD)
dementia 189, 198–9
deontological ethics models 27–9
Department of Public Health, Welfare and Sports (VWS) (Netherlands) 149–50, 149n1–2

descriptivity *see* normativity and descriptivity
diagnosis-related groups (DRG) 192
discourse ethics 29–30, 59–62

Eastern European countries 93–4, 139–40
  see also Bulgarian ethics consultation study; Croatia; Georgia
economic considerations 87, 162–3, 167–8, 198
education
  of clinical ethicists 18–19
  of health care providers 19n, 144–5, 166–7, 195
  of patients 144
embryo, status in stem cell research 112–13
empirical research 21–4, 21n
  in ethics 30–1
  and ethics consultation 31–33
empiricism 22–4
  in consequentialist ethics model 26–7
  in deontological ethics model 27–9, 27n
end-of-life care 192–3, 196–7
ethical decision-making *see* decision-making
ethical dilemmas (Bulgarian ethics consultation study) *179, 180*
ethical reasoning 13–14, 17–19
ethical theory 11–16, 53–5, 59–61
  person-centred case report 120–25
ethicist *see* clinical ethicists
ethics as a method 15–18
ethics café (Switzerland) 195
ethics consultants *see* clinical ethicists
ethics rounds (USA) 195
euthanasia debate 26
evaluation
  of bedside rationing process 169
  CEC study
    background 203–5
    methodology 205–9
    outcome criteria 209–10
    study discussion 210–13
  of ethical theory 11–15
  of moral case deliberation 155–8
  of moral problems 16–17
expert knowledge 18–19, 55–6, 108–11, 114–16

Index

facilitators
  ethicists as 48–9, 107, 107n
  facilitation approach 58–9, 152
  in moral deliberation projects 19n,
    40–1, 43–4, 151, 153–8
financial considerations 87, 162–3, 167–8,
    198
Fromm, Erich 66
fusion of horizons 44–5

Gadamer, Hans-Georg 39
games, role of 196
Georgia
  clinical ethics committees study
    aims and functions of 133–4
    and CEC 134–5
    establishment of 133
  health care system 131–3
Germany
  ethical discourse in 27n, 61
  German Medical Association
    (Bundesärztekammer) 61, 203
  nursing in 79–80, 79n1–2
  and rationing decisions 167
GGNet (Netherlands) 41–2, 49, 158

Habermas, Jürgen 29, 56, 59–60, 62
Hardin, Russell 81–2, 81n
health care providers
  attitudes towards ethics consultation
    181–3
  education 144–5, 166–7, 195
  experience of ethics consultation 178–81
Heidegger, Martin 38–9
hermeneutic philosophy 38–40, 49–51
  model of relationship of normativity
    and descriptivity 30–31
  moral deliberation project 40–42
  perspectives 43–5
  phronesis 46–8
  play and ritual 45–6
  role of ethicist 48–9
Hippocratic Oath 67–8
Hobbes, Thomas 28
homo oeconomicus 83
hospital management, role in
    implementation of CEC 98–9, *98*
Hurst, Samia A. 165–6

implementation of CEC 71–3
  bottom-up approach 74–5, 92–4
  common objections to 95–7
  existing problems with 92–4
  objectives and tasks 94–5
  steps toward 97–104, *98*
  top-down approach 73–4, 92–4
Institute of Bioethics of the Catholic
    University of the Sacred Heart
    119
institutional review boards (IRBs) 141
International Code of Medical Ethics 65,
    65n
'is-ought' 25, 25n3, 31–2
Italy, moving towards CEC
  health care system 119
  methodology 120
  mucopolysaccharidosis (MPS) case
    121–5

Kant, Immanuel 12–13, 12n, 16, 30, 67

LaFollette, Eva and Hugh 68
Lahno, Bernd 82
legislation of health care system
  in Croatia 141, 144
  in Georgia 132–5
  in transitional countries 139–40

MCD *see* moral case deliberation (MCD)
medical ethicists *see* clinical ethicists
Meyers, Christopher 58, 61–2, 113
mission, as motivational resource 127
moral authorities
  conscience in relation to 68–70
  external 70–1, 71n, 75–6
  internal 75–6
moral case deliberation (MCD)
  defining 151
  discussion of case 156–8
  and patient perspective 157, 157n
  reasons for 152
  role of research 153
  theoretical background 152–3
  training for health care providers 19n,
    153–4
  method of evaluation 155
  organization 154–5

pilot training 154
results 155–6
moral conflicts, terminology used 112
Moral Deliberation Group 154–8
moral deliberation project 40–42
moral deliberation sessions 49
moral judgement 110n, 114–16
moral philosopher, role in ethics
consultation 109–13
'moral rigorist' 83
morals, phenomenology of 55–7
mucopolysaccharidosis (MPS) case
120–25

Nagel, Thomas 115
Nazi regime 69
Netherlands
and clinical ethics 149–51
and moral case deliberation (MCD)
151–8
NJ SEED programme (USA) 195
normativity and descriptivity 25–31, 25n2
norm compliance 84, 86, 86n5
normative ethics 60, 62
professional norms 85–6, 86n6
Norway, nursing home study 189–99
nursing
and norm compliance example 84
preventive seclusion case 41–2
staff duties (Germany) 79–80,
79n1–2
nursing home study (Norway) 189–90
discussion of study 196–9
elderly person's perspective 192–3
ethical challenges within 190–92
strategies for handling ethical
challenges
clinical ethicists 194
ethics café and ethics rounds 195
ethics committee 194–5
games and role-play 196
informal discussions 193–4
reflection groups 194
three-step approach to decision-making
198
organizational ethics theory 72–3
organizational-level ethics consultation
92–3

palliative care 121–4, 196–7
patients
artificial nutrition case narrative 54
case-specific ethics consultation 92–3
communication with 16–18, 56
and concept of trust 80–83
education 144
equality of treatment 111–12
and palliative care 192–3, 197
physician-patient relationship 96, 126,
163–4
preventive seclusion case 41–2
rights legislation
in Croatia 141, 144
in Georgia 132–5
in transitional countries 139–40
see also person-centred ethical theory
case report
Peile, Ed 190, 196
person-centred ethical theory case report
120
contextual factors 124–5
medical indications 121–2
mucopolysaccharidosis (MPS) case
121
patient's preferences 122–3
proportionality 123–4
see also casuistry
phenomenology of morals 55–7
phronesis 46–8
Powers, Bethel Ann 190
practical discourse 29–30, 59–62
practical wisdom *see phronesis*
preventive seclusion case 41–2
principle ethics 11–13
principlism 14–15, 14n4, 57–9
professional ethics in changing hospital
environment 80–88
proportionality 123–4
prudence 17–18, 127
see also phronesis
psychiatric hospital case study 40–42
rationing *see* bedside rationing (BSR)
reasoning 13–14, 17–19
reflection 40, 49, 85–6, 143
groups 194
relational ethics 126
Republic of Croatia *see* Croatia

resources, allocation of scarce 162–3, 191
role conflicts in bedside rationing 164–5
role-play 196

Sabin, James E. 165–6, 169
Savulescu, Julian 68–9
septicaemia case 111–12, 111n
Singer, Peter A. 110n, 193
specification method 14–15, 14n3
stem cell research 112–13
sterilization, compulsory 69
suicide 12, 13
supererogation 86n5
'suprapersonal standards' 56–7, 59

terminal illness 11n, 120–24
top-down approach to CEC 13, 73–4, 92–4, 133, 136

training *see* education
transitional countries 93–4, 139–40
    see also Bulgarian ethics consultation study; Croatia; Georgia
trust, concepts of 80–83, 81n, 87, 96

Universal Declaration of Human Rights 65
Universal Declaration on Bioethics and Human Rights 65
utilitarian ethical approaches 12–13, 16, 26–7

virtues in clinical ethics 126–7

Willigenburg, Theo van 114–15
working groups, role in implementation of CEC 98, 100–101
World Medical Association (WMA) 65, 65n